THE TERROR BEFORE TRAFALGAR

By the same author

Nelson and His World
Chelsea Reach
Fighting General
Remember Nelson
The Young Nelson in the Americas
1945: The Dawn Came Up like Thunder
East and West of Suez
Horatio Nelson
Alan Moorehead
Sailor King
Rider Haggard and the Lost Empire
Norfolk
A Thirst for Glory
Travels of a London Schoolboy (ed.)
Battle for Empire
Nelson's Women
Captain Marryat
London Walks
Essential Venice

THE TERROR BEFORE TRAFALGAR

Nelson, Napoleon and the Secret War

Tom Pocock

JOHN MURRAY
Albemarle Street, London

First published in 2002
by John Murray (Publishers) Ltd,
50 Albemarle Street, London W1S 4BD

A catalogue record for this book is available from the British Library

ISBN 0–7195–6280–5

Typeset in Monotype Bembo 12/13.5
by Servis Filmsetting Ltd, Manchester

Printed and bound in Great Britain by
Butler and Tanner Ltd
Frome and London

For Daniel Thorndike

Contents

Illustrations

The author and publisher wish to thank the following for permission to reproduce illustrations: Plates 1, 5, 28, 29, 31, 34 and 36, Trustees of the British Museum; 2, 8, 9 and 17, National Portrait Gallery, London; 3, 4, 27 and 33, Musée National de la Marine, Paris; 6, 11, 12, 13, 14, 16, 22, 24 and 25, Private Collection; 10, Royal Academy of Arts; 18, 20 and 35, National Maritime Museum, London; 26, Musée de l'Armée, Paris; 30 and 32, courtesy of the Director, National Army Museum, London. Plates 7, 15, 19, 21, 23 and 37 are from the author's collection.

Preface

When its bicentenary falls, on 21 October 2005, the Battle of Trafalgar will be commemorated as a dramatic and pivotal event in European history. But it cannot be seen in isolation from the upheaval that brought it about, which began years before. This was the 'Great War' between Britain and France and, specifically, Napoleon Bonaparte's threat to invade England. There had been other such threats in the past and there was to be another in 1940 but what was called the 'Great Terror' – with its echoes of the recent 'Reign of Terror' in the French Revolution – was the longest and most intense since the Dark Ages.

This narrative begins in 1801, when the danger was first perceived as real, and continues until 1805, when it ended, but it also includes the dreamlike interlude following the Peace of Amiens when, for more than a year, the war must have seemed like a faded nightmare. The story is told largely through the actions and experience of those involved and often in their own words. It features not only the great men of action – Napoleon, William Pitt and Horatio Nelson – but also many others who were caught up in the storm, including women such as Fanny Burney, Emma Hamilton and Betsey Fremantle. Other, less familiar, names recur: Fulton, Congreve, Wright and Johnstone, and, across the Channel, Moreau, Pichegru and Cadoudal. These fought a parallel, secret war of espionage, subversion and the evolution of weaponry far removed from the stately lines of sailing battleships that fought off Cape Trafalgar and closer to the warfare with which we have become familiar in the twentieth and twenty-first centuries.

Visits to sites of the events described were, as expected, rewarding, particularly staying in the Hamiltons' rooms at the Royal Hotel at Deal, visiting the headquarters of the secret cross-Channel operations at Walmer Castle, exploring Juniper Hall and Fanny Burney's other haunts in the Mole valley of Surrey, finding the cleft in the cliffs at Biville, near Dieppe, where Captain Wright landed the conspirators who planned to overthrow Napoleon, and visiting Brest and Rochefort. There has even been an echo of the Peace of Amiens. My great-great-great-grandfather John Kennedy, the horticulturist, brought home mementoes of his dealings with the Empress Josephine, after whom a granddaughter was named; his family maintained friendships made in Paris and Malmaison and his grandsons and great-grandsons were sent to study in France.

Assembling this collage of past experience has been intriguing, and I am grateful to many who have helped, particularly Captain Allan Adair RN, Capitaine de Frégate Jean-Claude Bertault, Sir Murdo MacLean, John Munday, Michael Nash, Richard Ollard, John Pelly, Elizabeth Sparrow (author of the ground-breaking *Secret Service: British Agents in France, 1792–1815*), Anna Tribe, Michael Weigall, Alex Wills and Samantha Wyndham. For help with research and visiting historical sites I must thank Alan Giddings of the National Maritime Museum, the librarians and staff of the Archives Nationales, the Musée National de la Marine and the Musée de l'Armée in Paris, the British Museum and the British Library, the London Library, the National Maritime Museum and the National Army Museum, and Andrew Wedl of the Royal Hotel, Deal. Dan Cruickshank's television series *Invasion* for BBC2 usefully showed some of the remarkable fortifications built to counter a French landing. For advice and help with the preparation of this book I am grateful to Caroline Knox, Roger Hudson, Gail Pirkis, Andrew Lownie, David Crombie, Christine Highmoor and my wife, Penny. My father, the late Guy Pocock, kindled my interest in the theme of this book during walks along the sea wall at Dymchurch in Kent when I was a child, and he explained the purpose of the Martello towers, while my beguiling cousin Russell Thorndike talked of smugglers and the once-feared French beyond the horizon.

Tom Pocock
Chelsea, 2002

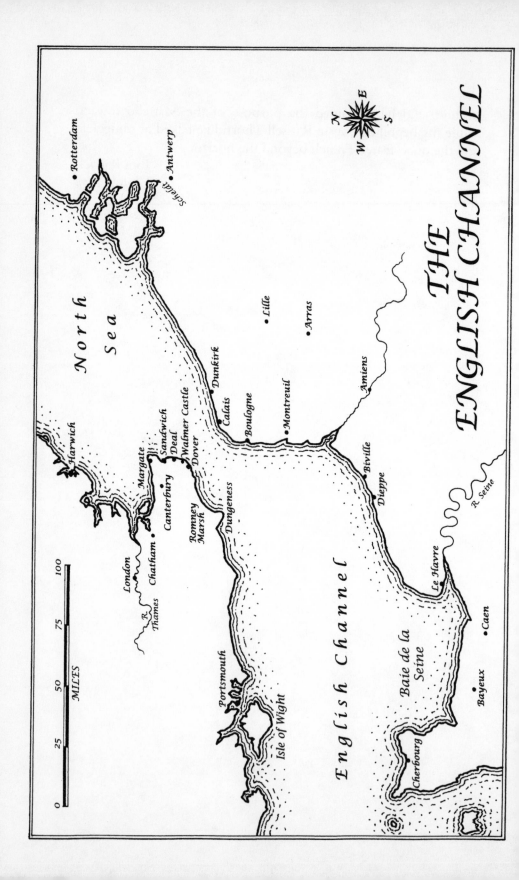

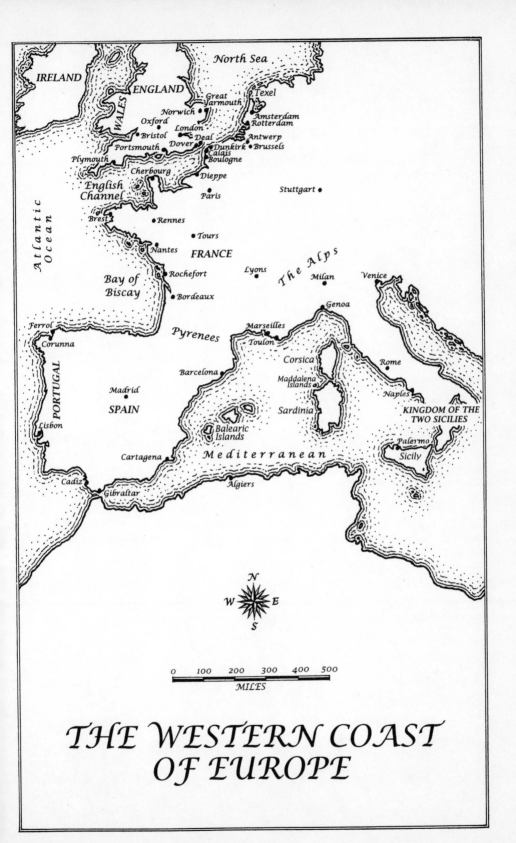

THE WESTERN COAST
OF EUROPE

Prologue

A SMELL of burning – charred wood and burnt gunpowder – still hung over Copenhagen. The fires had been dowsed by rain but their intended effect was being achieved. Six days after the gunfire had stopped, a banquet was held in the Amalienborg Palace and the principal guest was the British naval officer responsible for the smoke, which had long since been dispersed by the breeze. Vice-Admiral Lord Nelson, who had destroyed the line of Danish warships, armed hulks, floating batteries and forts that had defended their capital, had come ashore to reap the political reward for his victory.

A British fleet had been sent to the Baltic to destroy the Armed Neutrality of the North, of which Denmark was a member. The alliance forced on the Danes and their Norwegian territories, Sweden, Prussia and Russia by Napoleon Bonaparte, the First Consul of France, had closed the Baltic ports to British shipping. This had deprived the Royal Navy of its principal source of timber and hemp for rope and canvas, the price of which had doubled as a result, and cost the City of London much revenue in lost trade. The Danes had been reluctant to join the embargo but had been told by the French that, if they did not, Sweden would take Norway from them while Prussia took Jutland and Schleswig-Holstein; indeed, Denmark might be absorbed by Russia. To force them to abrogate this treaty, the British fleet under the command of Admiral Sir Hyde Parker, now in his flagship away to the north of the city, had Copenhagen at its mercy.

It was Parker's second-in-command, Lord Nelson, who had brought this about. Six days earlier, a fighting squadron of the lighter British ships of the line under his command had attacked the city's seaward defences. All day flame and smoke had rolled across the shallow sea and shoals beyond the city; each side had lost a thousand men or more until finally the Danes had been unable to stand the pounding by broadsides of 74-pound roundshot and had agreed to a truce. Today Nelson had come ashore to deliver the ultimatum to Crown Prince Frederick of Denmark in person. His deep-lined face and spare, one-armed figure, hung with stars and orders, attracted curious stares when he accompanied his host to the banqueting hall. As he climbed the wide, wooden staircase Nelson turned to a British officer beside him and, in the hearing of the Crown Prince, said, 'Though I have only one eye, I see all this will burn very well.'[1] In the negotiations that followed dinner, the Crown Prince agreed to Nelson's initial terms: a truce of fourteen weeks.

This may not seem the expected fruit of the total victory that Nelson claimed, but it was a beginning and it was enough. Soon after the agreement was signed, after dinner, news arrived of the assassination of Tsar Paul I of Russia, the keystone of the Armed Neutrality. He had been killed by his own courtiers on 24 March, ten days before the Battle of Copenhagen, which would never have been fought had this been known at the time. His successor, Tsar Alexander I, held opposite views and the alliance fell apart.

When news from Copenhagen reached Britain, expectations were fulfilled; decisive victory was what the British expected of their hero Lord Nelson, who could now sail into the Baltic to destroy the Russian fleet at Revel and the Swedish at Karlskrona. On 16 April, deep in rural England, the wife of one of his captains, Betsey Fremantle, wrote, 'This morning's post brought me most delightful news from off Copenhagen, where the English have gained a most complete victory. It seems to have been a most dreadful engagement but, thank God, Fremantle is safe.'[2] A fortnight later she was writing again: 'Glorious news from Egypt in this day's paper. The French have sustained a complete defeat. I wish all these victories may lead to peace.'[3]

The news from Egypt was of an assault landing in Aboukir Bay by the whole of the British army's strategic reserve on 8 March, followed two weeks later by a victorious battle outside Alexandria. This broke the French army, which had been led by General Bonaparte into Egypt in the summer of 1798, but then marooned there when the supporting French fleet was destroyed in Aboukir Bay by Lord Nelson. Subsequently Bonaparte had tried to lead his troops back to France overland, by way of Constantinople and Vienna, only to be thwarted by another British naval officer, Captain Sir Sidney Smith, who held the coastal fortress of Acre, which the French dare not leave in their rear. Now it was only a matter of time before the remaining French in Egypt surrendered and the threat they presented to the Ottoman Empire and India was eliminated.

Now, as then, victory was needed. Since war with revolutionary France had begun eight years earlier, there had been few enough. A succession of European alliances had not only failed to over-throw the aggressive republic but had themselves been worsted on military and political fronts; France commanded most of Italy. The first major success for the British had come when Bonaparte's unexpected and melodramatic eastward lunge had been halted by Nelson's destruction of his fleet at the Battle of the Nile. Lesser successes and failures had followed for both sides but the strategic balance was clear: France dominated the Continent, Britain the sea. Neither seemed to be able decisively to harm the other; stale-mate ensued.

These brutally effective actions by the British in Egypt and at Copenhagen were what was required. Yet in the weeks that fol-lowed the taste of victory soured. As spring turned to summer, it became apparent that neither had been necessary. It was now real-ized that the killing of Tsar Paul had shown the slaughter off Copenhagen to have been needless. In any case, the British had not wanted to fight the Danes, whom Nelson himself had described as 'the brothers of Englishmen'[4]; it had been an unpopu-lar victory and not even newspaper accounts of Nelson's heroism – 'Nelson, the most heroic of human beings, was all soul, purely ethereal, for his little body was scarcely visible in the fire'[5] – could rouse enthusiasm.

Soon after news of victory in Egypt had reached London word spread that that, too, could have been avoided. A year earlier

Captain Sir Sidney Smith, the victor of Acre, had negotiated with General Kléber, who had succeeded General Bonaparte on his return to France, and he had offered to withdraw from Egypt without further bloodshed. Through the diplomatic skill of a multilingual liaison officer, Lieutenant John Wesley Wright, an agreement known as the Convention of El Arish – after the coastal fort where it had been signed – had provided for the peaceful expulsion of the French from Egypt. But once this became known to Smith's superiors – notably Nelson and the commander-in-chief in the Mediterranean, Admiral Lord Keith – there was outrage. Only the unconditional surrender of the French was acceptable; the agreement was revoked and the war continued. Yet now, at the cost of many hundreds of British and French lives, the British government was about to agree to the same terms for the return of the French to France.

So nothing had changed; the stalemate continued after all. Only by crossing the narrow seas between the British Isles and continental Europe could one adversary get to grips with the other. The British army was not strong enough to attempt an invasion of France, but for the French it was different. Bonaparte would only need to move his invincible armies across the Channel – which he saw as little broader than some of the rivers he had crossed – and he could be confident of victory in a matter of weeks. Not only was the British army too weak to withstand the French face to face, but the nation was tired of war.

Throughout Britain the early ideals of the French Revolution maintained their hold on liberal imaginations and were expressed not only by the sophisticated politicians of the Whig faction but also by a widespread network of 'corresponding societies' and even revolutionary cells that occasionally broke surface. There was fear of subversion; it was, after all, only four years since the Royal Navy itself had mutinied at Spithead and the Nore. The British army was in no state to fight the French in Europe, or even to defend the British Isles. Its best troops – the 16,000 who had been fighting in Egypt – were only beginning to return, while those at home had little or no experience of active service and were poorly trained, many of their officers having purchased their commissions for social standing rather than martial ambition. Inflation and a run of six bad harvests had brought hardship, labour unrest and food shortages. Allies on the Continent had fallen away. The second coalition against France, which William Pitt, the Prime Minister for sixteen years, had laboriously rebuilt, had collapsed. Disputes between Russia and Austria had caused the former to withdraw from the alliance; in February Austria had followed suit.

At the beginning of the year the British Isles may have seemed united, with the Act of Union with Ireland coming into effect in January; but it was only three years since the Irish rebellion had been crushed and there was still active resistance to the rule of London. Pitt had realized that Ireland would remain a danger to the kingdom unless the Catholic majority could share political rights with the Protestants. However, the King, the Hanoverian Protestant George III, had refused to ratify Catholic emancipation and Pitt had resigned. His successor was the Speaker of the House of Commons, Henry Addington, who soon showed himself to be amiable but inadequate; certainly not the man to inspire a tired and apprehensive nation.

The nation seemed leaderless. King George, now past sixty, was losing the common sense that had earned him the affectionate nickname 'Farmer George' and was showing the eccentricity that would descend into insanity. Addington and his ministers lacked command and decision. The most able generals – John Moore and Arthur Wellesley – were still too junior to have caught the public eye, and the most capable admiral, Lord St Vincent, was nearly seventy and known for his harsh discipline as much as for his victories. Only one person could match the charisma of Napoleon Bonaparte and that was Horatio Nelson. This was a clash of symbols, a confrontation of icons: Bonaparte, the inheritor of the bloody tradition of the French Revolution, might be lampooned as 'Boney', but he was also viewed with apprehension as the 'Corsican Ogre', who must be defeated by a valiant champion. Nelson was a hero, celebrated for his originality and dash and for leading his men sword in hand, as the missing right arm, the scars and the dimmed eye proved. He had won two great victories in Aboukir Bay and off Copenhagen and, before that, had fought many actions that had become the stuff of legend, heroic paintings and popular song, including the battle off Cape St Vincent, when he had boarded and taken two Spanish ships. The excitingly theatrical Viscount Nelson of the Nile and Burnham Thorpe – his Norfolk birthplace – signed himself Duke of Bronte, after the Sicilian dukedom awarded for exotic services in the Mediterranean, and was aglitter with foreign decorations. He had also titillated the public appetite for scandal, for everyone knew of his abandonment of his dutiful wife for the once beautiful, vivacious Emma Hamilton, whose husband was his friend Sir William Hamilton, the ambassador in Naples. This showed him to be human and as fallible as he was brave and successful.

The nation was, as the poet Samuel Coleridge put it, 'wearied out . . . sick of hope long delayed and uncertain as to the real objects and motive of the war from the rapid change and general failure of its ostensible objects and motives . . . an unmanly impatience for peace had become almost universal'.[6] So, despite the ringing of church bells to celebrate the victories at Copenhagen and Alexandria, there was growing apprehension that the war might literally be brought home to the British. This possibility concentrated all minds in the spring of 1801.

I

Nelson speaking to the French

WATERMEN ALONG the steep shingle beach at Deal always watched the shifting pattern of sails and masts out at sea. The skippers of the luggers and the boatmen who manned the high-sided galleys that could breast the surf steadied their telescopes on the capstans, which hauled the heavier boats up the beach, to look for signal flags.

Deal earned its living by attending to the needs of ships in the great anchorage of the Downs, twelve miles long and sheltered by the Goodwin Sands. The sandbanks, notorious to seamen, lying some four miles off the coast of Kent and shifting on the chalk sea-bed, emerged from the sea at low tide. Here big Indiamen, bound for Bombay, Madras and Calcutta or for the Caribbean and the ports of North America, lay at anchor, along with traders for the Baltic, passenger packets for Hamburg and troopships for the Mediterranean − all awaiting the wind that would carry them down-Channel or across the North Sea. Here they could replenish their stocks of food and water and embark passengers, who had chosen a day's coach journey from London to Deal rather than join their ships in the Thames for wearisome days of working down-river to the sea.

Here convoys assembled to brave the French privateers from Boulogne, Le Havre, Cherbourg and Brest and their heavy warships in the Atlantic. Here, too, towering pyramids of sails could sometimes be seen as battleships of the Royal Navy swept slowly across the horizon. This August the telescopes were looking for a flag flying from the mizzen peak of a little frigate, the flag of Vice-Admiral Lord Nelson. The presence of the nation's hero on board a small ship in the anchorage charged the familiar scene of sea, sky and shipping with excitement.

At the beginning of August 1801 Nelson had assembled a squadron off Deal. This was nothing like the array of 74-gun ships of the line he had led with such style in his great victories. He now flew his flag in the frigate *Medusa* of thirty-two guns, commanded by Captain John Gore, and with her were some thirty smaller craft. The aggressive and impatient spirit of the squadron was even suggested by the names of its gunboats: *Boxer, Cracker, Flamer, Haughty, Attack, Bruiser, Conflict, Archer, Bold, Jackal* and *Charger* and the gun-brigs *Hasty, Biter, Defender* and *Bouncer*. Some were specifically designed for bombardment: heavily built bomb-vessels mounting mortars amidships, or gun vessels such as the little *Scourge*, a shallow-draught sailing barge, sixty feet in length and twelve in the beam, mounting a long 24-pounder gun in her bows and a broadside of three 32-pounder carronades to deter attack by boarders. It was obvious to the watchers along Deal beach that these were intended for a specific purpose.

Since July there had been signs that the French were planning the invasion of England. Bonaparte had commanded an *armée d'Angleterre* in 1798 but had realized it was impossible to cross the Channel with the force then available and had turned his attention to Egypt and a march on India; now that he was First Consul and virtual dictator he seemed to have returned to this unfulfilled ambition.

This suited the British government, since fear of invasion could give Henry Addington the air of command that his predecessor, Pitt, had had in such abundance that Nelson's friend Lord Minto had described him as 'the Atlas of our reeling globe'.[1] Indeed, the Lord Mayor of London had been told by the government that 'His Majesty's Ministers FULLY EXPECTED the French would attempt an IMMEDIATE DESCENT upon the island.'[2] It was believed that an army of some 75,000 men was encamped between Flushing and Le Havre, and that at least 100 shallow-draught barges had been assembled at the ports between in readiness for the invasion and another 250 had been built or were on the stocks. When Nelson was appointed to command the counter-invasion forces from Orfordness to Beachy Head, he had written a memorandum to the Admiralty entitled *Observations of the Defence of the Thames*.

> Supposing London the object of surprise, I am of opinion that the enemy's object *ought* to be the getting on shore as speedily as possible for the dangers of a navigation of 48 hours appear to me an insurmountable objection to the rowing from Boulogne to the coast of Essex. It is therefore most probable . . . that from Boulogne, Calais and even Havre, the enemy will try to land in Sussex, or the lower part of Kent; and from Dunkirk, Ostend and other ports of Flanders to land on the coast of Essex, or Suffolk . . . I will suppose that 40,000 men are destined for this attack, or rather surprise, on London; 20,000 will land on the west side of Dover, 60 or 70 miles from London, and the same number on the east side . . . In very calm weather, they might row over in 12 hours . . . If it is calm when the enemy row out, all our vessels and boats appointed to watch them must . . . meet them as soon as possible . . . If a breeze springs up, our ships are to deal *destruction*; no delicacy can be observed on this great occasion.[3]

Boulogne was known to be the keystone of the French deployment for there was the headquarters of the admiral commanding the invasion forces, Louis-René de Latouche-Tréville. A former officer of the royalist navy, he had survived the Revolution by his quick thinking, both political and professional, until he had won the reputation of being the only French admiral able to face Nelson with any degree of optimism.

So, as Nelson was certainly not prepared to swing round an anchor in the Downs, offensive action was certain. At the beginning of August he began a series of reconnaissance patrols along the French coast, particularly off Boulogne, which was now defended by a line of twenty-four brigs and gunboats anchored across the harbour mouth and ten batteries of heavy guns ashore. From his advanced headquarters by the site of a Roman lighthouse on the east cliff above Boulogne, Latouche-Tréville watched the *Medusa* sail past, just out of range, trailing a flotilla of bomb-vessels and gunboats. At five o'clock on the morning of 4 August the British, now accompanied by a ship of the line, suddenly closed to within a mile and opened fire. The bombardment and counter-fire continued until nine that night, hiding the coast in rolling clouds of smoke. It was a clear day and on the cliffs above Dover it was being said among the watching crowds that this was 'Nelson speaking to the French'.[4]

Yet next morning, when the smoke had cleared, the line of French ships was still there. Several had been damaged but the masts of landing craft still clustered as thickly as ever in the harbour. All that Nelson could claim was, as he wrote to his friend the Duke of Clarence (the son of King George III), who had been a naval officer, that 'The whole of this business is of no further moment than to show the enemy that with impunity they cannot come outside their ports.'[5]

Everybody knew that Nelson would not be content with that, and that a more determined attack was inevitable, probably by night and involving the boarding of the line of moored French ships. Meanwhile he had a duty, less agreeable to him, to carry out in England. He was responsible for the Sea Fencibles, the naval auxiliaries raised for coastal defence, who were proving unenthusiastic: another symptom of war-weariness. Of 2600 fishermen, bargees, smugglers and waterfront loafers who had enrolled so far, fewer than 400 had agreed to man ships offshore. As Nelson reported to the Admiralty: 'These men say, "our employment will not allow us to go from our homes beyond a day or two and for actual service"; but they profess their readiness to fly on board . . . when the Enemy are announced as actually coming on the sea.'[6] This was partly because many feared that this was a form of impressment and that they would find themselves aboard some taut ship of the Royal Navy, perhaps for years; as Nelson himself put it, 'they were always afraid of some trick'.[7] Realizing that he had been appointed to the counter-invasion command to bolster national morale, he now saw himself as having to chivvy reluctant watermen instead of giving orders to smart seamen, and he confided in his old friend Admiral Lord St Vincent, 'This service, my

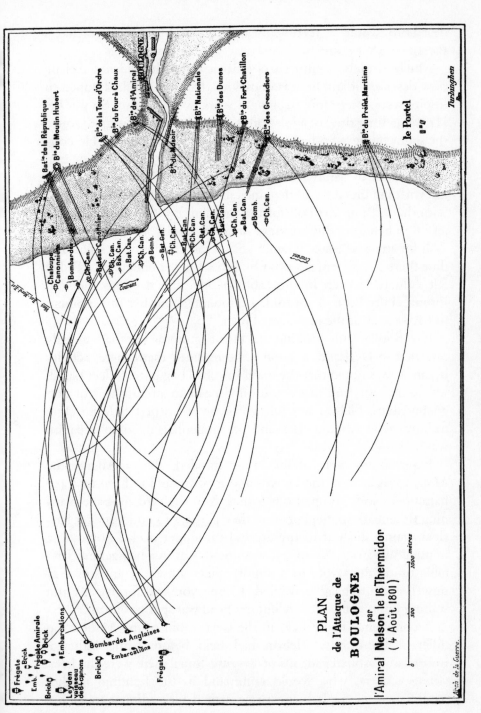

A French plan of Nelson's attack on Boulogne on 4 August 1801

dear Lord, would be terrible for me: to get up and harangue like a Recruiting Sergeant!'[8]

Much as Nelson enjoyed popular acclaim, he did not feel he now deserved it and he was conscious that those he had hoped to inspire were, after more than eight years, weary of war. So was he. He was getting tired of adulation too, for all England wanted to see the slight figure who had fought for them so dauntlessly. He confided in a letter to his lover Lady Hamilton, 'The Mayor and Corporation of Sandwich, when they came on board to present me with the Freedom of that ancient Town, requested me to dine with them. I put them off for the moment but they would not be let off. Therefore, this business, dreadful to me, stands over, and I shall be attacked again when I get to the Downs. But I will not dine there . . . if I can get off. Oh! How I hate to be stared at!'[9] He felt vulnerable even in the cabin of his little flagship, and told Emma, 'Fifty boats, I am told, are rowing about her this moment to have a look at the one-armed man.'[10]

His flotilla, still reeking of burnt gunpowder, had already returned to Deal and, as soon as he rejoined them there, activity began. It was noted that the naval yard had begun to collect oared, sea-going boats and that could only mean an attempt to 'cut out' enemy ships. Nelson was known to be at his best fighting close inshore, as in Aboukir Bay and off Copenhagen, so anticipation was high.

Expectations were about to be fulfilled. By 13 August the *Medusa* was back in the Downs and it was noted in Deal that 450 hammocks were shipped out to her from the yard: was she planning to embark soldiers or were they perhaps to build thicker barriers against small arms fire around the upper decks? Something unusual was afoot. Nelson, it was noted, was in a belligerent, irritable mood; he wrote to a senior officer ashore, 'I am still very unwell and my head is swelled. I hope you will forgive my not waiting upon you yesterday but my head was split with pain.'[11]

A conference being held in the stern cabin of the *Medusa* was different from those Nelson had held before battle hitherto. Instead of seasoned captains of 'seventy-fours' there were the keen young officers, who would command in the fighting; neither would there be a place for a one-armed vice-admiral in such a scrimmage. There was, as Latouche-Tréville had foreseen, only one way to attack Boulogne and that was to grapple with the defensive lines of ships moored across the harbour mouth. It would have to be launched at night, when the shore batteries might not dare to fire blindly at gun flashes for fear of hitting their own ships: a traditional cutting-out expedition, but on a grand scale.

The little flagship was officered by the pick of the younger breed. The admiral himself was attended by Captain Edward Parker, who had become both aide-de-camp and friend and had accompanied Nelson and the Hamiltons on fishing expeditions along the Thames. Others were equally well connected, such as Lieutenant Charles Pelly, aged twenty-two: 'a better officer is rarely, if ever, to be met with', as Nelson was to tell the young man's father, an Elder Brother of Trinity House and thus important in the business of the City.[12]

The plan of action was simple. There would be five attacking divisions, each commanded by a young captain. Four − led by Captains Somerville, Parker, Cotgrave and Jones and each of about fifteen boats − would board and the fifth − of eight flatboats, commanded by Captain Conn − would give supporting fire from eight-inch mortars. In each of the four assaulting divisions there would be two boats equipped with axes and grappling irons to penetrate the enemy line, cut their moorings and tow any that could be captured out to sea. On 14 August the *Medusa* and her consorts sailed and the next day they were off Boulogne.

Even at this moment Nelson could not concentrate fully on the task in hand. He was longing for Emma Hamilton and their infant daughter Horatia (their shared secret, whose twin sister was said to have died at birth), and he dreamt of an idyllic pastoral life with them (with Sir William hovering benignly in the background). Already he had asked Emma to look for a country house and had heard she had found one at Chiswick, on the Thames to the west of London. On this day he wrote to Emma about the immediate prospect at sea:

As you may believe, my dear Emma, my mind feels at which is going forward this night; it is one thing to order and arrange an attack and another to execute it. But I assure you, I have taken

much more precaution for others than if I was to go myself . . .
After they have fired their guns, if one half of the French do not
jump overboard and swim on shore, I will venture to be hanged
. . . If our people behave as I expect, our loss cannot be much.
My fingers itch to be at them.

But in the same letter he wrote:

From my heart I wish you could find me out a good comfortable house, I should hope to be able to purchase it. At this
moment, I can command only £3,000; as to asking Sir William,
I could not do it, I would sooner beg. Is the house at Chiswick
furnished? If not, you may fairly calculate £2,000 for the furniture . . .[13]

Across the Channel, Latouche-Tréville had been expecting such
an attack. He reinforced his line with bigger ships and embarked
more infantry. At night small boats patrolled, ready to signal early
warning. On board the moored ships heavy netting was triced up
to the yard-arms to keep boarders from their decks; loaded
muskets with bayonets fixed and cutlasses stood ready in racks.
Realizing that, even if boarders were repelled, anchor cables could
be cut and the ships towed away, he ordered the moorings to be
strengthened, the keels to be moored to the sea-bed and the hulls
to be made fast to anchors and to each other with chains, which
no axe could cut.

On the afternoon of 15 August Latouche-Tréville noticed
increased activity among the British ships, which constantly
patrolled a few miles offshore. A 'seventy-four', the *Leyden*, was
there but the centre of activity was a frigate, which might well be
Lord Nelson's flagship, and telescopes were trained upon her as
eagerly as they had been at Deal. With her were two other frigates,
while around the big ships swarmed cutters, barges and flatboats.
Such a combination could command only one interpretation: an
attack that night. Captain Gore of the *Medusa* jotted in his log,
'Light airs and cloudy weather. Employ'd fitting out the flatboats
to attack the enemy.'[14] The blades of the oars were muffled with
sacking and grappling irons were loaded into the boats. The

boarding parties buckled on white belts, borrowed from the marines, for identification in the dark. Freshly sharpened cutlasses, pikes and tomahawks were issued; pistols and muskets were loaded.

As it grew dark, Latouche-Tréville, watching from his command post on the bluff above the harbour mouth, ordered full alert and sent out his patrols. In the *Medusa*, Captain Gore recorded, '8.10, hoisted all the boats out and dropped them astern in two sub-divisions. Made signal for boats to assemble. 11.20, the boats were in position.' Six lighted lanterns were then hoisted in the rigging of the flagship and Gore concluded, 'At 11.30, the boats proceeded to attack the Enemy's flotilla.'[15]

In the darkness the boats of each division, their thwarts packed tight with armed men between the rowers, the officers seated in the bows, were linked loosely with tow ropes so that they should not be separated by the powerful tidal current. If they were, the password between them was to be 'Nelson' and the reply 'Bronte'. Nelson himself would be a distant spectator of the action he had set in motion; in any case, a one-armed admiral would be unable to board an enemy sword in hand. As it began all that he, and those watching and listening on the frigate's deck, could see and hear were gun flashes, the reports of cannon and carronades and the sputter of musketry. A burst of firing was followed by a more intense darkness and silence and then it would break out again.

On board the *Etna*, the senior officer's ship in the French line, Capitaine de Vaisseau Pévrieux had heard musket fire from one of his boats anchored ahead of the line to give early warning. The French mustered on decks to meet an assault and the loud reports of the British mortars showed that this was imminent.

On the racing tide the British swept towards the enemy, gun flashes illuminating the first to arrive. Somerville's first division lost contact with the others and saw they were being carried past the enemy line, as was Jones's fourth. Cotgrave, leading the third division, saw a French brig silhouetted against the flash of the guns and made for her, running his own boat against her and into a volley of musket fire. As she bumped alongside, French sailors above heaved a cannon-ball over the side to smash through the boat's bottom. Cotgrave saw his men collapse in convulsive heaps; the boat was

sinking, so he shouted for another to come alongside and the survivors scrambled aboard. Then they pulled out into the darkness to
prepare for another attempt.

The second division was commanded by young Captain Parker,
who ordered a lieutenant to attack the French ships at the northern end of the line to create a diversion while he, in a flatboat, led
a barge and cutter to the biggest ship he could see in the enemy
line, the *Etna*. 'The boats were no sooner alongside that we
attempted to board', Parker was to tell Nelson,

> But a very strong netting, triced up to her lower yards, baffled
> all our endeavours and an instantaneous discharge of her guns
> and small arms from about 200 soldiers on her gunwale knocked
> myself, Mr Kirby, the master of the *Medusa*, and Mr Gore, a
> midshipman, with two-thirds of the crew upon our backs in the
> boat, all either killed or wounded.[16]

Midshipman Gore was the captain's nineteen-year-old cousin.

On board the *Etna* the soldiers, secure behind the heavy
netting, fired, then stabbed with bayonets and pikes. As British
sailors grasped the bulwarks to heave themselves aboard, their
hands were axed with tomahawks and those who managed to
spring into the netting above the bulwarks were shot or speared.
Captain Pévrieux himself saw a sailor clambering over the top of
the netting, ran him through with his sword, seized him by the
hair and dragged him to the deck but was then stabbed in the
shoulder by the dying man.

As Somerville's scattered division reformed and ran alongside
other ships, the scene was repeated. The French infantrymen
fought ferociously: Fusilier Joseph Aubert of the 46th Démi-
Brigade, fighting on the deck of *La Surprise*, had an arm shot off,
paused while a tourniquet was lashed round the stump then fought
on with the other; Fusilier Nicolas Sarry of the 8th threw grappling irons back into the British boats and killed sailors clinging to
the netting. When a bullet smashed a French officer's arm, he continued to shout orders 'with the greatest *sang-froid*'[17] while an
infantryman was 'injured in his face by a grenade thrown by the
English, having previously received a pike wound in his leg, none

of which prevented him from remaining on deck and fighting with intrepidity'.[18]

As fighting spread along the line, Conn's mortar crews had to hold their fire for fear of hitting the British boats and so shifted their aim to the shore batteries. Somerville boarded a brig, which, he later reported to Nelson,

> after a sharp contest, I carried. Previous to so doing, her cables were cut; but I was prevented from towing her out by her being secured by a chain and, in consequence of a very heavy fire of musketry and grape-shot that was directed at us from the shore, three luggers and another brig within half a pistol-shot, and not seeing the least prospect of being able to get her off, I was obliged to abandon her.[19]

Cotgrave had to report that 'finding no prospect of success . . . [he] thought it for the good of His Majesty's service to withdraw the boats between two and three in the morning as we could not board her although every effort was made'.[20] Jones's division, having been swept down-Channel by the tide, struggled back towards the gun flashes and, as dawn was breaking, joined Somerville's as it was pulling away from the enemy line.

In the second division Parker's boat, filled with dead and wounded, would have been captured had not Lieutenant Cathcart's cutter towed her away from the enemy's blood-stained side. As the sun rose, he was joined by Lieutenant Williams's crews, who had fought hard and suffered as heavily. Parker's thigh had been shattered by a shot and Lieutenant Pelly, who commanded the *Medusa*'s launch, had also been wounded. 'At 3.00, the two flatboats, launch and one cutter returned,' noted Captain Gore in the *Medusa*,

> Captain Parker, Lieuts. Pelly and Langford, Mr Kirby, Master, Hon. Anthony Maitland, Mid., being wounded, Mr Gore, Mid., killed and several seamen and marines killed and wounded . . . Another attack commenced upon the enemy from another division. Employ'd getting the wounded on board. At 4, the firing ceased. Saw the boats returning from the attack.[21]

From the quarterdeck of the frigate Nelson watched the slow procession of boats return in the growing light of morning, noting that some were missing. They wallowed alongside the frigate, filled with bloodied bodies, some lying prone. A few French prisoners could be seen among them: a lieutenant, eight seamen and eight soldiers. As the summer morning became lighter, he could see the coast of France and Gore wrote in his log, 'Enemy's flotilla as before'.[22]

Soon after midday the British squadron made sail and steered away from Boulogne and at eight that evening it anchored in the Downs. 'Sent 18 killed and 20 wounded to the hospital', Gore recorded. 'Employ'd cleaning the ship. Four men deserted from the boats while on shore landing the wounded.'[23] Immediately the captains commanding the divisions wrote their reports for Nelson to forward to the Admiralty. The losses were counted; they amounted to 44 killed and 128 wounded. Several boats had been lost and no prizes taken. The attack had failed. The French line still lay off Boulogne, albeit much shattered aloft; several craft had been beached. But Pévrieux reported to Latouche-Tréville that all could be salvaged and that his casualties had been ten killed and thirty-four wounded. The defence had been an unqualified success.

Delighted by victory, the French began to celebrate with toasts and songs, one of which ran:

> Devant Boulogne,
> Nelson faisait un fer d'enfer!
> Mais ce jour-là, plus d'un ivrogne
> Au lieu de vin, but l'eau de mer
> Devant Boulogne![24]

(Off Boulogne,/Nelson poured hell-fire!/But on that day, many a toper/Instead of wine, drank salt water/Off Boulogne!)

Nelson meanwhile sat at his writing-table in the stern cabin of the *Medusa* and wrote to Lord St Vincent. 'I am sorry to tell you that I have not succeeded in bringing out, or destroying the enemy's flotilla moored in the mouth of the harbour of Boulogne. The most astonishing bravery was evinced by many of our officers and men.'[25] In another letter to the Secretary of the Admiralty, accompanied by his captains' reports, he added, 'I beg to be perfectly understood that not the smallest blame attaches itself to any person.'[26] He described how three of the four assaulting divisions had made their attacks and that 'more determined, persevering courage I have never witnessed'.[27]

He put the blame for the failure on what he saw as the disgraceful behaviour of the French in taking the sensible precaution of anchoring their ships with chains. 'The moment the enemy have the audacity to cast off the chains, which fix their vessels to the ground,' he wrote, 'that moment Lord Nelson is well persuaded they will be conducted by his brave followers to a British port, or sent to the bottom.'[28] There was no disguising the bad news. Even the *Morning Chronicle*, a newspaper generally sympathetic to Nelson ('I like the *Morning Chronicle*', he told Emma), was blunt, even when exaggerating his own part in the action. 'Our readers will lament to hear that the second attack on the enemy's flotilla has produced only a melancholy carnage', it reported on 18 August. 'The object of the attempt has not been gained and the gallant Admiral, after displaying desperate valour, has been obliged to return to the Downs, leaving the enemy's assembled force animated by a fresh proof of the security of their position.'[29] He had, however, been successful in implying that the French had behaved dishonourably by mooring their ships with chains, and he was gratified by a piece of doggerel in the monthly magazine the *Naval Chronicle*:

> Baffled, disgraced, blockaded and destroyed,
> The Gallic Navy a skeleton remains,
> And as a scare-crow is now employed,
> To frighten babies as it hangs in chains.[30]

But Nelson himself received a letter enclosing a pamphlet, 'Remarks by a Seaman on the Attack at Boulogne', violently criticizing his personal conduct and accompanied by a note reading, 'Should Lord Nelson wish the enclosed not to be inserted in the newspapers, he will please to enclose by return of post a bank note of £100 to Mr. Hill, to be left at the Post Office till called for, London.'[31] Nelson replied with a brisk note:

Very likely I am unfit for my present command and, whenever
Government change me, I hope they will find no difficulty in
selecting an officer of greater abilities; but you will, I trust, be
punished for threatening my character. But I have not been
brought up in the school of fear and, therefore, care not what
you do. I defy you and your malice.[32]

The blackmailer's letter was forwarded to the Admiralty and the
messenger who collected Nelson's reply from the Post Office was
arrested but denied knowing the name of whoever had sent him.

Such criticism took effect and Nelson wrote an agonized letter
to Evan Nepean, the Secretary of the Admiralty.

A diabolical spirit is still at work. Every means, even to posting
up papers in the streets of Deal, has been used to set the seamen
against being sent by Lord Nelson to be butchered and that at
Margate it was the same thing, whenever any boats went on
shore. 'What, are you going to be slaughtered again?' Even this
might be got over but the subject has been fully discussed in the
wardrooms, midshipmen's berths, etc . . . as I must probably be,
from all the circumstances I have stated, not much liked by
either officers or men, I really think it would be better to take
me from this Command.[33]

Accustomed to adulation, Nelson took all such criticism to
heart. Confiding in his friend and prize agent Alexander Davison,
he wrote, 'I agree with you and all my friends that this is not a
service for me, beyond the moment of alarm; but I am used and
abused.'[34] He blamed himself for not accompanying the attack,
then made the justifiable excuse that it had, as he had told Lady
Hamilton, not been an occasion for the 'personal exertions of a
vice-admiral'.[35] Yet he found it necessary to write a guilty letter to
St Vincent, protesting, 'I own I shall never bring myself again to
allow any attack to go forward, where I am not personally concerned; my mind suffers much more than if I had a leg shot off in
this later business.'[36] Any comfort in such confessions, or self-
justification, turned to ashes when he had to attend the funerals of
two midshipmen killed off Boulogne, one of them Captain Gore's

young cousin. He and eight captains had followed the coffins and it was reported, 'His Lordship was sensibly affected during the funeral and was seen to shed tears.'[37]

A particular worry was the condition of the three wounded officers from the *Medusa*. Charles Pelly, who had been shot through the collarbone and shoulder blade, had been taken, together with Midshipman Maitland, up the Thames to Guy's Hospital in a yacht belonging to Trinity House, sent by his father. The two others – Langford, Nelson's flag-lieutenant, and Parker, his aide-de-camp and friend – had been landed at Deal and lodged in a small house in Middle Street,★occupying rooms on the ground floor. Although both had been wounded seriously, their recovery was expected and both were cheerful and grateful for twice-daily visits by Nelson.

Meanwhile the admiral was putting forward new plans for offensive operations, including a major attack on Flushing with a landing by 5000 troops and an attempt on the harbour at Boulogne with a fireship. Living on board the frigate, he spent his days writing letters – on one occasion for seven hours – that reflected his swings in mood. Writing to his friend Nicholas Vansittart, the Secretary of the Treasury, he enclosed a letter to Henry Addington, saying, 'I am so miserably seasick that I can scarcely hold up my head but my last wish shall be down, down with the French . . .'[38] Nelson knew there was only one cure for his depression: the presence of Emma Hamilton, to whom he had, of course, been writing constantly: 'You ask me, my dear friend, if I am going on more expeditions . . . I go out if I see the enemy and can get at them, it is my duty: and you would naturally hate me if I kept back one moment. I long to pay them for their tricks the other day, the debt of a drubbing, which, surely, I'll pay.'[39]

On 19 August he was thrilled by a letter from Emma, recommending a house for them at Merton, a village in Surrey to the south-west of London. He replied immediately: 'I entreat, my good friend, manage the affair of the house for me.'[40] He begged her to join him at Deal, suggesting she and Sir William stay at an

---

★Tradition has it that this was number 71, which still survives, internally adapted as a shop.

inn that he could see from his cabin windows. 'The Three Kings,★ I am told, is the best house (it stands on the beach), if the noise of constant surf does not disturb you', he wrote.[41] In the hope that they would come, he wrote three days later giving details of the provisional bookings he had made for three large rooms 'with a gallery before them next the sea'.[42] He added hopefully, 'You would benefit by the jaunt. You can bathe in the sea that will make you strong and well . . . I hate the Downs but if my friends come it will be a paradise.'[43]

Nelson's enthusiasm was not shared by many of his naval friends, particularly those who knew and liked his wife, Fanny. When they had married on the Caribbean sugar island of Nevis in 1788 after a two-year courtship, she had seemed the ideal captain's wife. During his five years of unemployment in Norfolk, all had seemed well and he had written loving letters to her when recalled to sea in 1793 and sent to the Mediterranean. But she had fussed over his health and safety when he craved applause, and Lady Hamilton showered him with flattery in Naples after his triumph in Aboukir Bay. On his return to London with the Hamiltons in 1800 her hopes of a reconciliation had been dashed. Now officers who appreciated Nelson's brilliance shared the opinion of Captain Thomas Fremantle's wife, Betsey, who knew all the participants in the affair, and declared, 'Lady Nelson is suing for a separate maintenance. I have no patience with her husband, at his age and such a cripple to play the fool with Lady Hamilton.'[44]

But of course Emma took to the idea with characteristic enthusiasm, writing to Sarah, the wife of Nelson's elder brother William – now, thanks to his brother's fame, a senior clergyman at Canterbury Cathedral – 'Could you not come to Deal with us? Lord, that would be nice, as the children say.'[45] So when his new flagship the *Amazon* returned from sea at the end of August, Nelson was delighted to find that the rooms he had reserved were occupied by his lover, her husband and his sister-in-law. Although Emma called Deal 'this dreary place', she exulted. 'I can only say we are as happy as possible with our dear, invaluable Nelson. He

---

★The inn was renamed the Royal Hotel after Princess Adelaide stayed there in 1818 on her way to marry the future King William IV.

will go soon again on the coast of France . . . I tremble for him, but think Sir William has made an impression on him not to risk his dear, precious life without *greater* necessity.'[46] Her enthusiasm and breezy chatter immediately cheered Nelson and she appeared to be enjoying herself. Sarah Nelson, acting as Emma's lady-in-waiting, wrote happily, 'My lady call'd me this morning soon after six to go to bathe and a very fine dip we had; our maids do the same.'[47]

Both accompanied Nelson to visit Parker and Langford at the house in Middle Street. The former's thigh bone had been splintered and it was feared that only the amputation of the leg close to the hip might be able to prevent gangrene. Meanwhile Emma and Sarah fussed over him; they had a sofa moved into the house, although he himself had to lie flat on his back, and ordered as special delicacies jelly and port wine. It was to no avail. 'Poor dear little Parker had his thigh taken off,' wrote Emma to William Nelson,

and what he suffered is not to be described . . . The operation was long, painful and difficult . . . his groans were heard far off. If Nelson had been his father, he could not have suffered more . . . the leg and thigh were buried in the grave with Gore and Bristow, the two mids. that died in the glorious and brave attack.[48]

The prospects of his survival lessened and Nelson was left to worry alone when, on 20 September, the Hamiltons and Mrs Nelson departed for London because, as Nelson put it, 'Sir William's business forces him to London and mine irresistibly forces me to remain in this miserable spot.'[49] He paid their bill for £265 at the Three Kings and in his daily letters to Emma lost no opportunity to solicit sympathy, even telling her, 'Yesterday, if I could have enjoyed the sight, passed through the Downs 100 sail of West Indiamen.'[50]

Then Captain Parker died and a grieving Nelson attended his funeral at Deal parish church. The thud of minute guns from the flagship and, ashore, muffled drums, set the pace and solemnity of the slow march of soldiers with reversed arms escorting the coffin borne by six captains and followed by Nelson. At the graveside he was so racked with sobs that he had to steady himself by holding a tree trunk. When it was over, all that was left of his surrogate son was, as he wrote to Emma, 'dear Parker's hair, which I value more than if he had left me a bulse [bag] of diamonds. I have sent it in the little box, keep some of it for poor Nelson.'[51]

Such sentiment over what was presented by newspaper editors as a glorious failure off Boulogne did little to ease public weariness with the war. In France the action of 15 August was not only acclaimed as a glorious victory over the hated Nelson but was also seen, among those privy to the First Consul's strategic planning, as a brilliant sleight of hand. In 1798 Bonaparte himself had decided that the invasion of England was then beyond French capabilities. Now, three years later, he only intended the invasion force to sail in the unlikely event of exceptionally advantageous strategic and meteorological conditions coinciding, but he was concentrating on convincing the British that he had, indeed, every intention of invading them. He might have failed in the Middle East and in the Baltic, but if he could frighten the British with a threat of invasion, they might agree to peace terms favourable to himself. Meanwhile the Pas de Calais was a good holding ground for troops: healthy, rich in produce and well placed if there was any attempt by the British against France.

The stalemate continued. In the Downs there was little activity, but ashore one seemingly insignificant arrival was noted: that of a Captain Tom Johnstone. A tough, independent, humorous seaman of twenty-nine, he was handsome with bright blue eyes and dark hair, stood more than six feet tall and was famously attractive to women. Either wanted by the law enforcers or held high in official esteem, Johnstone attracted almost as much attention hereabouts as Nelson. Equally at ease among the shoals of the Goodwins or off the Dutch coast as in the tide-race of the Straits of Dover, and as comfortable in the company of Kentish smugglers as of French privateers, Johnstone was prized as a source of information. He had been in both French and British prisons as a smuggler, had escaped from a Royal Navy press-gang in Southampton and been posted as a deserter. But, following a stay in the Netherlands – where he had seduced his host's wife, who fled with him to

England – his knowledge of that coast became useful. In 1799 he had been invited by Vice-Admiral Andrew Mitchell to pilot the troop-carrying convoy to anchor off Den Helder for the landing of the Duke of York's expeditionary force. He had also landed a renegade French officer, assumed to be a royalist counter-revolutionary or a spy for the British, on the French coast.

In the autumn of 1801 there was one current rumour that prompted questions to Johnstone and all who might have heard news from Le Havre and the mouth of the Seine. Throughout the year there had been reports from Paris that the First Consul had authorized and financed a series of experiments with underwater weapons. These were variously known as the 'submarine bomb', the 'torpedo', the 'plunging boat' or the '*bateau poisson*' and were the inventions of an American resident in France, named Robert Fulton. A personable, confident man of thirty-six, he had been a jeweller's apprentice in Philadelphia and an art student, hoping to specialize in landscapes and miniatures. After coming to London in 1793 to study painting under the tuition of his fellow American Benjamin West, he had been so attracted by the ideals of the French Revolution that, four years later, he had visited Paris, where he had been invited to paint a vast panorama of the city. But he was more interested in promoting republicanism, and, depressed by the effects of the British blockade of France, had put his inventive mind to the design of a new maritime weapon in the form of a submersible warship. At the end of that year he wrote to the French government, 'Having taken great interest in all that would diminish the power of the English Fleet, I have planned the construction of a mechanical engine, in which I have the greatest confidence, for the annihilation of this Navy.'[52]

Fulton was said to have actually built a submarine boat, which had undergone trials in the Seine and then at Le Havre. Named the *Nautilus*, this had a fish-shaped, copper hull twenty-one feet long and with a diameter of seven feet; powered by a sail on the surface and, when submerged, by a hand-cranked propeller four feet wide, she was manned by a crew of three and designed to dive to twenty-five feet, where she could remain submerged for about forty-five minutes. The first trials had apparently been so successful that the boat had been hauled overland to Brest for more detailed evaluation. In September the submarine boat had used explosive 'torpedoes' – named after a stinging fish – either attached to a target ship and detonated by a timing device, or moored to the sea-bed to explode on contact. The *Nautilus* had actually cruised off Brest in a vain search for a British warship to attack and, as rumours reached the Admiralty in London, men such as Johnstone were employed to give early warning.

Benjamin West, Fulton's former drawing master, was fascinated by his plans for what he described with some exaggeration to his fellow artist Joseph Farington as 'the machine for diving and blowing up ships'. Fulton told him of the trials off Brest, when the submarine attacked a target ship anchored half a mile offshore, and West told friends

> When the diving-boat approached within a quarter of a mile of it, Fulton, who was in it with eight men, at once sunk his boat. In about a quarter of an hour, the vessel was blown up so entirely that nothing was left of her and, sometime after, Fulton's boat appeared again upon the surface of the water in an opposite direction from where she had sunk. The manner in which he blows up a ship is by enclosing a certain quantity of gunpowder in a small machine, which appears extremely like the back of a porcupine, having small pipes, or quills, standing out in every direction, any one of which, being touched, occasions a fire-piece something like the lock of a gun to go off and the powder blows up.

The submarine could remain submerged for eight hours, cruise at three knots and, he claimed extravagantly, dive to forty fathoms or more. When fresh air was needed, it was only necessary to break the surface so that induction valves were above it. 'This most dangerous and dreadful contrivance is said to be fully understood only by Fulton', said West. 'He will show the machine but there are certain mysteries about it, which he has not and says he will not, but in America.'[53]

But the British appetite for more battles and new weapons was slackening, as was the enthusiasm of the Sea Fencibles and Nelson's own seamen. Peace was in the air. The realization that the victories in the Baltic and Mediterranean had been needless only deepened the longing. Bad harvests combined with the effects of the stopping of grain imports from Germany, the Low Countries and, until recently, the Baltic had brought near famine to parts of the British Isles and discontent was spreading. The coalition against France had disintegrated. Among politicians, the Whigs had never wanted war with France but now the Tories, too, would welcome a peace settlement.

Knowing his own strength and sensing Addington's lack of global, strategic vision, Bonaparte presented what Pitt would have seen as demands rather than terms. All French overseas territories taken by the British were to be restored: the islands in the Caribbean (including Martinique) and in the Atlantic and the Indian Ocean, and the trading stations and forts on the coasts of India, West Africa and at the Cape of Good Hope, although the latter had belonged to the subservient Dutch. In the Mediterranean, Elba was to be returned to France, Minorca to Spain and Malta to the Knights of St John, from whom it could be retaken by the French whenever required. For his part, Bonaparte agreed to withdraw from southern Italy, guarantee Portuguese sovereignty and restore Egypt to the Ottoman Empire, without mentioning that the rump of the French army in Egypt had been about to surrender in any case. All that the British would gain would be Ceylon, which they had taken from the Dutch, and Trinidad, which had belonged to Spain. Meanwhile, the French dominated the northern shore of the Mediterranean – having annexed Piedmont and occupied the Neapolitan ports – and the Continent itself.

Acceptance of the terms meant peace and on 1 October Lord Hawkesbury, the Foreign Secretary, who had been negotiating with the French emissary Louis Otto, signed the provisional agreement. After more than eight years the war seemed to be almost over. Exhaustion and fatalism turned to relief and joy. That night the windows of London were bright with candles and illuminated transparencies. Celebrations concentrated on the Portman Square residence of Louis Otto, which was the most brilliantly lit of all. The word 'Concorde' blazed across its façade but when two British sailors read this as 'Conquered' they shouted, 'They conquer us!

They be damned!'[54] hammered on the door and protested, where-upon Monsieur Otto tactfully had the sign changed to 'Amity'. In response, a shop across the street decorated its window with a flattering illuminated transparency of Napoleon Bonaparte.

The news was swept through the country by mail coaches festooned with flags and laurels, the coachmen sounding their horns and shouting to those they passed that the war was over. But in London Addington realized that the terms demanded by the French would, once they had been calmly assessed, not be popular; it might be seen as peace at any price.

2

A great surprise indeed

WITH THE coming of peace, lives changed and new expectations arose. Lord Nelson drove through the gates of Merton Place to begin realizing his fantasy of life as a gentleman farmer with his mistress and her husband in the house she was already fashioning as a shrine to his fame. As he inspected the lawns and gravel paths among flower beds, ornamental trees and the little canal, freshly stocked for fishing, which he called 'The Nile', he exclaimed, 'Is this, too, mine?'[1] He toured the charming house lit by French windows opening upon graceful verandas and a profusion of mirrors within. Nothing could have been in more delightful contrast to the cramped, lurching cabin of a frigate, smelling of hemp and tar. 'We are all so joyous today, we do not know what to do', wrote Emma Hamilton to Nelson's sister-in-law Sarah. 'Believe me, my heart is all convulsed seeing him again safe on shore, safely moored with we – I must not say *me*.'[2] Ahead she could imagine months, perhaps years, of bliss.

As this rural idyll began, another was ending. An unemployed French general, Alexandre d'Arblay, was returning from exile to his native France to face an unknown, possibly dangerous, but exciting future. His English wife, the novelist and playwright Fanny Burney – as prominent in the public eye as Emma Hamilton but in all else her opposite – was dreading leaving the charming home they had shared for nine years in the leafy seclusion of West Humble in the Surrey hills. She was now aged forty-nine, charming and intelligent rather than beautiful, and she had been looking forward to middle age amid such pastoral tranquillity as Nelson now sought.

In the valley of the little river Mole, near the village of Mickleham, a handsome country house, Juniper Hall, had been rented by a group of French *émigrés*. In November 1792 they had been joined by another refugee, the former Lieutenant-General the Comte d'Arblay. A good-looking, cultivated man of forty-seven, he had been born into the rural gentry and brought up in a château south of Paris. He had become an army officer when still a boy, although more inclined to the arts and writing poetry. He had continued to serve after the start of the Revolution and had been on guard in Paris on the night of King Louis's abortive flight to Varennes in 1791; the following year he had been second-in-command to the Marquis de Lafayette in the war against Austria. He was, however, seen by his own men as an aristocrat and a royalist and, when mutiny threatened, had had to escape to the enemy lines, then through the Netherlands to the coast and a ship for England.

Fanny Burney had been staying with her sister Susan and her husband at Mickleham, and she had become a frequent guest at tea parties on the lawn and soirées in the gilded salon of Juniper Hall, where she met this intriguing *mélange*, including the newly arrived general. As powerful intellectually as socially, the group had all been involved in the beginnings of the French Revolution, and some of them were also bound together by political or sexual intrigue. The dominant few included Madame Germaine de Staël, the daughter of a Swiss financier and wife of the Swedish ambassador to France, who had become the leading literary hostess in Paris and was now, in exile, writing novels; after meeting her at Mickleham, Fanny delighted in her 'zest of wit, deep thinking and light speaking of almost unexampled entertainment'.[3] There, too, was Madame de Staël's former lover and a friend of General d'Arblay the Comte de Narbonne, said to be an illegitimate son of King Louis XV, who had been a royalist officer and Minister of War at the beginning of the Revolution until he was denounced by the Jacobins and escaped to England. A sinister visitor to Juniper Hall was the diplomat Charles-Maurice de

Talleyrand-Périgord, a former priest and Bishop of Autun, who had been in and out of favour with the Revolution and returned to serve as Foreign Secretary after the fall of Robespierre. A brilliant but devious diplomat trusted by none, Talleyrand, despite his repellent looks, fascinated all with the sharpness of his intellect and wit.

Fanny had eyes only for the handsome and intelligent Alexandre d'Arblay, and despite the opposition of her father, the musician Dr Charles Burney, she had married him at the parish church of Mickleham on 28 July 1793. Their joint income was small, in spite of her literary success, but her rich, cultivated friends the Locks of Norbury Park, a mansion on the hill across the valley, had given them a plot of land in their parkland near the hamlet of West Humble. This lay in a landscape that epitomized the cult of the picturesque: steep meadows, hanging woods with a winding stream below and the heights of Box Hill above; near by stood the Fox and Hounds inn, which Nelson and the Hamiltons were planning to visit. There d'Arblay designed, and they built, on the proceeds of Fanny's latest novel, *Camilla*, a pretty little house with its own library, whose bay windows commanded a view across the valley to Mickleham. They named it Camilla Cottage. He had seemed to forget his military ambitions and settled down to a modest social round, reading and gardening, although he did tend to trim the hedge with slashes of his sword. In 1794, as the Reign of Terror racked Paris, the couple's secluded contentment had been crowned by the birth of a son, also to be named Alexandre.

Then, early in October 1801, just as Fanny was completing a witty play, *A Busy Day*, her husband heard that an amnesty had been declared in France and that, if he returned, he might be able to resume his military career. Failing that, he might be able to collect a pension for his service before the Revolution and possibly retrieve his confiscated property. Although his host country was still officially at war with his own, he wrote excitedly to Paris, offering to serve as an officer in Bonaparte's own Garde Consulaire. Fanny was appalled for, if he succeeded, she would have to abandon Camilla Cottage and follow him. Despite her entreaties, he left for Paris to assess the prospects and apply for passports that would enable his wife and child to join him.

The journey by sea was long and stormy and, after arriving, d'Arblay seemed to vanish in the confused and dangerous country across the Channel. Realizing that, although the convulsions of the Revolution seemed to have ended, the leaders of France remained violent and their ideals egalitarian, she wrote to him in Paris simply as 'Citoyen Darblay', so as not to draw attention to his background. She said that his decision had 'made my heart ache heavily' and reminded him of the home they had created together:

Our hermitage is so dear to me – our book-room so precious and, in its retirement, its beauty of prospect, form, convenience and comforts so impossible to replace that I sigh, and deeply, in thinking of relinquishing it . . . Think, however, well, *mon très cher ami*, before you decide upon any occupation that robs you of being master of your now time, leisure hours, gardening, scribbling and reading . . . You are, perhaps, unable to appreciate your own value of those six articles . . . Weigh, weigh it well.'[4]

Fanny hoped that his visit to Paris would be fruitless, and in any case he was due to return to tell her what had transpired. So she read with horror his letter explaining that his old friend the Marquis de Lafayette, with whom he had also served as adjutant-general, had introduced him to the Minister of War, General Berthier, and that he had been offered command of a brigade. There was also the probability that he would be allowed a pension and to retrieve some, at least, of his property in France. This brigade was due to join an expedition to Santo Domingo to put down the rebellion led by the formidable black leader Toussaint l'Ouverture, a campaign that promised as much danger from tropical disease as from battle. She replied tartly, 'This is a great surprise indeed.'[5] As an Englishwoman and a former member of the Queen's household – she had been Second Keeper of the Robes from 1786 to 1790 – she could hardly remain in her own country, which was still officially at war with France; she would have to follow him.

In January 1802 Alexandre d'Arblay returned to England and explained his situation. Fanny and their son met him at her brother's house in Greenwich and he told them that only his acceptance of

Berthier's offer could provide the income they needed. Miserably she agreed but made him promise that he would make his own condition that 'it was his inalterable resolution NEVER to take up arms against the British Government'.[6] She then set about letting Camilla Cottage, which she advertised in *The Times* as 'a small, modern country residence, fitted up in the cottage style, with 5 acres of garden, orchard, pleasure and meadow land . . . in the centre of many romantic and extensive prospects'.[7] So as one household in Surrey was established, another was destroyed by the political negotiations still in progress between London and Paris.

Now Addington needed a popular national figure to persuade the British public that he was acting wisely. The choice fell upon Nelson. At Merton he had spent his first days realizing his dream of pastoral bliss. 'After clouds comes sunshine', the phrase he had once used to his wife when five years of unemployment had ended with his recall to duty on the outbreak of war in 1793, would have been appropriate. The Hamiltons had already settled in; Emma was practising her singing and Sir William was fishing and on Sunday they drove to the parish church to join their neighbours. It was already apparent that as a *ménage à trois* they would not be welcome at court, or in polite society, and would have to find new friends elsewhere. Several of their neighbours set the tone of their new circle – unfashionable but interesting and original – augmenting the naval friends they could expect to call. There was James Perry, the editor of the *Morning Chronicle*, at Wandle Bank House, and Abraham Goldsmid, a Jewish banker, at Morden Hall; other old friends returned from the West Indies and the Caribbean and there were still others to be met when attending literary and artistic gatherings in London with Sir William. There was no time to begin entertaining on the scale Emma had in mind before Nelson was called to London, where he was to take his place in the unfamiliar world of politics.

A week after arriving at Merton Place Nelson took his seat, formally robed, as a peer in the House of Lords. Next day he made his maiden speech, seconding a vote of thanks to his friend Admiral Saumarez, the Channel Islander, for success in action off Algeciras, while the other peers listened intently to Nelson's Norfolk voice, which few had heard. This was easy enough, but the politicians had already noted his lack of political skill and insight and his eagerness to please. Addington was worried that the peace terms were too favourable to France, although as yet there seemed little public awareness of this. On 3 November his predecessor, William Pitt, said in a lengthy *tour d'horizon* in the House of Commons that at the news of peace 'this particular joy was undiscriminating and that the people never stopped to inquire about the terms . . . It only proves that the people were so goaded by the war that they preferred peace almost upon any terms.'[8] Nelson's grand Norfolk neighbour William Windham of Felbrigg Hall, who had been Secretary for War under Pitt, attacked the government for giving too much for too little.

He was widely supported by Tory patriots, among them Charles Burney, who wrote to him from Chelsea:

> I had always seen the danger of making peace with France under her present rulers . . . With all Europe at her feet, except this country; in actual possession of half Germany, the Netherlands, Switzerland, Savoy, Piedmont, Lombardy, Genoa, the Ecclesiastical States . . . as are Naples, Spain and Portugal as well as Holland: and all this territory and its inhabitants under the direction of such Miscreants, Regicides, Assassins, Plunderers, Jacobins, Atheists and Anarchists! – what had we to expect?[9]

Before the nation could calmly consider the terms and the prospects, it was important that their veracity should be endorsed by unanswerable voices. These would best come from naval heroes, recognized as the saviours of the country: one would be Lord St Vincent, who as First Lord of the Admiralty could be expected to comply, although in the event he only agreed to answer criticism from his predecessor, Earl Spencer, who had said that 'the preliminaries were attended with circumstances of humiliation and disgrace to this country'.[10] To this St Vincent replied briefly, denying that this was so and claiming that 'by the peace two of the most valuable islands in the habitable globe, considered either in a political, or commercial view' had been gained; these were Trinidad and Ceylon, which were, of course, as valuable as he had said.[11]

It was given to Nelson to defend the concessions most open to criticism: the return of Malta to the Knights of St John, of Minorca to Spain and of the Cape of Good Hope to the Netherlands. Following St Vincent's terse address, 'Lord Nelson rose to say a few words respecting a point or two', as the parliamentary report put it.[12] He described Minorca and its great natural harbour as 'an island of little value to us as at too great a distance from Toulon to serve as a station to watch the fleets of France that put to sea from that port'.[13] Malta, he said, 'was of no sort of consequence to this country' and 'in any hands but the French it became immaterial to us'.[14] As for the Cape, it had been useful when Indiamen stopped there to refit but now 'since the India ships were coppered like our men of war and swift sailers, it frequently happened that they sailed out to India without touching at any port whatever'.* He 'considered it merely a tavern on the passage, which served to call at and thence often to delay the voyage'. When he had first been there, and it had been occupied by the Dutch, 'you could buy a cabbage there for twopence, but since it had been in our hands a shilling was obliged to be paid for a cabbage'.[15] Therefore, he maintained, 'it produced little that made it worth holding'. Finally he agreed with the government's view that peace could be ratified 'as soon as the government of France should wear an appearance of permanency'.[16] He then almost seemed to endorse the First Consul, whom he had always held in such contempt, claiming, 'Now, could any man say that the republic of France was not as permanent as any other state governed by one man?' Finally, he concluded that 'the preliminaries on the table were honourable and advantageous to this country'.[17]

Although she was staying in London, Emma Hamilton could not, as a woman, attend the debate. However, she was thrilled by what she saw as a new and exciting world of politics and power in which her lover would excel. To Nelson's sister-in-law Sarah Nelson she wrote, 'Our dear Nelson came home at six o'clock, the House broke up at five.' He had made, she said, 'a famous good speech' and she had heard reports that

---

*The bottoms of these ships were now sheathed with copper sheeting to protect their timbers from the wood-boring teredo worm in the tropics, so increasing their speed.

he spoke firm, well, distinct and audible. Indeed, he succeeds in all he does . . . I am quite Nelson mad again for him as an orator . . . I think this is my hero's second speech. I have been making him say it to me as he said it to the House. I could hear him talk for ever and am just as anxious that he should be admired in this his new career as I was when he went out to battle.[18]

She was alone in her admiration. William Huskisson, the former Under-Secretary for War, wrote to Lord Dundas, the War Minister:

I was much obliged to Lord Nelson for giving me anything that could create a smile on such a grave and awful subject. His Lordship's experience might have convinced him that a seaman could find a tavern nearer home than the Cape of Good Hope and if Malta is not to be considered of importance because it does not serve to blockade Toulon, we must be obliged to conclude that no station in the Mediterranean is a good one. How can Ministers allow such a fool to speak in their defence?

Even Nelson's old friend Captain Thomas Hardy remarked, 'I see almost by every paper that Lord Nelson has been speaking in the House; I am sorry for it and I am fully convinced that sailors should not talk too much.'[19]

Nelson himself was aware that political oratory was not among his talents, and described his speech to a naval friend as 'bad enough but well meant – anything better than ingratitude. I may be a coward and good for nothing but never ungrateful for favours done me.' Defensively he put this down to his being a bluff sailor: 'My professional education will plead my excuse for the imperfect manner in which I deliver my sentiments but I should not have done my duty if I had not, even in this plain, seamanlike manner, seconded this present address.'[20]

More to his taste were the celebrations of his fame, although he sometimes pretended to find them demanding. That November he wrote to the captain of his flagship, the frigate *Amazon*, which was still tossing in the Downs, 'Yesterday was a fagging day: 150 dined at the London Tavern and I, being cock of the company, was obliged to drink more than I liked but we got home to supper.' Finishing the letter several days later, he added, 'Yesterday was a busy day, between gardening, attending the house, eating and hurra-ing.'[21] On the 9th he and Sir William Hamilton were guests at the inauguration of the new Lord Mayor of London; after joining the procession, they were quickly recognized and the crowd unharnessed the horses and dragged the coach, cheering, to the Guildhall.

Shortly before eight o'clock on the morning after Nelson's triumphant progress with the Lord Mayor's procession, a single horseman rode up Whitehall. Strangely, reported *The Times*, he was 'attired in the Turkish dress, turban, robe, shawl and girdle round his waist with a brace of pistols'.[22] Those few in the street – crossing sweepers, draymen and those making their way to government offices – would have been startled to learn that this apparent alien with a sunburnt face, high-arched nose and dark locks was a captain in the Royal Navy. Captain Sir Sidney Smith had come ashore at Portsmouth the day before, after a long and stormy voyage from the eastern Mediterranean during which he had indulged his eccentricities, including his enjoyment of dining on stewed rats. He had brought with him the official dispatch reporting the final victory of the British expeditionary force over the French in Egypt, only to find that duplicate dispatches sent in another ship had arrived a fortnight earlier. He also found that excitement over the coming peace overshadowed gratification in distant victories and he was further mortified to hear of the glorification of Lord Nelson. Yet he was determined to make his mark and did so by reporting to the Admiralty in Turkish dress.

Smith, aged thirty-seven, and Nelson, forty-three, had much in common. Both were vivid, brave and ambitious; both were slight of build but compelling in presence; both had made their reputation by dramatic action in war. But whereas Nelson was the essence of the naval officer and a master of naval strategy, tactics, seamanship and leadership, believing that in such skills lay the answers to the problems of war, Smith also led another, different life as an intelligence officer. Since youth his subtle mind, command of languages and love of excitement had taken him into the underworld of espionage and secret diplomacy. In this he was partnered by his brother Spencer Smith, who combined his intelligence work with that of a diplomat. In the Levant they had both held diplomatic appointments in the Ottoman Empire: Spencer had been minister at the embassy in Constantinople. Sidney's dual role had infuriated his superior naval officer Admiral Nelson, who disliked him intensely until his successful defence of Acre. There, by halting Bonaparte's intended march through Syria on his way back to France via Vienna, he had proved that he was a fighting officer after Nelson's heart; they had become friends, albeit warily.

Riding into the cobbled forecourt of the Admiralty, Captain Smith gave his horse to a groom and entered for the first of several interviews with admirals and politicians there and in Downing Street. Unabashed by his exotic appearance, he explained the double military and diplomatic game he had played in the Middle East, pointing out that, had his advice been taken, the British invasion of Egypt at the beginning of the year would have been unnecessary and many lives saved. The Smith brothers' orders had been to expel the French from Egypt and they could have done so far sooner by diplomatic means. Nelson and his superior Lord Keith had believed only in the use of force.

Although aware that in London he had been upstaged by Nelson, Smith was accorded some honours: he was awarded an annuity of £1000 by the House of Commons and the freedom of the City of London. He too loved acclaim and was even more of a self-publicist than Nelson, delighting in the striking of silver medallions commemorating his achievement at Acre and the publication of a popular composition to mark his return, 'Sir Sidney Smith's Hornpipe'. This was an addition to several country dances already published in his honour – 'Sir Sidney Smith's Delight', 'Sir Sidney Smith's Escape', 'Sir Sidney, or, Bonaparte's Defeat' and 'Sir Sidney Smith's Triumph' – and was soon to be followed by 'Sir Sidney Smith's March' and 'Sir Sidney Smith's Strathspeay'.

Those familiar with Smith in the Mediterranean noted the absence of a young officer who had often seemed like his shadow. This was Lieutenant Wright, who had gone ashore dressed as an Arab and speaking Arabic to make contact with allies, or as a French-speaking European on missions to meet enemies. The Admiralty was deciding to promote him to command the sloop

Cynthia to follow Smith back to England. Several of Sir Sidney's officers had been similarly unconventional, also speaking foreign languages and growing whiskers *à la Turque*. Ashore Smith and his circle had long been suspect in polite society. Although a cousin of William Pitt, his family background was questionable: his father, a former army officer, had been a rake and a spendthrift, while his friendships outside the navy tended to be among the louche and eccentric. Now he sought to renew that with his first cousin the notorious Lord Camelford, who was also a cousin of Pitt and brother-in-law of Lord Grenville, the former Foreign Secretary.

At twenty-six Captain Lord Camelford of the Royal Navy was, to the surprise of his brother officers, still on the active list. A rich, hot-tempered, spoilt aristocrat, he had shot dead his first lieutenant five years earlier for apparently refusing to obey an order. The subsequent court martial acquitted him on the spurious grounds that the dead officer had been mutinous; there had also been reports of duelling and, in one encounter, another naval officer was said to have been killed. Wild and dangerous as Camelford was, Smith liked him and had tried to involve him, as captain of a frigate, in the operations he was now planning in the Levant. As the war ground to a halt, it had seemed that Camelford would turn to other diversions: he was courting his cousin, a niece of William Pitt, the striking and intelligent Lady Hester Stanhope. As an amateur boxer, he had become a patron of the boxing ring.

Whatever hopes Sir Sidney Smith had of rejoining his cousin's exciting circle, enquiries as to his whereabouts drew a blank. The swarthy, brutal face of the young peer had not been seen at Camelford House in Oxford Street, nor at his mansion in Cornwall, nor in the gaming rooms and clubs of London for two or three weeks and nobody seemed to know where he was. This was no surprise because he revelled in plotting and planning bizarre adventures – one had been a scheme to subvert and conquer the Spanish empire in South America – and now nothing would surprise his friends. 'I have not yet seen Lord C.', wrote Lady Hester. 'Lord C. certainly does not go to India.'[23] Then a rumour began to circulate that he had secretly travelled to France. It was known that he had friends among French royalist *émigrés* and so the possibility arose that he had become involved in plotting against the former enemy, perhaps even against the First Consul himself. The British government became worried, because whatever schemes they might consider hatching themselves would be compromised and endangered by quixotic freelance activities by the preposterous, violent peer.

Whether or not Camelford had disappeared into France, a general move across the Channel was gathering momentum on all sides. Other naval officers were returning home as their ships were recalled from now peaceful seas; usually they arrived at Portsmouth or Plymouth, where most of their ships' companies were discharged and the officers sent home on half pay. There was, of course, a more cheering prospect for those manning merchant ships, particularly the great West and East Indiamen, whose trading would continue and increase without the impressment of their crews for service in the Royal Navy. It would be different again for those in the murkier reaches of seafaring, such as Captain Johnstone. Now there would be no piloting of military expeditions and raiding parties, or the landing of secret agents on enemy coasts.

There might, however, be scraps of information to sell to the officers in civilian clothes, who visited the ports to ask questions, perhaps about the latest news of Mr Fulton. There was, in fact, little news of Fulton because the trials off Brest had ceased and no stories of the whale-shaped plunging-boat had been passed on by fishermen or smugglers. Johnstone would not have known it, but in Paris the Minister of Marine, Pierre Forfait, who had encouraged Fulton's experiment, had been replaced by a 'blue-water' admiral, Denis Decrès, who had dismissed the American's ideas, saying, 'Go, sir, your invention is good for the Algerians, or corsairs, but learn that France has not yet abandoned the ocean.'[24] His opinion had been supported by the First Consul himself, who declared, 'Bah, these projectors are all either intriguers, or visionaries. Do not trouble me about the business.'[25] But a disappointed Fulton had had to destroy his submarine to prevent French marine engineers from copying it.

So for Captain Johnstone it was back to smuggling and the most promising contraband was now gold, available in the City of London but banned from transhipment to France. Before joining the 'Guinea Run' Johnstone realized that, with the end of the war, plenty of fast ships would be available as revenue cutters, so he evolved a new type of smuggling craft, built to a design based on the Deal galleys. This was some forty feet long, with a beam of seven feet, powered by both sail and oars pulled by between thirty and forty rowers. When pursued by a King's ship, the smuggler could turn into the wind and use oars to escape, and of course he could do the same when becalmed.

French *émigrés* and royalist conspirators no longer needed the likes of Johnstone to smuggle them back into France since amnesties had been declared, such as that of which General d'Arblay had taken advantage. As his wife contemplated the end of her pastoral paradise at West Humble, her neighbours, the French *émigrés* at Juniper Hall, were also packing. Some had already judged it safe to return to Paris; one of the first had been Madame de Staël who was now followed by the Comte de Narbonne.

Alexandre d'Arblay had returned to France in February 1802 to join the expedition bound for Santo Domingo. Fanny was anxious that this would surely mean death by the 'pestilential climate'; her husband had, as she put it in a letter to her father, 'hardly a chance for safety, independent of tempests in the voyage and massacres in the mountains'.[26] It was to be a huge undertaking: an army of 35,000 men and a fleet commanded by Admiral Latouche-Tréville, the victor of Boulogne. Then, a month later she received a letter from her husband giving her the news that he would not, after all, be going on active service because of his refusal to fight against his wife's country.

But Fanny would still have to follow him to France and in April she, accompanied by her child, set out with a heavy heart. She had reserved seats on the Dover coach for the morning of the 13th and boarded it before dawn at the White Bear inn off Piccadilly. Her journey into exile had begun. The coach left London in the dark at five o'clock in the morning so as to reach Dover within a day and next morning they embarked in the Calais packet. Although the sea was calm, Fanny determined to remain on deck throughout the crossing to avoid seasickness. 'Scarcely, however, were we out of the harbour, when my poor Alex was taken sick . . . the contagion of his example so suddenly prevailed that I was compelled to take a side view of the vessel, not to shock the party by a front view of my poor self.' She was helped below and into a hammock, where, she remembered, 'I was unable to utter a single word from a sickness without a moment's intermission that tore me to pieces'.[27] She was becoming one of many discovering for the first time what it was that had protected their country from the invader across the Channel: the sea.

Now, as one Parisian was to put it, 'All the idle captives of the land of fogs shook their damp wings and prepared to take their flight towards the regions of pleasure and brightness.'[28] The travellers were to land on what for nine years had been enemy soil, the lair of bloodthirsty revolutionaries and now of the tyrant who had threatened their lives; within it lay the heart of darkness itself: Paris. Their newspapers had been so filled with reports of massacres that the city still seemed a bloody morass over which stood the guillotine; the beheading machine, which had killed the King and Queen of France and thousands of others – men, women and children of all social classes – had become the symbol of what had once seemed the civilized country across the narrow sea. The caricaturist James Gillray had added the shocking imagery of the guillotine set up outside St James's Palace as an example of what could be expected if Lord Nelson could not save them from invasion.

So at Calais Fanny d'Arblay and her little son hardly dared venture outside, even after being received with courtesy by the port officials and served dinner at a comfortable hotel, while a local band played 'God Save the King' beneath the dining-room windows. She wrote to her father, 'I had not the courage to think of walking in France . . . I had conceived an horrific idea of the populace of this country, imagining them all transformed into bloody monsters.'[29] However, a Scottish officer with whom she had travelled reassured her that 'Calais was in the hands of the English so many years, that the English race there is not yet extinct'.[30] So she ventured out and found 'a very clean and pretty town and so orderly'.[31]

Paris, of course, might be another matter. The road south, running through Abbeville and Amiens, was busy with heavy diligences – coaches slung on wide straps above huge, iron-bound, wooden wheels – and carriages hired by wealthier visitors. Staring out of the windows, the travellers were surprised to see the land well cultivated and the villages neat. One new arrival noted that 'the only buildings that wear a melancholy and ruined appearance are the poor churches, all of which, even in the little villages, have their windows broken, the tops of their spires knocked off and, with most of them, their roofs falling to pieces.'[32]

The peace treaty had been ratified at Amiens on 27 March 1802, three weeks before Fanny had landed, and already the trickle of wary travellers from England was becoming a torrent. The curious wanted to inspect the enemy's heartland, the artistic wished to see the looted treasures of Europe now in the Louvre; the sociable anticipated the ballrooms, dance halls and the two dozen theatres; the morbid sought scenes of horror in the Reign of Terror; libertines, the *cocottes* in the arcades of the former Palais Royal; gourmets anticipated delicate cooking and rare wines; and men of business looked for new, hitherto unexploited trade. Above all, Paris was again becoming a fashionable destination for the rich and the aristocratic; it was estimated that, in that year, two-thirds of the House of Lords arrived, including five dukes, three marquesses and thirty-seven earls.

But it was not only the well-to-do. When the Admiralty halted its shipbuilding programme that spring, unemployed English shipwrights crossed the Channel on hearing that there was work in the French ports. Bonaparte had accelerated his own naval construction and soon Englishmen from Portsmouth, Plymouth and Chatham were at work in dockyards of the recent enemy, not only on battleships and frigates but also on small, sturdy craft, which they may not have known to have been designed to ship French soldiers to English shores.

In October 1801 the First Consul had ordered Joseph Fouché, his Minister of Police, to admit all British citizens, and regular cross-Channel packets began running a month later. For most the journey began in London, where tickets to Paris could be bought for less than £5 at Charing Cross, or in the City. Passengers were advised to bring a picnic for the Channel crossing from Dover of about eight hours, or from Brighton to Dieppe of ten to fifteen; those arriving off Boulogne at low tide had to be carried ashore through the surf by French fishwives. From Calais and Boulogne stage-coaches and three-horse mail coaches now reached Paris in between fifty and sixty hours, while faster carriages, or chaises, were for hire; the British were not allowed to bring their own horses. It was a tiring journey but senses were sharpened by the *frisson* of travelling through a country so recently feared and hated.

The travellers' anticipation mounted on passing the ransacked cathedral at St Denis, where the kings of France had been buried. Roadside cottages multiplied and the road passed the windmills of 'a small village situated on a small hill' named Montmartre.[33] These were the suburbs of Paris, which began well before reaching the peripheral road outside the fortifications of earthworks and four-teen-foot wall, pierced by guarded gateways. That of St Denis, through which the road from Calais ran, opened on to a warren of narrow streets, where 'from a variety of causes, the air was so impregnated that the smell was intolerable'.[34]

On 20 April Fanny's coach rumbled into Paris, through these gates and into streets below leaning cliffs of tall houses and into the terminus at the Rue Notre Dame des Victoires. There her husband, waiting in the expectant crowd, embraced her and their son – 'seized with speechless fondness to his father's breast', she said[35] – and then hurried them into a waiting cab and deeper into the maze of streets. Their destination was the long, straight, quiet Rue de Miromesnil – near the Faubourg St Honoré and not far from the Champs-Elysées – where he had taken rooms.

Another arrival in Paris had been the eccentric and violent Lord Camelford. It was believed that he had entered France illegally, under an assumed name, but his whereabouts were unknown. The French police had feared that he might be involved in one of many plots they knew, or imagined, were being hatched to assassinate the First Consul. But Camelford had proved a slippery quarry, travelling under the name of Rushworth and apparently flitting in and out of Paris and indeed beyond the French frontiers at will. It was said that he was making contact with royalist subversives and that he carried a newfangled repeating pistol capable of firing nine shots without reloading.

It was as important to the British as to the French that General

Bonaparte's life – and so the peace – be preserved, so it came as relief to both when Camelford was finally identified in the arcades of the Palais Royal, gazing into the window of a cutlery shop and then arrested in the Tuileries gardens. Under interrogation he protested that he was a friend of France and had had nothing to do with royalists, or plots. Fouché, the Minister of Police, and the First Consul himself knew, of course, that Camelford was a cousin of William Pitt and had no wish to create a diplomatic crisis at this time. Being unable to prove Camelford's guilt and knowing of his instability, they decided to deport him. He was sent to Boulogne under escort and his arrival in England was reported by *The Times* on the day Fanny d'Arblay arrived in Paris.

But Camelford was to return the following year, surprisingly with a visa. On landing at Calais, however, he made a flippant remark about planning to assassinate the First Consul and officials searched him and found a second passport, again in the name of Rushworth. He was sent to Paris and the Temple prison while his files were reopened. But Bonaparte had no plan to antagonize the British for the time being and Camelford was bundled out of the country as a tiresome eccentric. Within a year he was killed in a duel.

Meanwhile, in the spring of 1802, Paris was becoming crowded with those who a year earlier could never have imagined themselves there.

3

A young man intoxicated with success

FOR THE British visitors Paris came as a surprise. It was smaller than expected. One young Englishman walked round the walls in four and a half hours – including two crossings of the Seine by ferry – and reckoned its circumference as eighteen miles. Within, it was an extraordinary mixture of squalor and splendour, with washing hung out to dry, flapping like banners from poles thrust from the windows of the tall houses, and muddy streets opening on to noble squares, avenues, churches and palaces. Some of the latter were derelict, or occupied by squatters, while others had regained their magnificence under the *nouveaux riches* of the republican and military regime of Bonaparte. There was a surprising amount of open ground within the perimeter – including the Champs de Mars parade ground – and the suburbs sometimes spilled beyond. The smells were different from those of London; while the air of both cities was tainted with sewage, horse manure and unwashed bodies, Paris was scented by cooking, the steam from its kitchens pungent with herbs and garlic.

'The appearance of Paris was to me pleasing', wrote one young Englishman, John Trotter,

> though the narrowness of the streets and the want of footways on each side were unpleasant symptoms of a former disregard to the health and comfort of the people. As yet, no liveries upon servants, or arms upon carriages, were seen; a republic and

46

respectable plainness met the eye, the contrast of glaring opulence and decent mediocrity was not manifest and this agreeable effect of the Revolution remained, whilst returning good sense had also corrected that frightful extreme of slovenliness and negligence of dress, which a republican mania had consecrated as a test of principle and a mark of patriotism.[1]

He had mixed feelings about the sights of Paris, and considered the cathedral of Notre Dame 'venerable but by no means magnificent'. He thought the city looked at its best when viewed from a vantage point such as the top of the Panthéon, from which he admired 'a beautiful panorama of Paris and its vicinity; and, as the air is not loaded and darkened with coal smoke, everything looks distinct and cheerful'.[2]

The society of Paris was as mixed as its architecture. Old friends were reunited, and Fanny d'Arblay was welcomed by several who had been refugees at Juniper Hall. The Comte de Narbonne was a neighbour in their street but, although Madame de Staël called, the d'Arblays were out and had no wish to resume the friendship. She might be a celebrity in Paris – her new novel *Delphine* was an immediate success – but Fanny avoided her company, not so much because of her morals – she had taken another lover – as because she was openly hostile to Bonaparte's dictatorship and renewed intimacy might harm Alexandre's prospects of employment. A particular welcome came from another old acquaintance, the former Princesse d'Hénin d'Alsace (now plain Madame d'Hénin). Fanny told her father that she 'came almost instantly to welcome me to Paris – amply supplying me immediately with tea, sugar, urn, teapot, etc., *à l'Anglaise*'.[3] Moreover she introduced Fanny into the Parisian society composed of survivors from the *ancien régime*, which was as genteel as any in London or Bath.

It was possible, too, to hobnob with former enemies. There was a delicious *frisson* in meeting the fierce and glittering officers of the republican armies, including Murat, Masséna, Kellermann, Marmont and the dashing Androche Junot, the Governor of Paris, nicknamed 'La Tempête'. Even more exciting was to converse with sinister figures such as General René Savary, who commanded the special police guarding the First Consul, and the

Minister of Police, Joseph Fouché. Cruel in looks, with thin lips and hooded eyes, Fouché had during the Revolution attended the massacres in Lyons on horseback with a pair of human ears dangling from either side of his hat.

Of this array the most interesting, it was agreed, was General Jean Victor Moreau, whose father had been guillotined during the Terror but who had himself risen to command the French army in Germany. Moreau was handsome, witty and indiscreet, and one visitor he charmed was Lady Bessborough, the daughter of the first Earl Spencer and sister of Georgiana, Duchess of Devonshire; at forty she was handsome, sharp-witted, cultivated and gregarious. 'I am bound to like and praise Moreau,' she said, 'for he has been very flattering to me',[4] adding, 'his first appearance marks only extreme simplicity, a look of great sweetness and bonhomie . . . When he talks on subjects that interest him (which he does very freely) his countenance animates, his eyes sparkle and he is quite a different creature.'[5] After another meeting she admitted, 'I am accused of having flirted unmercifully with Moreau . . . I certainly had a great deal of very interesting conversation with him for near an hour and I was surpris'd and pleas'd at his talking too much and so freely with me.'[6] Moreau introduced her to his elegant wife and celebrities, including General Jean-Baptiste Bernadotte (the future King of Sweden and Norway) – whose 'tremendous countenance'[7] she noted – and Admiral Latouche-Tréville. There were even rumours that Moreau might see himself as a rival to Bonaparte.

As the hotels – notably the fashionable Grange Batelière and the Richelieu – filled with the affluent English, they also formed their own society, so avoiding problems with language or, for some, worries over fraternizing with the recent enemy. An Englishman named Rudd had been introduced to a woman artist, who was studying under Jean-Jacques David, the most celebrated painter of the new republic, but found that she had been 'the dear friend of Robespierre', the instigator of the Reign of Terror. He was relieved to move into the company of such familiar compatriots as the Whig politician Charles James Fox – the leader of the opposition and and an opponent of war with republican France – and his wife, and Benjamin West, the President of the Royal Academy. 'In short,' he concluded, 'the only Society that is to be had in Paris is English. The race of French gentlemen is extinct.'[8]

Joseph Farington, too, was disillusioned. A landscape painter with alert, perceptive eyes, he watched eagerly for the telling detail and the prevailing moods. 'The French have long had the character of being a gay people', he wrote in his diary.

> That they are volatile is certain; and that they are impetuous and energetic is equally so. But if the French may be said to be gay it is not, in my opinion, to be understood that they are cheerful . . . If I were to judge of the state of the heart from the visage, I should associate with the look little of that complacency and ease which proceeds from content.[9]

Another Englishman, Bertie Greatheed, a robust, shock-headed Warwickshire squire of cultivated tastes, complained of the French he met, 'Is this Society? The old evils are returned, or returning, without the old elegance. Take away the foreigners from this town and what remains?'[10] His social expectations of French officers were not met, despite the splendour of the parades he watched. 'The officers seemed to me just as coarse fellows as the soldiers, I saw no difference; and how should there be since they have arisen from the ranks, which is the reason why they are so tremendous.'[11] He too turned to his fellow countrymen and called on the d'Arblays, who had moved from the Rue de Miromesnil to the cleaner air of the suburban village of Passy on the escarpment above the Seine overlooking Paris. It was peaceful, but even here there was no escaping the city: one of their neighbours, who had taken refuge from the Terror in Passy, remembered that he had 'often in a calm day, or evening, heard distinctly the *chop* of the guillotine'.[12]

In Alexandre d'Arblay, Greatheed found a welcome change from the new breed of French officer, noting that 'the husband of Miss Burney is a pleasant and handsome man, very intelligent and bears a most excellent character . . . They live at Passy very poor and keeping but one maid.'[13] Barred from an active command because of his refusal to contemplate fighting against his wife's country, d'Arblay was lucky to be granted a small pension in recognition of his twenty-six years' service in the army but could only

49

hope for some insignificant administrative post; in the event, this proved to be in the department of the Ministry of the Interior, dealing with buildings, particularly prisons. Yet he was aware that his inhibition had probably saved his life: while the expedition to Santo Domingo had succeeded in suppressing the slaves' rebellion, the cost had been terrible; two-thirds of the expeditionary force of 35,000 men had died, mostly of disease, and many survivors resumed broken in health, among them Admiral Latouche-Tréville. Alexandre at least had his health and his family, if little else.

Not all the visitors formed a low opinion of the Parisians, notably those who remembered the *ancien régime*. Among these was the American Benjamin West, who thought 'the people of Paris appear in a much better state since the Revolution'. Another artist from London added that

> West said that when he was in Paris thirty-nine years ago . . . he found the streets crowded with fine coaches with servants in rich liveries, two, four or six, standing behind on footsteps raised above each other, religious processions moved in every direction; but the mass of the people abject and ragged. Now there appears to be but one order of people, a middle class as they may be called.[14]

The greatest surprise for the visitors was to find that Paris, far from being in a state of shock, was enjoying a reaction to the years of horror and deprivation. Theatres and restaurants were crowded. The British had to learn that, in egalitarian Paris, a waiter's attention in a busy restaurant could not be caught by shouting '*Garçon!*' but by tapping a glass with the blade of a knife. Bibliophiles were excited because, 'The shops now overflow with books; the poverty of the *ancien régime* has brought them to the market and the illiteracy of the *nouveau riche* leaves them there. Were it not for the heavy duties on entering England, this would be the place to stock one's library from.'[15] Visitors were particularly attracted to the windows of the *charcutiers*. One noted that 'these shops contain every cold dainty of the salted or pie kind, game, dried fruits, wines, liqueurs; their turkeys stuffed with truffles, their *pâté aux foix gras* . . . their partridge pies with truffles . . . it really requires some resolution not to be gluttonously expensive.'[16] Those invited to dine at the grandest private houses enjoyed rare imported delicacies: turbot and eels from the Netherlands, pike and perch from the Rhine, game from Provence.

For the young bucks the Palais Royal was a principal attraction. There they could be 'amused by the variety of shops', as one noted:

'Booksellers, jewellers, milliners, shops for blacking shoes with a covered seat and a newspaper to read during the operation, coffee houses, restaurateurs, gaming rooms, night cellars, etc., abound. A narrow piazza runs round three sides of the great square of the building, in which people of all sorts are perpetually moving. Many loose women parade the piazza, who by their dress and manner sufficiently express their character but are under a proper restraint so far as not to interrupt, or molest, or address any person who does not give them encouragement. I was told the police was very strict in this respect.[17]

For most tourists there was a list of half a dozen sights they needed to see: the Tuileries, the Louvre, the Panthéon, the Invalides, the Palais du Luxembourg and the Place de la Concorde, while, for strolling, there were the Champs-Elysées and the Jardin des Plantes. For artists and the artistic the draw was, of course, the Louvre. Benjamin West, Henry Fuseli and Joseph Farington were joined by the portrait painters John Hoppner and John Opie, who complained that Paris was so dazzling in the sunlight that he might have to leave or be blinded, by the sculptor John Flaxman and the collector Samuel Boddington. Deprived of continental art for nearly a decade, they arrived well aware that the paintings and sculptures they would enjoy were not only French, for Bonaparte had filled the galleries with the loot of Italy, where he had particularly admired the heroic statuary of Greece and Rome. They compared and discussed Florentine and Venetian painting far more vigorously than did the French, whose concentration was primarily on the merits of David and his portraits of Bonaparte. West was so excited that he began to discuss plans for young British artists to travel cheaply to Paris for educational visits to the Louvre. It was not only the artists who were thrilled; the young Mary Berry gushed:

> Such a gallery! But such a gallery!!! as the world never saw, both as to size and to furniture! So long that the perspective ends almost in a point, and so furnished that at every step, tho' one feels one must go on, yet one's attention is arrested by all the finest pictures that one has seen before in every other country, beside a thousand new ones.[18]

All were aware that much had been looted. Squire Greatheed recounted how he 'sauntered down to the Seine and saw them unloading, and drawing into the Louvre, large cases of pictures, or statues, of which there are a great quantity in barges still to be housed. Poor Italy! How does this differ from the plunder of *banditti* but the magnitude of it?'[19] In the Place du Carrousel, near the Tuileries, he saw, mounted on the triumphal arch, 'the antique bronze horses, once the pride of Venice'.[20]

Some hired coaches to visit the palace at Versailles to admire the art and architecture and were shocked by what they found. On arrival Greatheed saw, 'Versailles, once the gay, the proud, the brilliant, now a desolation'. Within, he found 'the furniture all sold, except some old porphyry tables and Etruscan vases, etc., which appear to have been overlooked'. There was some consolation in pondering lost glories, musing that 'perhaps there never was a place so much the child of art. Nature was absolutely banished here . . . and it became a magnificent monster, which corrupted the senses and perverted the understanding by pomp and bluster and gaudy trappings.' What was still occupied had been put to different uses: 'the great building, where the officers of the court lived is converted into a manufacture of arms . . . and, close by the Petit Trianon, a very pretty imitation of an English villa built by the late Queen . . . is now a restaurateur's, where we dined.'[21]

English women were fascinated and a little shocked by the prevailing fashions, which favoured diaphanous dresses of classical cut and a display of bosom. Fanny d'Arblay felt frumpish in her English clothes but did not feel, in middle age, ready to conform to the *costume Française* and confessed to a compatriot, 'I gave over the attempt and ventured forth as a Gothic *Anglaise*, who had never heard of, or never heeded, the reigning metamorphoses'.[22] The more sophisticated followers of fashion studied the latest colours of fabrics, such as *Terre d'Egypte*, *Mameluke* and *Fumée de Londres* and a coiffure called *à la Cléopatre*, all inspired by Bonaparte's campaign in the Middle East, as was the opera *Les Mystères d'Isis*. Englishmen admired the fashions and those that wore them, whom the artist Robert Smirke considered 'generally much thinner than the English women', although he 'saw but few such complexions as are common in England and much less beauty'.[23] Their lightness of figure and dress made them graceful dancers and when Farington visited the Tivoli pleasure gardens he noted that, when waltzing, 'the women were light and airy and easy in the motions and their persons, in general well formed for the purpose', whereas their male partners 'appeared in comparison to much disadvantage; inelegant in their dress and as below the class and rank of the women'[24]; although wigs were no longer worn, knee-breeches and shoe-buckles were again in fashion.

Only occasionally could British women rival the French in elegance and sexual allure, for a visiting British officer remarked, 'The Bishop of Durham would expire at seeing the dresses . . . The ladies are almost quite naked . . . There cannot be anything so profligate, so debauched, or so immoral as the ideas or manners of all ranks of people, particularly the higher class.'[25] But the Duchess of Gordon was accompanied by her daughter Georgina, who made up for bad teeth with a fine figure displayed in diaphanous dresses and her grace as a dancer. Soon she was dancing with Bonaparte's dashing stepson Eugène de Beauharnais, and it was said that they were in love. Gossips went far further, hinting that she had her eye on the First Consul himself, and eventually it was reported in *The Times* that

it is certain that some of our travelling Nudes of Fashion intended to conquer the Conqueror of the Continent. What glory would it have brought to this country if it could have boasted of giving a Mistress, or a Wife, to the First Consul. How pretty would sound Lady G – (we mean Godiva) Bonaparte?[26]

It was generally agreed that the most fashionable hostess in the city was the beautiful young Madame Récamier, who regularly held court in her exquisite small house and whose invitations were highly prized. Male visitors were more rewarded than female and Lady Bessborough told a friend

an indelicate story, how distress'd I was at Mad. Récamier's . . . We went there and found her in bed – that beautiful bed you saw prints of – muslin and gold curtains, great looking-glasses at the side, incense pots, etc., and muslin sheets trimm'd with lace, and beautiful white shoulders expos'd perfectly uncover'd to view – in short, completely undress'd and in bed. The room was full of men.[27]

The gaiety was recognized as a reaction to the horrors of the recent past, particularly the Reign of Terror. One excitement was to hear stories of that time, particularly of last-minute escapes from the guillotine. Lady Bessborough was particularly thrilled to hear 'a little, weak old woman' talk 'in the softest voice and gentlest manner' of the slaughter and of having had to 'walk miles surrounded by assassins thro' the streets of Paris'.[28]

Most gruesome of all were the sites of the guillotines. Lady Bessborough remarked 'that shocking place Place de la Concorde with the remains of the guillotine . . . makes my blood run cold'[29] In the Place de Grève, outside the Hôtel de Ville, executions were still carried out, and several visitors chose to watch. Sir Samuel Romilly immediately recognized the scene from Gillray cartoons and mused:

The ideas which the guillotine must awaken in everybody's mind naturally render it an object of horror . . . the large, slanting axe, the hole through which the sufferer is placed, smeared round with a different colour and seeming yet to be stained with blood . . . a most hideous instrument of death.[30]

Greatheed was also a spectator, and then wished he was not. He saw the guillotine, 'the same horrid, dirty thing, which was employed during the whole Revolution and . . . the scaffold on which it stood is of much greater age and has been the theatre of misery for some generations.' The condemned man was a murderer, rather than an aristocrat, but the procedure was the same and the Englishman noted that 'the axe fell with the sound of cutting through a cabbage'.[31]

One story of a remarkable escape from such a death was being told among the visitors about a compatriot, but not one whose company was generally sought. An Englishman with a hooked nose and glittering eyes, who spoke with a Norfolk accent, he was said to have been a provincial stay-maker and to drink too much, particularly in the company of Irishmen – some of them members of the revolutionary United Irishmen Society, of which he was an honorary member – in the Irish Coffee House in the Rue de Condé. This was Thomas Paine, who had achieved international recognition as a radical pamphleteer. An inspiration of American republicanism, his celebrated polemic *The Rights of Man* and his declared admiration for the French Revolution had brought him to Paris, where he had been elected to the Convention. But he had opposed the execution of the King and in 1794 was imprisoned in the Luxembourg and sentenced to death. When prisoners were condemned, gaolers chalked a sign on the doors of their cells, from which they could be collected for the procession of tumbrils to the scaffold. It was said that Paine's door was mistakenly marked on the wrong side, just before he was to be summoned, so that the fatal sign was hidden and the gaolers passed him by. Immediately afterwards Robespierre's regime was overthrown and he himself sent to the guillotine.

Now Paine could sometimes be seen dining out with an American friend. Their conversations were often political, discussing republicanism and touching on theories of free trade and the need to maintain the peace by naval disarmament as well as libertarian topics such as the iniquities of the press-gang. But they also talked about engineering and particularly the use of iron in bridge-building and the construction of ships. This was of interest to Paine, but especially to the American, who was Robert Fulton, the disappointed designer of the submarine. Fulton was still working on this but had another, equally revolutionary, project: the steamboat. When he explained steam power to Paine, and the difficulty of using it in a submerged plunging-boat, the latter suggested that gunpowder might make a suitable propellant. Fulton must have mocked him for years later Paine was to enquire of a mutual friend, 'What is Fulton about? Is he taking a whale to draw his submarine boat?'[32] Paine was to return to America in 1802, leaving Fulton to develop his ideas both for the submarine and for the use of steamships in war.

The more worldly and sophisticated British visitors soon became aware that, although Paris seemed a stable city, there was an uneasy atmosphere. As they were increasingly taken up and entertained by the French, words of warning circulated as to who was regarded with suspicion by the regime, notably by Fouché's agents. Madame de Staël and her circle were still among those best avoided, and several senior army officers seemed dangerously frank in their criticism of the regime.

The vortex of uncertainty and speculation was the new British embassy, housed in the Hôtel Caraman in the Faubourg de Roule, where Lord Whitworth arrived on 14 November 1802 to relieve a temporary chargé d'affaires as the first post-war ambassador. Recently the ambassador in St Petersburg, he was tall, patrician, charming – a long, sharp nose gave him a commanding, inquisitive air – and, thought the French, 'a clever *politique*'[33]; his wife, the widowed Duchess of Dorset, seemed the embodiment of what they expected in a haughty aristocrat, with tight lips and a square, determined jaw. The numbers of British visitors in Paris – many of them influential political, financial and social figures – added hugely to his responsibilities. A particular concern was that they might become involved with French critics, or opponents, of the regime, as had Lord Camelford. Then they might inhibit the double role Whitworth was trying to play. His principal task was, of course, to keep open communications with Bonaparte and his Foreign Secretary, Talleyrand; this was particularly important since, in August 1802, the former was declared First Consul for life and confirmed in his absolute dictatorship. But Whitworth, also secretly, had charge of a key element in the British intelligence network established by William Wickham, who was ostensibly head of the Aliens Office in Whitehall. Both Whitworth's first secretary and his private secretary were experienced intelligence officers, skilled and discreet in watching, listening and enquiring. But there were others who seemed likely to draw attention to such activity.

One was Whitworth's friend the Comte Antoine Viscovitch, who became an embarrassingly frequent visitor to the embassy. He was of Venetian ancestry and was thought to have become involved in espionage while living in Switzerland, from where British intelligence operations were sometimes mounted. Believed to be motivated by a desire for revenge for Bonaparte's extinction of the Venetian Republic in 1797, Viscovitch had moved to Paris and become more deeply engaged, though his personal friendship with Whitworth might be given as the reason for his visits. Then the arrival at the embassy of a new attaché, a British naval officer wearing civilian clothes, increased French suspicions. This was Captain John Wright, who was constantly out and about in the city.

As Fouché and his agents were aware, Viscovitch and Wright were old friends. They had met four years earlier, when Wright and his commanding officer, Captain Sir Sidney Smith, had been in the Temple prison, an unlikely place of confinement for officers of the Royal Navy. They had been taken prisoner in a scrimmage at sea off Le Havre, when Smith had approached the port in an apparent attempt to seize a privateer sheltering there, though perhaps he had had another, more secret, objective. Suddenly becalmed and swept inshore by the tide, the British had been attacked by oared gunboats and finally forced to surrender. Neither Smith nor Wright had been treated as a prisoner of war. Smith, it was known, was, like his brother Spencer Smith, the former minister at Constantinople, involved in what Sir Sidney described as an 'occupation of a superior sort'[34] and, as the French also knew, so was Wright.

At first Captain Wright might have been taken for a conventional officer, a well-educated son of the middle class. Lancastrian by ancestry, he had been brought up in Minorca, the trading island with a deep-water harbour in the western Mediterranean, where his father had been in business involved with military supplies and a paymaster. At the age of ten he had been entered for the army but changed to the navy, which he joined as a 'volunteer' – a boy under training as a potential officer – and he had seen active service at Gibraltar. He had drifted from the navy back to school in the village of Wandsworth, near London, and then found work as a clerk in a City merchant's office. Commerce had taken him to Russia and he had spent five years in St Petersburg, where he became fluent in several languages. On returning to London he had met Sir Sidney Smith, who had earned his Swedish knighthood as a mercenary in the Baltic but had returned to the Royal Navy and who, early in 1794, a year after the outbreak of war with revolutionary France, had been given command of the frigate *Diamond*.

Recognizing Wright's value as an interpreter, and knowing of his brief naval training, Smith had invited him to become his secretary, although at the age of twenty-six only rated as a midshipman. He was to be far more than a secretary, however, his main task being liaison with French royalists ashore. These were the Chouans, dissident countrymen, often peasants and smugglers, angered by the republican government's interference in their lives, but sometimes royalist gentry and sometimes led by ambitious army officers. They had risen *en masse* in the Vendée in the west in 1793 and were being repressed with ferocity. Midshipman Wright was put ashore by Smith to assess their need for arms and to open lines of communication with the coast, but he also travelled far inland and had become involved in fighting in the Vendée.

Then, on 19 April 1796 Smith and Wright had been captured off Le Havre, but whether they were, as they claimed, conventional officers had been questioned. Smith had been accused of planning arson in the dockyard and sent to Paris under armed escort, accompanied by Wright; with them was a manservant, who claimed to be French Canadian but who, as both his companions knew, was a French royalist officer, Lieutenant François de Tromelin, in disguise. They were imprisoned in the Temple, from which King Louis XVI had been taken to execution, and it was feared that Smith was in similar danger. Indeed, Bonaparte was later to say to his doctor, Barry O'Meara, while in exile in St

Helena, that Smith 'was arrested and confined in the Temple as a spy; and, at one time, it was intended to try and execute him.'[35] After two years the prisoners were rescued. French royalists, disguised as republican officers but acting on Wickham's orders, presented a forged order for their transfer to another prison and, once outside the Temple, whisked them into hiding and then to the coast and a waiting British frigate. John Wright had then followed his patron to the Mediterranean and the Middle East.

On 18 March 1803 Whitworth had written in cipher to Lord Hawkesbury, the Foreign Secretary, complaining about this new embarrassment.

Captain Wright arrived this morning by way of Havre with your Lordship's letter of the 16th. I shall, of course, be very happy to avail myself of this gentleman's aid and information. But I fear he is too well known to be of any material service; and I will confess to your Lordship that I am not without apprehension that, in a moment of irritation like the present, it may be recollected that he was a prisoner here and that he escaped from prison. I cannot but help think a less remarkable person, however intelligent Captain Wright may be, might have been equally useful without the risk of adding another *pierre d'achoppement* to the many which we may expect to find in our way. I have, however, told him that he might remain here for the present and see his old friends, if they are willing under the present circumstances to renew their acquaintance – which I very much doubt. For the rest, he has seen nothing at Havre which can be construed into an armament and I verily believe this is the case in every port of France. They doubtless will now begin.[36]

Early in March that year, when Captain Wright had arrived in London from the Mediterranean, Captain Sir Sidney Smith had mentioned his various talents to the Prime Minister, Addington, who had invited them both to lunch. So it was with embarrassment that Sir Sidney had to apologize to Addington that his friend would not, after all, be able to attend, explaining that 'Captain Wright, by this time in Paris, trusts me to make his excuses by thus accounting for him'.[37] What was awkward for Lord Whitworth was that no passport had been issued in Wright's name; he had landed secretly at Le Havre and reached the capital travelling under an alias. There he had entered the embassy and reported to the ambassador, who had hidden his irritation by expressing his 'considerable admiration'[38] for his ingenuity. Whitworth's embarrassment was increased when his unexpected visitor disappeared into the streets of Paris, and was sometimes reported at expatriates' parties and calling at the embassy. Soon Bertie Greatheed was noting after one evening's entertainment, 'I have not had such a pleasant English dinner for some time past', adding that among the company had been 'a Captain Wright of the Navy, who had been two years in the Temple with Sir Sidney Smith'.[39]

Yet when Smith's brother Spencer Smith, now British minister in Württemberg, attended a levee, Bonaparte asked after Sir Sidney, remarking, 'He is a good fellow and a good officer'.[40] Other British naval officers were made welcome, including Nelson's friends Captains Sir Edward Berry, Eliab Harvey and William Hoste; military officers included the two sons of General Abercromby on their way home from Egypt, where their father had been killed defeating the French outside Alexandria. Other British visitors included bankers, merchants, architects, actors, clerics and doctors, including Dr Benjamin Moseley of Chelsea Hospital, who had known Nelson in the West Indies and was still his doctor in London.

But visitors soon became aware of the watchfulness of the regime, even if they could not name the various agencies of security and counter-espionage. Soldiers were much in evidence – 20,000 were said to be quartered in and around the city – and, as John Trotter put it, one had 'above all a knowledge that the system of espionage was carried to an incredible height, making suspicion of the slightest indisposition to government sufficient cause for individuals to be hurried away at night – many of them never to be heard of again'.[41] Yet Captain Wright, despite his air of mystery, continued with what appeared to be a busy social life.

Above all, British visitors to Paris wanted to see the First Consul, the conqueror of Italy and Austria, the invader of Egypt. Although portrayed in English caricatures as a malevolent Corsican dwarf, he towered over Europe. There was no difficulty in seeing the man who had haunted their dreams for so long. Curiosity was mutual: Napoleon Bonaparte was fascinated by the islanders who had fought him with such determination; so intrigued was he by their contradictions that he kept busts of his apparent supporter Charles James Fox and his arch-enemy Horatio Nelson on a mantelpiece. He spoke no English so, to keep abreast of British opinion, he had *The Times* and the *Morning Chronicle* read to him by a translator as soon as they reached Paris. The British were welcomed at monthly receptions in the Tuileries palace and at military parades. Despite this, one of his generals told an English visitor that 'he hates the English from the bottom of his heart'.[42]

Among the first arrivals Fanny d'Arblay was an early guest, and she described the occasion at length in a letter to her father. 'Two human hedges' were formed to either side of the room; there was a hush and then

the door of the audience chamber was thrown open with a commanding crash, a vivacious officer-sentinel . . . nimbly descended the three steps into our apartment and, placing himself at the side of the door, with one hand spread as high as possible and the other extended horizontally, called out in a loud and authoritative voice, 'Le Premier Consul!' You will easily believe nothing more was necessary to obtain attention; not a soul spoke, or stirred, as he and his suite passed along.

Fanny was standing by the door, so had

a view so near, though so brief, of his face as to be very much struck by it. It is of a deeply impressive cast, pale even to sallowness, while not only in the eye but in every feature, Care, Thought, Melancholy and Meditation are strongly marked with so much of character, nay, Genius and so penetrating a seriousness – or, rather, sadness, as powerfully to sink into an observer's mind . . . He has by no means the look to be expected from Bonaparte, but rather that of a profoundly studious and contemplative man.[43]

Another Englishwoman, Mary Berry, was less impressed, finding him

not much like his busts. All I saw was a little man . . . with a sallow complexion, a highish nose, a very serious countenance and cropped hair. He wore the dress of some infantry regiment, blue with a plain, broad white lapel and a plain hat with the very smallest of national cockades in it.[44]

A young English girl – the future Countess Brownlow – was as excited as Fanny d'Arblay had been:

How grand was his face, with its handsome features, its grave and stern and somewhat melancholy expression! A face, once seen never to be forgotten. It fascinated and acted upon me like a rattlesnake, for though a mere child, I felt all the English horror of the man and yet could not look at him without admiration mixed with awe.[45]

The most celebrated British visitor to Paris was an unusual figure: an untidy, blue-jowled, hard-drinking, clever and affable politician aged fifty-two, whom Madame Junot likened to a Devon farmer. This was the Whig leader of the opposition in the House of Commons, Charles James Fox, who had opposed war with republican France. He had arrived ostensibly for some research at the national archives into Jacobean links with France in the seventeenth century for a historical book he was writing. But he was curious to see something of the regime for which he had sympathy and was accompanied by his wife, anxious to see the city reputed to be the 'centre for everything interesting and elegant'.[46] Enjoying Paris that August, they dined in the garden of their hotel and visited the deserted palace of Versailles, noted as a 'grand and, indeed, an awful monument of the ostentation of a haughty dynasty . . . this cumbrous pile seemed little to suit Mr Fox's taste'.[47] He was surprised to be recognized so often in the street, but became aware that the newspapers had presented him as an ally of France. Attending a performance of *Phèdre* at a theatre, he was, as his secretary, John Trotter, reported, 'very soon recognized by the audience in the pit: every eye was fixed on him and every tongue resounded, "Fox! Fox!" The whole audience stood up and the applause was universal. He alone, to whom all this admiration was pain, was embarrassed.'[48]

He was received by Talleyrand, of whom Fox's secretary said, 'there is a want of what is noble and elevated in his air and countenance . . . it is evident, however, that he possesses great acuteness and pliability . . . alert, indefatigable and completely conversant with the ways of men.'[49] Most of the British who met Talleyrand were impressed by his intellect but not his looks: Greatheed described him as 'a nasty-looking dog in a coat embroidered with silver'.[50]

Then, at a reception in the Salle des Ambassadeurs at the Tuileries, Fox met Bonaparte himself. Diplomats and important visitors stood in a semicircle as the First Consul entered, 'a small and by no means commanding figure, dressed plainly, though richly, in the embroidered consular coat – without powder in his hair, [he] looked at the first view like a private gentleman, indifferent as to dress and devoid of all haughtiness', as Fox's secretary noted.[51] English noblemen were presented to him first, and then Fox.

At this Bonaparte 'was a good deal flurried', and, after indicating considerable emotion, said rapidly in French,

Ah! Mr Fox! I have heard with pleasure of your arrival. I have desired much to see you. I have long admired in you the orator and friend of this country, who, in constantly raising his voice for peace, consulted that country's best interests, those of Europe and of the human race. The two great nations of Europe require peace; they have nothing to fear; they ought to understand and value one another. In you, Mr Fox, I see with much satisfaction, that great statesman who recommended peace because there was no just object for war; who saw Europe desolated to no purpose and who struggled for its relief.[52]

Fox remained silent but did reply briefly when Bonaparte asked him about his visit to Paris before passing on. He then questioned a young Englishman dressed in the elaborate uniform of his local militia and, through an interpreter, questioned him about his rank and prospects of promotion.

Fox was particularly shy of the new, smart French society that was beginning to evolve. Persuaded to attend one soirée, he was so overwhelmed by the flattery with which he was received that, a friend reported, 'he look'd round to see if he could jump out of a window, or run downstairs again, but . . . thinking so large a body attempting quick motion might throw the company into confusion,'[53] he remained and found the conversation 'so extremely amusing, so brilliant and clever . . . and so good humour'd, stayed the whole evening and has returned several times since. He says he had no idea Frenchmen could be so pleasant.'[54] Later Fox told English friends that he had thought Bonaparte

> easy and desirous to please without effort . . . In one particular only he noticed the manner of a man who acts as a superior, which was that he sometimes put questions and did not wait for the answers before he proposes other questions. It has been observed that he smiles with his mouth but that his eyes never have a corresponding expression.[55]

A similar impression was made on others. Benjamin West saw the First Consul at an exhibition of French art and noticed that 'though Bonaparte looked at the different objects and asked questions, his countenance expressed that his mind was elsewhere'.[56] John Kemble, the actor, said that 'his face in respect of expression is divided into two characters. The upper part never indicates pleasure but the lower part is often smiling and agreeable.'[57] Farington attended a reception and reported that Bonaparte 'looked me full in the face, which gave me an opportunity to observe the colour of his eyes, which are lighter, and more of blue-grey, than I should have expected from his complexion . . . I thought there was something rather feverish than piercing in the expression of his eyes.'[58]

Fox was to be invited to private meetings with Bonaparte but for the majority of British, who did not attend the receptions, there were regular opportunities to see the First Consul review his soldiers. These monthly parades in the Place du Carrousel outside the Tuileries, or on the Champs de Mars, just across the river from the d'Arblays' house at Passy, were inspected by the general on horseback. Again Fanny wrote to her father:

> Bonaparte, mounted on a beautiful and spirited white horse, was closely encircled by his glittering aide-de-camps and accompanied by his generals, rode round the ranks, holding his bridle indifferently in either hand and seeming utterly careless of the prancing, rearing, or other freaks of his horse . . . he . . . appeared to me as a Man, who knew so well he could manage his Animal when he pleased that he did not deem it worth his while to keep constantly in order what he knew . . . he could subdue in a moment.[59]

But her sensitivity was touched by the implications of the spectacle. 'The review . . . was far more superb than anything I ever beheld,' she wrote, 'but while – with all the "Pomp and Circumstance" of War – it animated others, it only saddened me! – and all of past reflection and all of future dread, made the whole of the grandeur of the martial scene, and all the delusive seduction of the martial music, fill my eyes frequently with tears but not regale my poor muscles with one single smile!'[60] Farington recorded a less fulsome impression after attending a parade inspected by Bonaparte, noting the contrast between the 'very showy appearance and the dress of the officers particularly fine and glittering' and his plain blue uniform with white coat and breeches and 'his hat quite plain with a very small cockade'. As the parade marched past Bonaparte, mounted on his white horse, Farington 'noticed that he picked his nose very much, sometimes took snuff and would take off his hat and wipe his forehead in a careless manner'.[61]

One Parisian admitted, 'Paris was infatuated with the arrival of these foreigners. It was a scramble among all classes to give them the best reception. It was the height of fashion to dine and amuse them and give them balls; the women especially were enamoured of the English and had a rage for their fashions. In short, France seemed to eclipse itself before a few thousand unprofitable foreigners.'[62] Even the First Consul's secretary remarked, 'The appetite for luxury and pleasure had insinuated itself into manners, which were no longer republican, and the vast numbers of English, who drove about everywhere with brilliant equipages, contributed not a little to this metamorphosis.'[63] Paris teemed with the British and, indeed, there were at any one time at least five thousand there.

British women particularly wanted to meet Madame Bonaparte, the beautiful Creole, Josephine. She had been married to the Vicomte de Beauharnais, who had been guillotined during the Reign of Terror and by whom she had a son, Eugène. Becoming the mistress of the revolutionary leader Paul Barras, she had married Bonaparte in 1796. Neither had been faithful during his absence in Egypt but the marriage survived in apparent happiness. The gossip attending these infidelities fascinated the visitors, and one reported hearing the Marquis de Lafayette telling the Comte de Narbonne that Josephine's style and manners reminded him of a rope-dancer, who might be either too high or too low, so that 'only time and practice give them ease and grace', to which the other added, 'provided they don't break their necks in the meantime'.[64] She attended her husband's soirées, but she herself also entertained lavishly at the Tuileries, at his country seat at St Cloud and at her own house, Malmaison, rivalling the beautiful young Madame Récamier herself.

Curiosity was mutual. Fox was an experienced, middle-aged politician and Bonaparte a successful military dictator twenty years younger; each had speculated about the other's motivations. The First Consul sought further meetings with the Whig leader for two reasons. He wanted to assess the depth of sympathy in his party for his plans to redesign Europe. He also needed to discover all he could, albeit obliquely, about conspiracies against him within France, which, he knew, had the tacit approval, or even the active support, of some in or close to the British government. There had long been plots against him, and several attempts on his life, either by French royalists, extreme Jacobins, or military and political rivals. But until Christmas Eve 1800 these had been foiled by the police and secret agents. On that day, as he and his wife had left the Tuileries by coach for an evening at the opera, the road ahead, the narrow Rue Niçaise, had been blocked by a horse and cart.

The commander of the cavalry escort ordered the carter to drive on but, as the cavalcade swept past, the cart exploded. The fuse of the barrel of gunpowder had burnt a fraction too long and the blast failed to destroy Bonaparte's coach, although the passengers were showered with window glass; some twenty passers-by were killed and sixty injured.

Fouché had then uncovered a royalist conspiracy to assassinate him and there were suspicions of links with London, a particular suspect being the Secretary for War, William Windham. Indeed, as the visiting lawyer Giles Romilly remarked two years afterwards, 'everybody here is firmly persuaded that it was suggested and paid for in England. Windham is universally considered as the principal machinator.'[65]

Bonaparte made his accusation on 23 September 1802, when he invited Fox to dine at the Tuileries following another levee. He began with small talk in French and random ideas, including inter-racial marriage, 'doing away with all differences between the inhabitants of the two worlds – of blending the black and white and having universal peace!'[66]; to this end, he added that 'in the East Indies it was right to allow a man several wives and it would be right to allow it in the West Indies, too, on account of the variety of persons.'[67] His mood then changed and he began accusing the British government and, in particular, William Windham and William Pitt, then Prime Minister, of having been plotting against his life. Romilly reported later that Bonaparte 'was astonished at Charles Fox for assuring him that there was not the least ground for the imputation'.[68]

Lady Bessborough reported the exchange in detail. Bonaparte began by saying that he understood Windham's 'talents were mediocre and that he was an unfeeling, unprincipled man'. Fox at once came to Windham's defence but Bonaparte replied, 'It is easy for you who only know public debate. But for me, I detest him [Windham] and that Pitt who together have attempted my life.'[69] 'Mr Fox stared', she continued.

Bonaparte went on saying he would have forgiven open enemies in the Cabinet, or the field but not cowardly attempts to destroy him, such as . . . setting on foot the infernal machine.

Mr F. again with great warmth assur'd him he was deceiv'd, that Mr Pitt and Mr Windham, like every other Englishman, would shrink with horror from the idea of secret assassination. 'You do not know Pitt,' said Bonaparte. 'Yes, I do know him,' replied Mr F., 'and well enough to believe him incapable of such an action. I would risk my head in that belief.' Bonaparte, after a moment, walked away in silence.[70]

Fox had confided in Lady Bessborough, but when his wife asked what had transpired, 'he only answered, "Oh, he was very civil", and immediately ask'd where she left off in the novel they were reading.'[71] However, the First Consul was better-informed than Fox probably realized. Throughout the months preceding the *attentat* the British government – Windham, and even Pitt – had been involved in financing French dissidents and helping transport them to and fro across the Channel. Among these had been two of the principal conspirators, General Charles Pichegru and the royalist Chouan commander Georges Cadoudal. Both had been in London that summer and Windham had written in his diary, 'Georges . . . predicts that Bonaparte will be cut off before two months, though he professes not specifically to know of such intention, seems to think such a course of proceeding legitimate and has thrown out the idea to Pitt as he has before to me. Not necessary to say that no countenance was given to it.'[72]

A month later he recorded a conversation with Pichegru, who 'talked of the design to cut off Bonaparte by assassination and of the general instability of the government, to which latter opinion I felt inclined to assent. On the other hand, having before expressed my opinion, I did not now say anything.'[73] A few days later a third dissident, Chevalier de Bruslart, 'made wild proposals of carrying off, or cutting off, Bonaparte, to which I pointedly declared that a British minister could give no countenance'.[74] Soon afterwards both Frenchmen returned to France taking with them large sums in British gold, leaving Windham and others well aware of their intentions.

Yet after his confrontation with Fox Bonaparte recognized the former's loyalty to his colleagues, and remarked to Louis de Bourrienne, his secretary, who had been present throughout, with a touch of sarcasm, 'Bourrienne, I am very happy at having heard from the mouth of a man of honour that the British government is incapable of seeking my life; I always wish to esteem my enemies.'[75] But he was also to describe Fox as having 'a noble character, a good heart, liberal, generous and enlightened views . . . an ornament to mankind'.[76]

Fox was a patriot as much as a peacemaker and, when one of the First Consul's staff pointed to a globe of the world and remarked that England was but a small country, Fox flung his arms round it, exclaiming, 'Yes, that island of England is a small one but, while Englishmen live, they fill the whole world and clasp it in the circle of their power.'[77] He was happy, however, to discuss peaceful projects with Bonaparte and when told that his host had been reviewing plans for building a tunnel to England under the Channel, cried, 'Oh! this is one of the great things that we will be able to do together.'[78]

Fox led a busy social life in Paris. On one occasion he was invited to a breakfast party by Madame Récamier, together with Lord Whitworth, two visiting duchesses and a variety of British notables, when his hostess was upstaged by Madame Bonaparte. As always, Jeanne Françoise Récamier was bewitching her guests: Fox's secretary, John Trotter, described her as a 'lovely phantom, breathing a thousand delicious charms . . . and so ingenuous and unaffected! Shunning the ardent gaze and, if conscious of her dazzling beauty, unassuming and devoid of pride; rich in the first of female virtues – a kind and noble heart!'[79] Yet breakfast had not finished when there was a clatter of hoofs outside and they were joined by the Madame Bonaparte's dashing son Eugène de Beauharnais, now an army officer. After apologizing to his hostess for arriving late, he turned to Fox, bowed and declared, 'I hope, sir, soon to be enabled in some measure to indemnify myself for the loss of your society I have sustained.' Then he got to the point: 'I am commissioned by my mother to attend you to Malmaison and precede only by a few minutes the carriages destined for you and your friends, when you can resolve on leaving so many charms as must detain you here. I shall have much pleasure in acting as your guide.'[80] With that he swept the cream of Madame Récamier's guests off to dine with Josephine.

At Malmaison, Josephine, as expected, 'made use of all her unrivalled powers of pleasing, which she could so well do without effort' so that Fox, as he later said, 'was enchanted by all he saw and heard'.[81] The young Trotter was less impressed. He noted that she was six years older than her husband, but that 'Madame, the disparity of whose age and appearance and that of the First Consul was ill-concealed by a great deal of rouge', charmed her guests. 'Mr Fox seemed to think extremely well of her. As she loved plants and understood botany, he found it agreeable to converse with her on this elegant and interesting subject. She had enriched Malmaison by a very fine and choice collection of plants.'[82] She had shown him the gardens, which were already revealing the influence of another, very different, English visitor, John Kennedy. He and his fellow horticulturalist James Lee owned the celebrated Vineyard Nursery at Hammersmith,* near London, which specialized in the importation and cultivation of rare and subtropical plants, some from as far away as Australia. When peace negotiations began to succeed in 1801, Josephine had written to Louis Otto of the French mission in London asking to be sent the nursery's latest catalogue. As soon as the peace agreement was ratified, Kennedy himself came to Paris to see Madame Bonaparte; a handsome, cultivated man of forty-two, he soon beguiled her with imaginative plans for her garden, and inspired her to place enormous orders for plants, costing £2600; after returning to England with the orders he sent his son Lewis to Malmaison to supervise the planting.† At first Bonaparte delighted in his wife's love of gardening because, as Bourrienne noted, one of his pleasures was 'to see a tall, slender woman walking beneath an alley of shaded trees'[83] but 'after paying Josephine's debts and the whole of the great expenses at Malmaison'[84] he had second thoughts. Josephine continued to place extravagant orders for plants from the Vineyard Nursery, which so infuriated her husband that he later 'uprooted all her famous plants from Lee and Kennedy'.[85]

Politically, however, the outlook was disturbing. The entente cordiale was no longer reflected in Anglo-French relationships.

---

*Its site is now occupied by the Olympia exhibition halls and railway lines.
†Lewis was to name one of his daughters Josephine.

On his return to London at the end of the year Fox was more wary of French intentions but still inclined to give Bonaparte the benefit of any doubt and, according the diarist Thomas Creevey, 'he talks publicly of Liberty being asleep in France but dead in England',[86] describing Bonaparte as 'a young man intoxicated with success'. Summing up his view of the likelihood of resumed war, Fox told a fellow Whig, 'First, I am sure Bonaparte will do everything that he can to avoid it. Second, that, low as my opinion is of this Ministry, I cannot believe them quite so foolish as to force him to it.'[87] His optimism was not widely shared and most were aware that the sky was darkening.

4

The buzz of war

EARLY IN 1803 return to war seemed inevitable. Neither government was fulfilling the conditions of the peace treaty: the British were suspicious of the French, and with reason as diplomatic reports came from the Mediterranean, the Levant and India of their intrigues with local rulers and their plans for expansion southwards and eastwards. In consequence, the British held back from fulfilling the last of their commitments under the treaty, the evacuation of Malta. This enraged Bonaparte because the strategically important island could become a British base for blocking moves he planned against the Ottoman Empire, the reoccupation of Egypt and then his old ambition to expel the British from India and replace them there. Yet it did not suit him to resume the war at this time because he had not completed his rearmament – particularly the building of major warships and the recall of his fleet from the Caribbean – and nor had he completed the rearrangement of alliances and of continental Europe.

Unease was driven by suspicion and speculation over the First Consul's intentions. While he was complaining that the British had yet to evacuate Malta, he himself had been realigning continental Europe. He refused to withdraw his troops from the Netherlands as he had promised, and in September 1802 annexed the north Italian state of Piedmont, followed by the duchies of Parma and Piacenza. In October he turned his attention to Switzerland, accused the governments of its cantons of hostility,

72

issued an ultimatum and ordered General Ney to invade. The Swiss appealed to the British for help but there was, of course, none that the Royal Navy could offer; only a new European coalition against France could be effective and of that there now seemed no possibility. The German states were dominated too and, with the exception of Malta, Bonaparte seemed to have used the time won by the Peace of Amiens to his political advantage. Yet he had failed in another, vital part of his grand design: rearmament.

Across the Atlantic, British maritime power had indirectly achieved major, if oblique, successes. The disastrous French expedition to Santo Domingo and British naval dominance had shown that the French fleet could not repeat its success in the western Atlantic during the American War of Independence. So Bonaparte realized that in wartime he could not expect to hold territory on the far side of the Atlantic, and that included more than 800,000 square miles of North America, especially as the Americans themselves were hostile to French ambitions on their continent. So early in 1803 he sold Louisiana and the whole Mississippi Valley as far as the Rio Grande and the Rocky Mountains to the United States for $15 million in what became known as the Louisiana Purchase. What had half a century before been seen as New France, stretching from the Gulf of Mexico to the mouth of the St Lawrence, was no more. India was another matter, as the Maratha princes were resisting British expansion and there was always the renewed possibility of a French army reaching the subcontinent overland. The British were powerful at sea but relatively weak on land; much of their strategic reserve was still in Egypt, and Ireland tied down some 20,000 regular troops.

Bonaparte needed more time to rearm and to consolidate his grip on Europe and he was convinced that Addington would not withstand the bullying at which he was so adept. The British feared the same and George Canning, a member of the opposition, called for the return of William Pitt, declaring, 'Whether Pitt *will* save us I do not know; but surely he is the only man that *can*.'[1]

As relations between London and Paris deteriorated, some of the British decided to go home. Already more than ten thousand of them had visited Paris during the peace but few were arriving

now. For Joseph Farington the experience had gradually soured
and when he left Paris in October 1802 he had noted that he 'had
trouble at our hotel before quitting it finally', although the
manager

> did not molest us with further application. He had, in every way
> which he could, fleeced us and, seeing no more was to be got,
> took no further notice of us; but François, our valet, the bed-
> maker and the waiters seemed to strive who should appear the
> most dissatisfied and we left them fully impressed with a feeling
> that if Frenchmen were to be judged by what we experienced,
> gratitude would not be found in the country.[2]

But many remained. In January 1803 the monthly parade in the
Place du Carrousel was held as usual, attended by Generals Junot,
Marmont and Masséna, 'all dressed extremely fine', while the First
Consul, in studied contrast, 'affected extreme simplicity – a hat
without any lace and plain blue uniform and, on the whole, the
look of a sea-captain in undress'.[3] But as he inspected the parade
Lady Bessborough was aware of undercurrents. 'He pass'd slowly
along the line, stopping and talking to many of the soldiers. I do
not know whether it was to save time, or from any apprehension of
danger, but I observ'd that as he came to the end of the line near
where the people stood, he set his horse at speed until he came
within the second line, and so on the whole way.'[4]

At the reception afterwards British visitors were presented to
Bonaparte as usual, but Lady Bessborough noticed that Lord
Whitworth appeared distracted and distant towards his compatriots
and frosty towards the French. Indeed, she was shocked by his
manner, and wrote that he did 'everything to offend and show
every slight . . . and this neglect extends to the English here as well
as to the government', adding, 'from something he said, I cannot
help suspecting their orders are to show slights to the government
here'.[5] The Russian ambassador noticed that Lady Whitworth was
even more icy than her husband, and remarked that he had 'never
seen such cool assurance . . . to say nothing worse'.[6]

Soon afterwards Bonaparte summoned Whitworth to the
Tuileries and demanded an explanation for what he saw as British

hostility. Why had the British not evacuated Malta, as they had undertaken? Why were they alarmed about his supposed designs on Egypt when he had none? Inevitably, Egypt would eventually belong to France but he had no intention of going to war to achieve that. He had nothing to gain by war, he declared. But if Britain was bent upon it – as the vilification of himself in the London newspapers and the hospitality given to royalist *émigrés* seemed to show – he gave a warning. France now had half a million men under arms and another half-million ready to be mobilized: these could crush the puny British. This bullying continued for two hours until Whitworth explained that the British government had a right to be concerned over French expansion in Europe. Bonaparte brushed this aside, describing Piedmont and Switzerland as 'two miserable bagatelles'.[7] When Whitworth withdrew, he knew what to expect.

Warned by their ambassador, the government in London ordered him to inform the First Consul that the evacuation of Malta was the only condition of the peace agreement that they had not fulfilled but they would do so if he honoured his undertaking by promising to abandon his expansion in Europe and the Mediterranean. By now thoroughly alarmed, the British began to rearm and on 8 March ordered the immediate recruiting of 10,000 more men for the navy. Five days later the climax of tension exploded in Paris. That month at one of the First Consul's customary levees at the Tuileries Lord Whitworth was, as usual, present to introduce British visitors. Then, as the ambassador told the Foreign Secretary in his dispatch, Bonaparte 'accosted me, evidently under very considerable agitation . . . He immediately said, "So you are determined to go to war." "Premier Consul," I replied, "we are too sensible of the advantages of peace".' The argument continued, in French, with Bonaparte replying, 'But now you mean to force me to fight for fifteen years more!' Turning to the Spanish and Russian ambassadors near by, he declared that the British were untrustworthy, then seemed to threaten Whitworth with his cane, shouting, 'If you arm, I shall arm, too! If you fight, I shall fight also! You think to destroy France; you will never intimidate her!' The ambassador protested that Britain only wanted to live in peace and Bonaparte shouted, 'Then you should respect treaties! Bad luck to those who cannot respect treaties!' Whitworth concluded his report, 'He was too agitated to make it advisable to prolong the conversation; I therefore made no answer and he retired to his apartment, repeating the last phrase.'[8]

The scene was witnessed by British guests and one, George Douglas, spoke to Whitworth later and reported that,

> Bonaparte either was, or pretended to be, in a rage. Never, throughout his life, a gentleman in his feelings or conduct, he now outraged a ceremony and a time of courtesy, coming up to Lord Whitworth and addressing him in the loudest tones of anger and even with gestures which suggested the possibility of an assault. Lord Whitworth was a tall, handsome man with great dignity of manner. He stood perfectly unmoved whilst the Little Corporal [Bonaparte's nickname] raged and fumed beneath him – now and then saying a few conciliatory words as to the desire of his government to secure an honourable peace. Yet so violent was the demeanour of Bonaparte that Lord Whitworth was compelled to think what he ought to do with his sword if, in his person, the Majesty of England was to be publicly insulted by an actual assault.[9]

This was a signal for a further exodus. Others, such as Bertie Greatheed, heard 'the buzz of war, the ambassador is selling horses and the Duke of Bedford says he goes on Wednesday'[10] and that Lord Granville had already left for Calais, but he hoped for the best and decided to stay. Whitworth himself took the outburst as a sign of weakness and continued to negotiate for a peaceful outcome. The continued British occupation of Malta being the principal French complaint, the ambassador now offered to accept a lease of ten years on the island, followed by evacuation. This was unacceptable to Bonaparte, who responded to British rearmament, and the stationing of Admiral Cornwallis's Channel Fleet off Brest, with the threat of reactivating his plans to invade across the Channel. Five hundred troop-carrying barges were ordered to the northern French and the Dutch ports while the British received reports of troop movements along the French coast. Bonaparte was still playing for more time, if only enough for his fleet to return from Santo Domingo, and he now staged what he believed to be a diplomatic coup. He persuaded the Tsar of Russia to offer mediation over Malta; since Russia seemed Britain's only potential ally on the Continent, the latter would surely be loath to refuse point-blank and this would gain time.

The British reaction was unexpected. On 10 May Lord Whitworth received orders from London to bring the crisis to a head: if the French did not agree to the British terms, he was to leave Paris in thirty-six hours. As Greatheed heard the news he noted that it 'fretted me and unhinged me a great deal . . . everything concurs to hasten us away', but he added, 'This day the rumour of peace is more strong than ever about Paris, why and wherefore I know not.' The city was almost empty of foreign visitors and, he continued, 'Now that the strangers . . . have done with their fine balls, all the gaieties have vanished.'[11] But still he lingered and, on the 12th he visited the d'Arblays at Passy, where, he wrote in his diary, he found Alexandre

> in great uneasiness. She [Fanny] had retired to her room, he was in the greatest agitation. This approaching war seems quite to overset them so linked are they to both countries that to separate from either is ruin and to hold both impossible. It was the most extraordinary first visit I ever made and affected me much; particularly as I am not able to assist. They have a nice little dwelling with a beautiful view of Paris, one maid their only servant, I believe; a fine boy was in the room. It is sad pity these modest domestic comforts should be disturbed.[12]

Fanny had just been writing to her father about 'the anguish of suspense and terror'[13] and to her sister Esther, 'How well do I know what you will feel for us at this cruel moment! I am so shaken, I can hardly hold my pen, for I had entertained hopes to this last . . . such here has seemed the unwillingness to renew hostilities and such has been my confidence in the love of peace and wish for it in England.'[14] Now her British friends were calling to say farewell, and she knew that she and her little family could not leave.

Security grew tighter and the remaining British were aware of being watched. One girl complained that Bonaparte 'has ears everywhere; I believe he spies on one's thoughts'.[15] But one particular Englishman was preparing to leave Paris: the elusive Captain Wright. He was seen at an expatriates' party in the city but then disappeared as mysteriously as he had arrived. He was, in fact, making his way secretly to Calais, accompanied by a friend from the embassy, Robert Clifford, and a huge, locked chest weighing more than two hundredweight. On 17 May they were able to embark, but with more risk than had attended Wright's arrival. They landed at Dover, where they were waved through by customs officers after Clifford presented an order from the Treasury that the chest was not to be opened until it reached London. There it was unlocked and shown to contain a large quantity of secret plans, maps and documents.

Bonaparte was still playing for time for he needed some weeks to redeploy his fleet, so on 10 May Talleyrand sent Whitworth another proposal: that the British should leave Malta, which would then come under the trusteeship of Russia. This was unacceptable. On 12 May the ambassador finally lost his cool detachment and wrote an exasperated note to Lord Hawkesbury:

> I have been delayed much longer than I wished by the infamous chicanery and difficulties which have occurred. I shall, however, set off in half an hour . . . I shall in all probability be at Calais on Sunday and I hope to find the packets ready to take me over immediately. I am so hurried and tormented that I scarcely know what I write. I shall not rest till l get out of this bustle, which has already lasted too long.[16]

As soon as he reached London, the Cabinet met and Parliament was informed of the only possible outcome. On 18 May 1803 Britain again declared war on France.

Ironically, Bonaparte had sought war but was not ready for it, while the British had hoped for peace and were ready to fight. Action began almost immediately when the Royal Navy captured two French ships. Bonaparte was furious and issued a shocking order. He summoned General Junot, the Governor of Paris, and ordered, 'All Englishmen from the age of eighteen to sixty, or holding any commission from His Britannic Majesty, who are at present in France shall immediately be constituted prisoners of war. I am resolved that tonight not an Englishman shall be visible in the most obscure theatre, or restaurant in Paris.'[17] Nothing like this had been experienced before, and at first those at risk could not believe the news. The next day Greatheed wrote in his diary, 'Went for my passport for England and was informed we were all prisoners of war and [to be] sent to Fontainebleau in twenty-four hours on parole.'[18] He at once appealed to Junot, with whom he had made friends, and was granted permission to remain in Paris, albeit under nominal arrest. Hundreds of others were rounded up, among them John Kennedy's son Lewis in the gardens of Malmaison. Even Lord Elgin was arrested, despite his diplomatic status as the ambassador returning to London from Constantinople. Women and older and younger males were not affected, and women had the choice of staying with their men, or returning to England, leaving some 500 of them under arrest in Paris alone.

Not all those detained were travelling gentry; also interned were students, visiting tradesmen, artisans and even the shipwrights who had been working on French slipways. Nobody seemed to know how many were sent to detention centres; Bonaparte claimed that 7500 had been interned but the actual number was found to be about 700, of whom 400 were merchants and tradesmen.

Their future seemed bleak because it might involve worse than internment. As the British minister to the Electorate of Saxony wrote home, they faced 'a long, tedious and unjust captivity under a madman, who considers them as hostages in his hands of which he will take advantage in any future rebellion in Ireland by declaring that he would put them to death for every Irish rebel who may be executed'.[19]

A few made lucky escapes. The 26-year-old Duke of Argyll had been in Geneva, which was under French control, but had moved closer to the Rhine and the border of the German state of Baden. Hearing that he was to be arrested but could remain moderately free within French territories if he gave his parole, he refused to do so. With the help of a French woman friend, he dressed as a maid-servant and hid in thick woodland near the border. After dark she drove past in her carriage, the coachman sounded his horn and

Argyll hitched up his skirts, scrambled out of the undergrowth and joined her to cross the frontier, undetected, as her *fille de chambre*.

After five more months in Paris the well-connected Bertie Greatheed was, thanks to his friendships with General Berthier, the Minister of War, General Junot and Talleyrand, finally allowed a passport to cross into Germany, from which he could make his way to England. When he reached the Rhine he noted,

> We felt extreme pleasure in crossing it. It seemed as if a load of dependence was taken off our shoulders; we are no longer liable to the caprices of a wayward despot, nor the obsequious moroseness of his creatures in office, both civil and military. We have now been for five months without claim, or right, in a state of uncertainty and exposed to every insult. I hope never to experience a similar situation.[20]

Those who straggled back to England at the outbreak of war felt a similar relief and echoed the feelings of Joseph Farington, as he had landed on the beach at Brighton and made his way to the Old Ship inn. 'In coming from disorder to order; from confusion to convenience; from subjection to freedom', he wrote, 'all appeared appropriate and substantial and every man seemed respectable because his distinct and proper character was consistently maintained. What must be the nature of that mind that would not feel grateful that it was his lot to be an Englishman; a man entitled from his birth to participate in such advantages as in no other country can be found.'[21] He had travelled with an American, who had been staying in France, Italy and Germany, and whom he now reported as saying that 'each of the countries had something to be admired and something to be approved, but there was but One England in the World'.[22]

In May and June 1803 the vortex of warlike activity in London was the Admiralty in Whitehall. Through the arch of the elegant stone screen built by Robert Adam and between the great pillars of the portico, poured a stream of naval officers seeking employment. Most had been on half pay for more than a year; others had come up from their ships at Portsmouth, Plymouth or Chatham in the hope of even more desirable appointments, or commands. They

A. STOPPAGE to s STRIDE over the GLOBE

1. The Great Terror: Napoleon Bonaparte, First Consul of France, seen in a cartoon of 1803 bestriding the world. 'Ah, who is it that dares interrupt me in my progress?' he demands. From the British Isles, a tiny figure replies, 'Why, 'tis I, little Johnny Bull, protecting a little spot I clap my hand on and d—n me if you come any farther, that's all.'

2. Attacking and losing: Vice-Admiral Viscount Nelson, commanding counter-invasion forces at sea, drawn by Henry Edridge

3. Defending and winning: Contre-Amira Vicomte Louis de Latouche-Tréville, Nelson's opponent at Boulogne; after V. Adam

4. Nelson's defeat: the fierce but fruitless British attack on the French ships moored off Boulogne on the night of 15 August 1801; engraved after Louis-Philippe Crépin

5. Peace at last: the residence of the French minister in London, Louis Otto, in Portman Square illuminated to celebrate the news of peace in October 1801

6. The road to Paris: a coaching inn at Calais, through which most British visitors travelled on their way to the French capital

7. The attraction: the British longed to see Napoleon Bonaparte, their enemy for so long. This portrait was brought home from Paris by John Kennedy, the horticulturalist, and his son

8. An early arrival: Fanny Burney, the novelist, and her son followed her French husband, General d'Arblay, to Paris; painted by Edward Burney

9. The visiting squire: Bertie Greatheed brought his blunt British attitudes to the exotic Parisian scene; painted by William Artaud

10. The visiting artist: Joseph Farington, RA, landscape painter and diarist, viewed the Parisians with a sharp artistic eye

11. The robust rebel: the Breton leader Georges Cadoudal, who was determined not only to overthrow Bonaparte but also to kill him; after a portrait by Gautier

12. The charming turncoat: the popular and successful General Jean Moreau, whose true loyalties left everybody guessing; after J. Guérin

13. The arrest of General Charles Pichegru in Paris early on 28 February 1804: the third of the counter-revolutionary leaders, he, like Cadoudal, had travelled to France from London

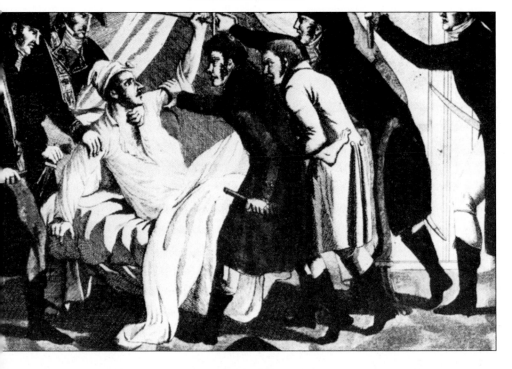

14. Naval officer and intelligence agent: the gallant Captain John Wright, who landed the dissident French generals in Normandy and paid a high price; after G. Galleia

15. Intelligence agent and naval officer: Captain Sir Sidney Smith, who divided his career between the Royal Navy, espionage and diplomatic intrigue

16. The capture of Captain Wright: attempting to rescue escaping rebels, his brig the *Vencejo*, becalmed off the coast of Brittany, was taken by the French on 7 May 1804

17. Treason in England, too: Colonel Edward Despard after his arrest in London with his fellow-conspirators on 16 November 1802

18. Lord Nelson in civilian dress such as he wore at the trial of his former friend, Colonel Despard; painted by Heinrich Füger

19. Conspirators arrested in the back room of a London tavern, as depicted by George Cruikshank in his drawing 'A Radical Parliament!'

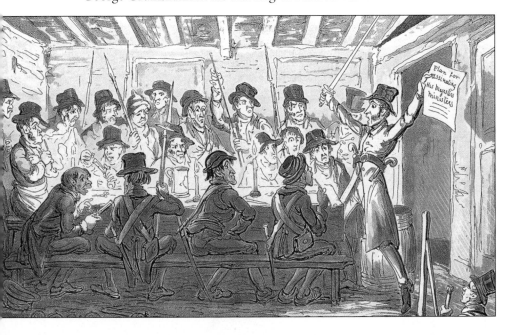

20. The pioneer: Robert Fulton, the American inventor of the submarine and the torpedo, who offered his weaponry to the highest bidder; after a drawing by Chappel and Emmett

21. The rogue: Captain Tom Johnstone, smuggler, pilot, spy and Fulton's collaborator and successor in British submarine development; regarded as both hero and villain

22. The deadly invention: Fulton's submarine the *Nautilus*, seen submerged and on the surface under sail in this late nineteenth-century engraving

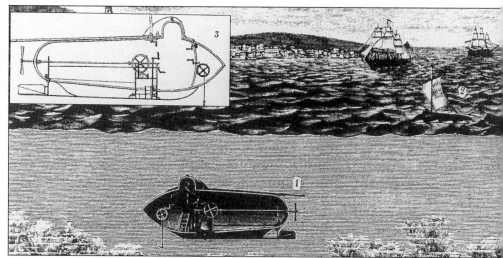

23. Conventional defence: a typical British gunboat under Nelson's command in 1801, the *Scourge* mounted a long 24-pounder gun in her bows and three short-range carronades

24. Conventional attack: boarding parties from British frigates 'cutting out' a French brig off Brest from under the guns of shore batteries in 1801

Le Camp de droite à Boulogne

25. The threat: Napoleon Bonaparte inspecting infantry of the Grande Armée on the cliffs east of Boulogne in 1803. Beyond can be seen the pavilions of his forward headquarters and the line of moored warships off the harbour mouth

26. La Gloire on parade: the Emperor Napoleon presented 2000 soldiers with the Légion d'honneur at a huge ceremonial parade near Boulogne on 16 August 1804, which was watched from distant British frigates; after a painting by Raffet

27. Off parade: soldiers of the Grande Armée settling into their camps along the Channel coast, which Napoleon considered a well-placed holding ground either for an invasion of England or for an advance into central Europe; after Joseph Bellangé

28. 'Little Ships, or John Bull Very Inquisitive': as war seems
imminent in 1803, John Bull asks Bonaparte about the 'thumping
in your workshop' and is told 'Don't be alarmed, Johnny, I am only
making a few little ships for my own private amusement.'

29. 'Boney's Peep into Walmer Castle': a cartoon of 1803 shows
Colonel William Pitt of the Cinque Ports Volunteers confronting an
inquisitive Bonaparte, who declares, 'I know his tricks of old!' Walmer
Castle was the forward base for clandestine operations against France

30. The defender: Lieutenant-General Sir John Moore, commanding the Light Brigade at Shorncliffe in Kent

31. The volunteer: Major Rolleston of the Loyal Pimlico Volunteers, a Londoner among the many civilians who took up soldiering

32. The militia: reserve soldiers of the Staffordshire Militia, drafted south in support of the regular army, at Windsor Castle

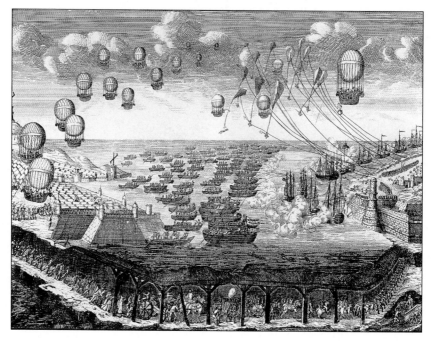

33. Pessimism: fearing the worst, the British imagined French invaders arriving in swarms of landing craft and even by a tunnel under the Channel or by balloon, as is shown in this French cartoon

34. Optimism: the British could also imagine the rout of the invaders and a humiliated Napoleon paraded in triumph through London, as in this cartoon in which a bystander cries, 'We may thank our Volunteers for this glorious sight!'

35. The Grande Finale: fears and rumours evaporated when Nelson engaged the combined French and Spanish fleets off Cape Trafalgar on 21 October 1805. The note of sublime triumph is captured in J.M.W. Turner's great painting of the battle

36. 'John Bull Exchanging News with the Continent': the victorious British broadcast the news of the 'Total Defeat of the combin'd Fleets of France and Spain', as shown in this contemporary cartoon

37. 'The Death of Nelson': even the caricaturist James Gillray solemnly reflected the loss of the nation's hero at Trafalgar, but he was unable to keep a totally straight face, showing Emma Hamilton as a distraught Britannia, King George as a grieving captain and the Duke of Clarence as a cheering sailor

crowded into the waiting-room off the entrance hall, sending messages to whichever senior officer or official they hoped might remember them, and their social, political or regional connections.

Two officers who entered the cobbled courtyard and the stately building beyond did not expect to join the crowd in the waiting-room. One was Vice-Admiral Viscount Nelson, who was ushered straight into the presence of the First Lord of the Admiralty, Admiral Earl St Vincent, at whose invitation he had called. The other was Captain John Wright, who had come to enquire about his next employment, a decision that would be made not only by naval officers in the Admiralty but also by others without naval rank in the discreet rooms of the Aliens Office near by.

Lord Nelson had arrived from Merton Place with mixed feelings. Since he had come ashore at Deal a year and a half before, his life had been a bizarre amalgam of the idyllic, the sad, the extravagant and the epic. The idyllic had been generated by his fulfilled love for Emma Hamilton, with whom he had been living, ostensibly as a friend of her and her husband. Their daughter, Horatia, could not be acknowledged as their child but only as a ward, living with a nurse in London and occasionally brought to visit them at Merton. While Sir William occupied his time fishing in the ornamental canal they called 'the Nile', the nearby Wandle, or the Thames, sometimes staying at the house he had rented in Piccadilly to attend meetings of the Royal Society, and visiting Mr Christie's saleroom, Nelson and Emma played out their fantasy as rural gentry. Her first ambition for her lover's political career had faded with the realization that those waters were too deep and treacherous for him; henceforth he would speak in the House of Lords only on naval and maritime affairs.

There had been the enjoyment of extravagance. As a clergyman's son, brought up in a simple Norfolk parsonage and then in cramped, wet ships of the Royal Navy, Nelson was still dazzled and impressed by the opulence he had encountered in the Hamiltons' residence and the Palazzo Reale in Naples. At Merton, Emma had recreated this for him; and his sophisticated friend Lord Minto described how 'the whole house, staircase and all, are covered with nothing but pictures of her and him, of all sizes and sorts, and representations of his naval actions, coats of arms, pieces of plate in his honour, the flagstaff of *l'Orient* [the French flagship at the Battle of the Nile] – excess of vanity, which counteracts its purpose'.[23] This had been the setting for Emma's lavish entertaining, about which Sir William complained: 'I by no means wish to live in solitary retreat, but to have seldom less than twelve or fourteen at table, and those varying continually, is coming back to what became so irksome to me in Italy.'[24]

There was a dark side to the bright scene: the shadow of Nelson's rejected wife, Fanny. A few weeks after his arrival at Merton she had written to him, saying:

> The silence you have imposed is more than my affections will allow me and in this instance I hope you will forgive me in not obeying you . . . I have now to offer for your accommodation . . . a comfortable, warm house. Do, my dear husband, let us live together. I can never be happy until such an event takes place . . . Let everything be buried in oblivion, it will pass away like a dream.

He had resealed the letter and given it to his agent, Alexander Davison, to return with the inscription, 'Opened by mistake by Lord Nelson, but not read'.[25] He hoped that this would be the end.

There had been much happiness, too. The summer had been memorable for the tour by what Nelson described as the 'Trio Juncta in Uno' of southern England, Wales and the Midlands. Ostensibly, the purpose of this had been to visit Sir William's estate in Pembrokeshire but it became a triumphal progress. It began at Oxford with honorary degrees for Nelson and Sir William and an honorary Doctorate of Divinity for William Nelson; then on to the Forest of Dean for a professional look at the stands of ship-building timber; next Ross-on-Wye and downriver to Monmouth, which was the greatest triumph of the tour. The trio proved such a success that the town worthies persuaded the party to return from Pembrokeshire via Monmouth for a civic banquet. There Emma sang patriotic songs in her loud and resonant voice with new words, appropriate to the West Country, to the tune of 'Rule Britannia'.

> Come hither all ye youths of Bath,
> Whose bosoms pant for glory . . .[26]

Nelson rose to praise the patriotism of the local youth:

If ever war was again to take place, I would send every ship, every Regular soldier out of the Kingdom and leave the nation to be protected entirely by the courage of her sons at home. Suppose the French were to land in England, they might plunder and destroy a village, they might burn Monmouth, but I will engage for it they never would advance as far as Hereford for they would always find Britons ready to receive them.[27]

This was a useful speech as it could be adapted to wherever it was delivered.

They returned through the Midlands, where they ordered a large dinner service painted with Nelson's coat of arms from the porcelain factory at Worcester. In Birmingham they attended a gala performance at the theatre at which a song was sung, ostensibly to celebrate peace with France:

> We'll shake hands: if they won't, why, what then?
> We'll send our brave Nelson to thrash 'em again!

The son of the theatre's manager noted that, 'The crowded house was frantic in its applause at this sublime effusion. Lady Hamilton laughing loud and, without stint, clapped with uplifted hands and all her heart and kicked her heels against the footboard of the seat, while Nelson placidly and with his mournful look (perhaps in pity for the poet) bowed repeatedly to the oft-repeated cheers.'[28] Then it was home to Merton.

Not all Nelson's public appearances were so successful. In June 1802 there had been the subscription dinner at the London Tavern in the City to raise money for a naval orphanage, at which there had been another guest of honour, his former *bête noire* Captain Sir Sidney Smith. Rising to address the 200 diners, Nelson spoke briefly, 'thanking them for their attention to these brave men, who had died in the service of their Country', as the *Naval Chronicle* reported; the orphanage was 'an institution that could not fail, for it must be grateful to the Deity, who would bless and prosper so charitable an undertaking'.

At this point, however, he was upstaged by the officer who had ridden up Whitehall to the Admiralty in Turkish robes and turban. The report continued that Sir Sidney had spoken of the orphans' dead fathers, saying that 'unfortunately for him, too many were in the list of his dearest friends. (Here Sir Sidney's feelings were too great for utterance – his head sunk – the big tear rolled down the hero's cheek.) A solemn silence prevailed for several minutes and soft sympathy filled many a manly bosom, until Sir Sidney was roused by the thunder of applause which followed.' He finally sat down to more applause, the choir sang 'Rule Britannia' and the national anthem, and a choirboy recited a poem beginning,

> Ah! not in vain, their gallant blood they shed,
> Since British bounty shrinks not from the dead . . .[29]

Nelson put a brave face on it, congratulating Smith and inviting him to visit him at Merton.

There had been causes for sadness too. In March 1802 Nelson's father, the Reverend Edmund Nelson, the elderly Norfolk parson, had died. He and his son had recently been reunited, since the latter's abandoning of his wife a year before had threatened to alienate them. The old man had remained loyal to Fanny and even suggested that they might live together, although she had demurred on the grounds that this would cause a break with his son. Eventually Edmund, while remaining friends with Fanny, had accepted an invitation to stay with Nelson and the Hamiltons at Merton. This had been only a qualified success, with Emma seeing his presence as a threat and almost an accusation, despite his tact. He had resumed to Bath, fallen ill and died. Nelson had been kept informed of his declining health but had not visited him. He had also given detailed instructions for the funeral in Burnham Thorpe and the burial itself, but he had not attended, giving his own poor health as an excuse. He had presumably kept his distance because he feared that he might meet Fanny, either in Bath or at the graveside.

Most events during the fourteen months of peace had been predictable, or nearly so. But in November 1802 something had happened that nobody — least of all Nelson — could have foreseen. Like all in public life, he had been concerned by the subversive political undercurrents that occasionally broke surface — most spectacularly with the great naval mutinies of 1797 and the Irish rebellion a year later. He himself had long been aware of the danger and, shortly before his five years' unemployment in Norfolk had been ended by recall to duty in 1793, he had written a long letter to the Duke of Clarence on the subject. Describing in detail the hard life of rural labourers and blaming their plight on their employers, he had nevertheless urged that inns which allowed 'improper Societies' to meet on their premises should lose their licences. He also advocated the arrest of agitators, particularly the radical Presbyterian minister Joseph Priestley, who had been active in East Anglia.

In November 1802 Nelson was as startled as all newspaper readers in London to see a report in the *St James's Chronicle*. This read:

> It is with much regret that we have to state that Colonel Despard and his associates have been apprehended for a conspiracy of the most atrocious and shocking description. Colonel Despard appears to have been at the head of the plot . . . One of the Bow Street officers at the head of a strong party of the London, Surrey and Kent patrols . . . proceeded on Tuesday night, about a quarter after nine, to the Oakley Arms in Oakley Street, Lambeth, where they found Colonel Despard and 32 labouring men and soldiers, English, Irish and Scotch; the whole of whom they took into custody . . . The leading feature of the conspiracy is of so shocking a description that we cannot mention it without pain and horror. The life of our beloved Sovereign, it appears, was to be attempted on Tuesday next by a division of the conspirators, while the remainder were to attack the Tower and other places.

Then details emerged. The plot had been nationwide. The Guards stationed at the Tower of London and Windsor Castle were said to have been subverted and planned to mutiny, seize weapons from armouries and storm St James's Palace and the Bank of England. They even intended to kill the King. The huge Turkish cannon brought back from Egypt and displayed on Horse Guards Parade was to be loaded with chain-shot and grape-shot and, as the King passed on his way to open Parliament, it was to have been fired at his coach. Their leader had been a Colonel Despard.

Nelson remembered a Captain Despard with whom he had shared a tent in the Nicaraguan jungle twenty years earlier, during the abortive campaign to cut Spanish America in two from the Caribbean to the Pacific. That Despard had been an ardent, patriotic officer. Surely this could not be the same man? During those twenty years Despard had become a minor colonial governor but then been recalled to London for a disciplinary enquiry, which was never resolved. Embittered, he had met dissident groups, the London Corresponding Society, the United Irishmen (Despard was part-Irish and brought up in Ireland) and the United Englishmen. For the last five years he had been active in expanding the conspiracy and a final meeting had been held in Lambeth on 12 November. The conspirators had been betrayed and police officers stormed the Oakley Arms. Despard was taken to Newgate prison.

That this was the man Nelson had known was proved when, soon afterwards, he wrote to Nelson, asking him to testify on his behalf in court. Nelson noted that he had been 'subpoenaed by him for a character . . . I could not resist'.[30] The trial began on 7 February 1803, and Lord Nelson was called to the witness box to see the ravaged face of his old friend looking at him. Asked whether he had known Despard, Nelson replied that he had, twenty years earlier. 'No man could have shown more zealous attachment to his sovereign and his country than Colonel Despard did', he continued, 'I formed the highest opinion of him at that time as a man and as an officer . . . If I had been asked my opinion of him, I should certainly have said. "If he is alive, he is certainly one of the brightest ornaments of the British Army".'[31] It was a courageous testament on behalf of a traitor and intending regicide.

Despard and six others were found guilty and sentenced to be hanged, drawn and quartered. Shortly afterwards the portrait painter Thomas Lawrence reported that when a friend had visited the Hamiltons' house in Piccadilly, 'Mrs Despard was in another room in great distress. She came to urge Lord Nelson to make further applications to Government for Colonel Despard.'[32] He did take action, but the sentence was only reduced to one of hanging followed by decapitation after death. Nelson tried to help Despard's Afro-Caribbean wife and Lord Minto wrote, 'Mrs' Despard . . . was violently in love with her husband . . . Lord Nelson solicited a pension, or some provision for her, and the Government was well disposed to grant it.'[33] In the event, the reformist MP Sir Francis Burdett gave her money and paid her fare to join the Despard family in Ireland.

The Despard melodrama had occupied Nelson briefly but intensively, yet he had been well aware that war was coming again. The Prime Minister was a friend and he tried to stiffen his resolve. He had made an encouraging speech in the House of Lords, stressing that the French expansion on the Continent must be countered and applauding the government's determination to 'pay due regard to the connection between the interests of Europe and the liberties of this country'.[34] Visiting Downing Street, he illustrated his ideas with the poker in the fireplace, telling Addington that if Bonaparte insisted that it lie in one direction it was vital – and here Nelson moved the poker – to make sure that it lay in another. There were more encouraging visits to the Admiralty and Nelson realized that it was time to put his private affairs in order. Sir William Hamilton died on 6 April in the arms of his wife and holding her lover's hand. But the untrammelled domestic bliss Nelson might have enjoyed with Emma and their daughter – Sir William had paid Emma's debts in his will and left her an annuity of £800 – was likely to be cut short.

On 14 May, four days before war was declared, it was announced that Admiral Nelson had been appointed to the command in the Mediterranean. There was just time for his daughter to be christened Horatia Nelson Thompson – the *nom de plume* he and Emma had used in their private correspondence – at Marylebone parish church before he left for Portsmouth. On 18 May he hoisted his flag in the *Victory*, the most powerful ship of the line in the Royal Navy, with 100 guns. Next day he wrote to the First Lord of the Admiralty, Lord St Vincent, 'If the devil stands at the door, the *Victory* shall sail tomorrow.'[35]

There seemed an inevitability about Nelson's departure. Not only was he the obvious choice to counter the enemy's main fleet, but he was the only British commander seen as capable of confronting Napoleon Bonaparte. The two men had much in common. Both had won dazzling victories, leading from the front; both exerted almost hypnotic powers of leadership, with Nelson generally showing himself to be the more humane; both were self-absorbed and vain, displaying high theatricality. Both were attractive to women, and had acquired exotic reputations as lovers. Bonaparte was more than a decade younger than Nelson but, although one was supreme on land and the other at sea, they appeared to their respective countrymen to be well-matched opponents.

Two other British sea commanders were of an older generation. Admiral Lord Keith, now nearly sixty, was a dour, efficient Scot, who had been Nelson's stern superior in the Mediterranean, while his own priorities had been at Naples and Palermo with the Bourbon court and the Hamiltons; he now commanded the North Sea Fleet and was responsible for direct defence against invasion. Nelson's old friend from early years in the Caribbean Admiral Sir William Cornwallis, also nearing sixty, commanded the Channel Fleet, blockading the French in their main base outside the Mediterranean, Brest, and the ports on the Bay of Biscay. Nicknamed 'Billy Blue' because of the frequency with which he hoisted the Blue Peter flag to make sail, and 'Coachee' or 'Mr Whip' because his florid face suggested a convivial coachman, he was loved by those under his command, despite his determination to keep them at sea in the worst weather off the dangerous, rocky coast of Ushant and Brittany.

Ships were brought forward for action, too. At the beginning of the year the Royal Navy had had only thirty-two ships of the line in commission. During the peace – or truce, as it had come to be seen – St Vincent, long regarded as the sturdiest bulwark of British sea power, had allowed the fleet to become dangerously weak. This was largely because his distrust of contractors and shipbuilders outside the royal dockyards had prompted him to impose stringent constraints on Admiralty orders. So when Pitt returned to office he replaced St Vincent as First Lord with the former Secretary for

War, Henry Dundas, now Viscount Melville. At once naval rearmament accelerated. By the beginning of May twenty more battleships had been brought out of reserve and commissioned; sixty
by the beginning of June. By the end of the year there were to be
75 battleships, 114 frigates and more than 200 other warships in
service.

At about the time Nelson sailed from Spithead another naval
officer was visiting the Admiralty to be told that he had been given
a new, very different command. This was Captain Wright and the
command under discussion was not classed as a ship but simply as a
boat. Although neither Nelson nor Wright realized it, they would
be linked through their respective commands by a grand strategy
that would span all Europe and its surrounding seas.

5

A fearful day is preparing

SIX WEEKS after Lord Nelson sailed for the Mediterranean in the *Victory*, on the evening of 29 June 1803, Boulogne was the scene of ceremonies and celebrations. Triumphal arches were erected and flanked with pyramids and columns of greenery, while the streets leading to the Place d'Armes were strewn with flowers. Outside the classical façade of the grandest house, the Hôtel des Androuins, paraded a guard of honour formed by Boulonnais youths in dashing uniforms to welcome the First Consul and his wife from Paris, cheering them as they drove up through the narrow streets. General Napoleon Bonaparte was coming to take personal command of the Grande Armée for the invasion of England.

Bonaparte was now supremely optimistic, despite his earlier doubts. He had, after all, once secretly assembled a large army for the invasion of Egypt and achieved surprise and success in landing it there; and if the Romans and the Normans could successfully invade England, so could he. The Channel, he declared, 'is a ditch which one can jump whenever one is bold enough to try it'.[1] The grand strategy of this plan was two-tiered. The first, of course, was to cross the Channel with an army of more than 100,000 men. As he had always known, it would be essential to command the seas between the Isle of Wight and the Thames estuary, and he believed this could be achieved by a combination of ruses to lure British squadrons away from the Channel, if only for weeks or even days.

As he had already found, the country around Boulogne was an ideal holding area for large numbers of troops: it was healthy, fertile and linked by roads with Paris and with other potential theatres of war. If he wished to march into central Europe for an attack on Austria, an army based here would not only enjoy these natural advantages but would also, by appearing to be bound for England, lull his possible victims elsewhere into a sense of false security. He could move either way.

Whichever option was taken, the main body of the Grande Armée would be deployed along this stretch of coast while other formations waited on the shores of the Low Countries to the north-east and, to the west, within a day's march of Cherbourg or Brest, while the principal reserve remained in Paris, a week's march by road. Eventually the whole army would number some 200,000 men, half of them waiting in four vast, tented camps around Boulogne. This force would make the initial crossing and, while he would try to convince the British that the landing would be along the coast of Sussex and the flat shores of Dungeness and Romney Marsh, his chosen beachhead would be to the north-east, on the equally flat, east-facing coast between Deal and Ramsgate. This would enable his invasion fleet to lie at anchor in the Downs, sheltered by the Goodwin Sands. On landing, he could then march directly to the naval base and dockyard at Chatham, through which reinforcements and heavy supplies could pass. 'Embark plenty of artillery', he ordered, 'I shall have to besiege Dover Castle, Chatham and perhaps Portsmouth.'[2] From there it should be simple to advance westward on London, while the bulk of the British defenders were still deployed along the Surrey hills to defend the capital against an attack from the south. There were also the options of diversionary attacks: one a landing in Essex and Suffolk by troops crossing from Flushing, the other, an invasion of Ireland mounted from Brest.

Accompanying the First Consul was Rear-Admiral Denis Decrès, the Minister of Marine. Born into an aristocratic family from Champagne, he had, as a young naval officer, fought against the British in the Caribbean. He had been lucky to survive the Reign of Terror, by virtue of his professional skills, and his career had again flourished. In 1798, at the age of thirty-six, he had been promoted to flag rank after more successful actions in the Mediterranean. Badly wounded a year later in defending the *Guillaume Tell*, the last survivor of the Battle of the Nile, against Nelson's friend Captain Edward Berry, he and his ship had been captured but he had soon been exchanged for a captive British officer. His reputation as a brave and efficient seaman and hardworking administrator was now established. There was also a hard-edged drive in his character, which the First Consul recognized as akin to his own, and there was even some physical resemblance between the two men. With their impassive, ruthless looks, the two could have passed as brothers.

Also with Bonaparte were Pierre Forfait, the engineer and marine architect who had been Decrès's predecessor and who was now Inspector-General of 'the flotilla' for the invasion, Vice-Admiral Eustace de Bruix, Generals Soult, Lauriston and Marmont, his stepson Colonel de Beauharnais and a large staff. Bonaparte worked with Decrès at the Hôtel des Androuins until one o'clock in the morning of that first night, then had a bath and went to bed, only to appear on the ramparts high above the port with Soult and Lauriston at a quarter to three to watch the dawn. After riding down to the harbour, where 1500 labourers were digging new docks and building jetties, he went on to inspect the coastal defences and asked which of them had shown most vigour in repelling Nelson's attack. He ordered a barrel to be towed out to sea as a target and required the shore batteries to demonstrate their skill and the range of their guns, firing both cold and red-hot roundshot. He told the gunners, 'Your shot isn't red enough. It ought to be nearly white and scintillate like stars all over.'[3] He then rode inland to inspect farmland that had been recommended as sites for new encampments to the east and west of the town. By ten o'clock that morning he was back at his headquarters in the Place d'Armes.

His stay in Boulogne was brief. After another day of inspections and meetings, he set out to tour the coast between Boulogne and Antwerp accompanied by Josephine and his staff. There was the constant urge to look north-east, where the view might only be of calm, grey sea and mist, or perhaps a British frigate tacking to and fro a couple of miles offshore; then perhaps a smudge like a low cloud on the horizon, which as the visibility cleared became the gleaming chalk cliffs of England. Bonaparte rode his little grey horse through the coastal villages of Wimereux, Ambleteuse, Audresselles, Wissant and Sangatte, seeing enough from the saddle to make decisions. More shore batteries should be deployed, particularly on the heights of Cap Gris Nez, and the little harbours at Wimereux and Ambleteuse should be enlarged to take more landing craft, as should that at Boulogne. He only dismounted at Ambleteuse to inspect the defences, notably Vauban's fort on the beach, and to meet a few prominent citizens. To these he delivered a short exhortation and presented their spokesman with a snuffbox from a store that he took on such tours as gifts.

The cavalcade – Bonaparte on his horse, Josephine and her ladies in their carriages – reached Calais at five o'clock in the afternoon of 1 July. 'His entry, as might be expected, was in a grand style', reported *The Times* in London three days later.

> He rode on a small iron-grey horse of great beauty. He was preceded by about three hundred infantry and about thirty Mamelukes formed a kind of semi-circle about him . . . As soon as he and his attendants had passed through the gates, he ordered them to be shut to prevent their being incommoded by the populace. The execution of this order very much dampened the ardour of the Corsican's admirers, who remained entirely silent, although the moment before the whole place resounded with *Vive Bonaparte!*[4]

Bonaparte inspected the harbour from a packet named the *Josephine* and himself fired one of the guns covering the harbour mouth.

One of Josephine's ladies thought the occasion 'strongly resembled the progress of a king'[5] as they drove to their hotels, Quillac's and the Angleterre, where the British delegations negotiating the Treaty of Amiens had stayed. He received the mayor, the commander of the citadel and civic worthies, presenting them too with snuffboxes, and offered his own snuff to others; it was estimated that he used about two pounds of snuff a week. In his determination to make a personal impact on those he met, he was in the habit of pronouncing proverbs he had learned as a boy, which, being Corsican, were unfamiliar in France. Among those recorded at Calais were, 'The world belongs to him who knows how to seize it', 'Who risks nothing, gets nothing', 'Who wants fire must put up with the smoke', 'Who cannot perform, cannot command', 'He is not a man who cannot say no', 'The coward increases the courage of his adversary', 'Who is firm, prevails', 'The sail must be set according to the wind', 'A hundred men may not have the value of one' and 'Who makes a good war is assured of a good peace.'[6] As a further bellicose and patriotic stimulant, he ordered that the Bayeux Tapestry, the great embroidered narrative of the triumphant invasion of England by Guillaume, Duke of Normandy, who became known as William the Conqueror, be publicly displayed.

The cavalcade continued to Dunkirk and Ostend but on crossing the French frontier a change of mood was apparent, as a member of the party noted, 'we detected some coldness in the popular greeting . . . they were curious but not enthusiastic'.[7] At Brussels, however, there was an extravagant welcome, with a succession of receptions and banquets before they continued to Antwerp. This Bonaparte recognized as having the potential to become as important a naval base as Portsmouth, which was vital to his plans because only Brest, far to the west, offered his ships of the line a secure anchorage and all they could require for refitting and replenishment. He therefore ordered that vast sums be spent on converting Antwerp's commercial port into a naval dockyard capable of servicing twenty-five large warships at any one time.

The Minister of War, General Berthier, was charged with assembling the army in the huge camps around Boulogne and new ones in the Low Countries and Germany, troops from the two latter to embark at Flushing. Initially one corps would be commanded by General Michel Ney, with his headquarters at Montreuil, near Boulogne, another by General Jean Soult, based at St Omer, while a third would be commanded by General Louis Davout at Bruges. It was hoped that more than 70,000 men would be encamped by the beginning of 1804. This total would be more than doubled during the year.

The whole force would, of course, be commanded by Bonaparte himself. As he could not devote all his time to this as First Consul, he would have to shuttle between Boulogne and Paris, a journey of twenty-four hours each way. He therefore chose as his main headquarters the château at Pont-de-Briques, a handsome, pedimented house of the eighteenth century with its own small park, two miles outside Boulogne on the road to Paris. This would have the advantage of enabling him to arrive unannounced to inspect his troops, who would never know whether or not he was near by and watching them; he could also take his friends and enemies in the capital by surprise.

As a forward tactical headquarters he ordered the construction of a complex of pavilions on the bluff above the mouth of the Liane to the east of Boulogne, from which he could see the harbour, the coastal defences, the open sea and, on a clear day, England. His own elegant *baraque* was to be built on the site of the Tour d'Odre, a well-known seamark on the foundations of a Roman lighthouse erected by the Emperor Caligula. Other pavilions were to be built near by for General Soult, Decrès and the naval commanders.

The next priority was the provision of enough landing craft to ferry the army across the Channel. This was particularly the responsibility of Forfait, as inspector-general of the flotilla. But while General Bonaparte commanded an instinctive, deep and perceptive understanding of land warfare, he had no experience of the sea and he did not take Forfait's limitations into account. The latter's education as a mathematician and scientist had won him a commission as an engineer before the Revolution and his early work had involved the digging of canals; his most successful ship designs had been for shallow-draught sailing barges for carrying cargoes up the Seine to Paris. Forfait knew little more of the perils of the open sea than did Bonaparte. So, when told to design and build hundreds of landing craft, those he ordered were more suitable for calm, fresh water than the Channel and for carrying farm produce rather than troops, artillery and ammunition and withstanding the recoil of guns. Yet the First Consul trusted Forfait, despite criticism from Decrès, who declared his plans to be 'monstrous ideas . . . which are as wrong as they will prove to be disastrous' and the invasion craft themselves as 'a heap of monstrous baubles'.[8]

There were to be four principal classes of invasion craft, designed specifically for the purpose by Forfait. The largest was the three-masted *prame*, 110 feet long and mounting 12 guns, then the two-masted *chaloupe cannonière* and the smaller *bateau cannonier* gunboat and finally the 60-foot *péniche*, armed with two howitzers. Two problems were inevitable, but not foreseen by their designer. One was that all were too small to provide a steady gun platform and their hulls were liable to be ruptured by the recoil. They were built as troop carriers and were expected to make the crossing to England in calm weather, possibly negotiate sandbanks and certainly have to be run as far inshore as possible, but they lacked a Channel packet's high sides, draught and keel. It was obvious to any seaman that they would be of use only under ideal weather and sea conditions.

The principal troop carriers were to be the *chaloupes* and the *péniches*; together, a pair could, it was estimated, carry nearly 200 men, their weapons and equipment. Added to these would be commandeered vessels – fishing boats, barges and flatboats – making a planned total of more than 2000, which were to be organized in divisions of twenty-seven vessels. In addition, Forfait, who enjoyed free access to Bonaparte imagined more unconventional designs, including a floating battery mounting sixty guns that could manoeuvre close inshore. Rumours of such craft reached England and were so exaggerated that reports circulated of huge landing rafts of 44,000 tons, measuring 2000 by 1500 feet, powered by windmills, mounting 100 guns and capable of embarking two infantry divisions together with cavalry and artillery; it was even reckoned that the building of each would require the timber of 216,000 trees.

The first orders for more than 1000 of Forfait's newly designed vessels were drawn up in May 1803, with 300 due for completion by the end of December; this deadline was then brought forward to September. Bonaparte decreed that not only coastal shipyards should be pressed into building them – including French yards in the Mediterranean – but also all cities on rivers and major canals, including Paris itself, as far east as the Rhine. Rich French citizens anxious for social or political preferment were to be asked to pay for the building of at least one landing craft each, which would bear their name. By August, more than 1000 vessels of all types were available, although Bonaparte himself claimed twice that number.

When the Flotille Nationale was ready, the first essential would be the command of the Channel itself. This had long belonged to the British, who could dominate the narrow seas from their naval bases at Plymouth, Portsmouth, Sheerness and Chatham and their secure anchorages in Torbay, Portland, Spithead, the Downs and the Nore in the Thames estuary. The French controlled no major base or anchorage between Antwerp and Brest, although Cherbourg was being developed as a deep-water harbour; there were modest harbours at Calais and Ostend and docks were being dug to take close-packed landing craft at Boulogne, Wimereux, Ambleteuse and Etaples.

That August the overall command of the flotilla was given to Admiral de Bruix. Aged forty-four, he had been, like Decrès an officer in the old navy; like most of the others, he had been arrested during the Revolution then returned to duty, and he had been promoted to rear-admiral in 1797. It was he who had carried out the disbanding of the Armée d'Angleterre after Bonaparte's departure for Egypt. A cultivated man – he dabbled in chemistry and writing opera – he was also tough, efficient and abrasive and had been a supporter of Bonaparte since the latter's return from Egypt to seize control of the government.

There was an equally vital naval command and that was of the heavy ships which would be needed to cover the passage of the flotilla. At last, Decrès and his admirals had been able to assemble a fighting fleet worthy of the name. In May 1803 there had been only five ships of the line and ten frigates in French ports and ready for active service. By the summer more ships had been recalled from the Caribbean while others, in reserve, under repair or still on the stocks, were made ready for sea so that the deep-water ports of France held thirty-two ships of the line and twenty-six frigates. The British might have fifty-two sail of the line at sea, but these were divided between the Channel and the North Sea, the approaches to Ireland, and more distant seas; it would, in theory at least, be possible to overwhelm any one of their fleets, or squadrons when the time for the invasion was chosen.

Plans were taking shape for luring away the British Channel and North Sea fleets to meet other dangers, perhaps an invasion of Ireland combined with another threat to Egypt, or British islands in the West Indies. Initial ideas of making a surprise crossing on a long, calm winter night or during fog had been abandoned as impractical, if only because it would be impossible for all the landing craft to leave port on a single tide; several tides would be needed. So an overwhelming naval force would be required to hold the British at a distance for perhaps weeks until the army had been put ashore. But the French fleet – and the Dutch ships of the line, which the French had commandeered – were, although available for service, scattered between Toulon in the Mediterranean (where the largest squadron was based), the Atlantic ports (notably Brest and Rochefort) and the Texel. The supreme naval command therefore had to be vested in an admiral capable of co-ordinating their departures from more than half a dozen ports, combining at sea into a single powerful fleet and sweeping up the Channel to dominate the Straits of Dover. For this command Bonaparte chose Nelson's adversary off Boulogne, Latouche-Tréville.

The grand strategy with which he would be entrusted was that he was to debouch from Toulon with ten ships of the line, make a feint towards Egypt to lure the British eastward, then go about and make a dash through the Straits of Gibraltar into the Atlantic. There the British fleet under Admiral Cornwallis was watching Brest and its huge almost landlocked, rock-bound anchorage, where twenty more French ships of the line were ready to transport 20,000 troops to Ireland. Latouche was to be joined by six more sail of the line from Rochefort – on the river Charente, its roads sheltered by the Ile d'Oléron – and, while the British were preoccupied off Brest, he was to steer to the north of them and take station off Boulogne. The British squadron in the North Sea would be assumed to be busy watching the Dutch ships at the Texel. Meanwhile the Channel fleet would still be watching the heavy French ships in Brest.

As a provisional date for sailing Latouche-Tréville was given January 1804, with his arrival off Boulogne to be a month later.

First, he would have to escape from Toulon and he realized how difficult that might be when in the summer of 1803 the masts of the *Victory* came up over the horizon off that port, flying the vice-admiral's flag of Lord Nelson. Although far from the scene of the immediate threat, Nelson was confident that he was in the right place. 'I believe that we are now so well prepared that the French will not venture the attempt at landing in England', he wrote to a friend at home, 'Ireland is their object, and Egypt'.[9]

Much remained to be planned by the French. The assembling of this mass of shipping – let alone the building programme – and the soldiery would inevitably take time. On 21 October 1803 Lord Keith returned to anchor off Broadstairs after a cruise along the coasts of France and the Low Countries and reported the results of his reconnaissance. Off Boulogne his lookouts, high in the masts of the *Monarch*, had scanned the harbour through their telescopes and counted only 'about fifty rowboats and two brigs, two schooners and one gallit, all armed', while ashore they saw 'two very extensive camps of huts, which I think might have contained sixteen thousand men – they seemed full of troops and then there are also small camps at all the batteries along the shore and soldiers in the towns'. At Calais he reported 'a very large barracks but saw no considerable number of troops', while at Ostend there were 'in readiness forty fishing boats and many open vessels of a smaller description – twelve thousand men are said to be about the place'. In addition, 'twenty-nine decked boats of some size, with two guns each, are said to have left Rotterdam for the purpose of proceeding by inland navigation to Dunkirk, where there are no doubt many other vessels of various descriptions'.[10] This, of course, was only the beginning.

Bonaparte divided his time between Boulogne, Paris and tours of inspections. He kept his movements secret to ensure that his field commanders were alert for an unannounced inspection and to allow potential rivals and dissidents less opportunity to act against him during his absence from the capital. He would suddenly appear at the Tuileries, or his country residence at St Cloud, along the Seine escarpment close to Passy – where the d'Arblays still led their quiet, restricted lives – to convene immediate meetings of ministers. A day later, without warning, his cavalcade of carriages and cavalry would sweep into the courtyard at the château of Pont-de-Briques, or he would arrive at his pavilion on the cliffs above Boulogne. The latter was a prefabricated wooden building, painted pale grey, erected in two days on a brick foundation. It was 100 feet long and 23 feet wide, with semicircular extremities and a rotunda, 30 feet in diameter, overlooking the harbour. Within, a passage linked three rooms, one of them a council chamber. This was papered in silver-grey and 'the painted ceiling represented golden clouds in an azure sky, in which an eagle and a thunderbolt was seen directing its flight towards England guided by Napoleon Bonaparte's star'.[11] A map of the Channel hung on a wall and at the large oval table, covered by green baize, was only one chair; this was for the First Consul, as all his officers were expected to stand in his presence. The pavilion was surrounded by lawns, flower beds and a formal pool, where swam a pair of black swans presented to him by the mayor of Amiens.

Further inland the encampments began to assume a more permanent character and tents were replaced by thatched huts standing within a grid pattern of roads with such names as Avenue des Pyramides and Rue de Valmy, after early victories by the armies of the Revolution.* As months passed, vegetable and flower gardens were planted around the huts, while veterans who had fought in Egypt set up 'small columns, pyramids, obelisks, statues or redoubts fashioned out of clay and shells'.[12] The officers' quarters were often made to look 'like charming country villas . . . some even had aviaries filled with birds of all kinds, or poultry yards abundantly supplied with fowls, ducks, geese, pigeons and rabbits'.[13]

Bonaparte's impromptu inspections were designed to build morale as much as to improve efficiency. Hearing that the leather straps of the infantrymen's equipment were chafing their shoulders, he dressed and equipped himself as a private soldier, marched up and down and then berated their officers in the soldiers' hearing: 'Ask her sons to shed their blood for the glory of France

---

* Respectively, the victories over the Mamelukes outside Cairo in 1798 and over the Austrians and Prussians in 1792.

and they will do it, but don't let my soldiers bleed shamefully, like ill-harnessed mules; steel alone makes honourable wounds.'[14] After tasting the sour wine issued to the troops he stormed at the provider, 'To make a few more *sous* profit, miserable man, you would poison my soldiers!'[15] The troops, too, were sometimes disciplined, once by ordering that the elaborate plaits in which some liked to wear their hair, or the use of hair powder, be forbidden and that all should wear their hair short, 'in some Roman style *à la Titus*'.[16] More importantly, in the summer of 1803, after watching three British frigates bombard his positions ashore and seeing the shots from the French batteries fall short, he found that the powder charges were only those used in saluting guns and 'flew towards the unhappy subaltern – upbraided him for his ignorance and neglect, and with his own hands tearing the epaulettes from his shoulders, told him that he was no longer an officer in the French army'.[17]

Bonaparte combined such attention to detail with the grandest strategic vision. Knowing that the Channel tides were strong and coastal navigation difficult, particularly off his chosen beachhead within the Goodwin Sands, he saw he would need pilots and, while these could be found among French fishermen and smugglers familiar with the coast of Sussex and the levels of Romney Marsh between Dungeness and Dover, they could not claim such intimate experience of the treacherous Goodwins. Twelve miles long and intersected by channels of varying depths, they were dangerous not only to shipping but also, at low water, to the shallow-draft boats in which most of his infantry would be embarked. He therefore made enquiries about enlisting English smugglers who had run gold coin into France during the Peace of Amiens and might not be averse to a little clandestine employment as pilots for their country's enemy. At once a name was suggested: that of Captain Thomas Johnstone of Deal.

In December 1802 Johnstone, who had been imprisoned in London for debt, had escaped from the Fleet prison and made his way to the coast near Brighton, where a cutter, owned by a smuggling friend, took him to safety across the Channel. Here, it was reported, he came to Bonaparte's notice and was said to have been summoned into his presence to be made an offer. If he would act as pilot to the Flotille Nationale in the invasion, he would be handsomely rewarded and given a pardon for all outstanding charges in England when it was occupied by the French. 'I am a smuggler', Johnstone was said to have replied, 'but a true lover of my country and no traitor'.[18] So, to encourage second thoughts, he was sent back to prison.

There he remained for nine months, after which his movements are unclear, varying according to newspaper reports and mythology. However, it seems probable that he was imprisoned in Flushing and escaped again. To elude his pursuers he dived into the harbour and swam to the American schooner *Lafayette*, which was about to sail for New Orleans. On arrival there he reported to the British consul as an unemployed Channel pilot, which was of course true, and was given work as a clerk in the consulate. This news must have reached London, because in due course he was to be offered a free pardon if he returned to England, on the condition that he work as assistant to an old friend. This was the American inventor Robert Fulton, who had himself arrived there.

Johnstone had first met Fulton in France – in Calais, it was said – and they had taken to one another. They had discussed submarines, because Johnstone could imagine their potential for smuggling; the American had enjoyed his enthusiasm, wit and openness to his own inventive ideas. Fulton had remained in France, despite the final rejection of his submarine by Bonaparte and Decrès, on the grounds that 'the English, so ingenious at creating destructive machines, would soon be doing the same thing'.[19] On the assumption that peace would continue, he had concentrated on the development of steam propulsion. Other inventors had been conducting promising experiments for the past fifteen years, some of them in Scotland and in the United States. Fulton himself favoured paddle-wheels at either side of his steamer rather than a stern-wheel and had built an eight-horse-power engine to drive them. This he fitted into a seventy-foot wooden vessel, which underwent trials on the Seine in Paris on 9 August 1803. She steamed up and down the river for an hour and a half, making way against the strong current, albeit slowly. Confident that this had come to the notice of the government, he asked his friend Pierre Forfait if he could arrange an audience with the First Consul to discuss his 'new endeavours'.[20] He wanted to propose the building of a fleet of steamboats to transport the Grande Armée across the Channel on a still day when the British squadrons would be becalmed, or when immobilized by contrary winds.

Bonaparte refused to receive Fulton but was told of his proposal. He was not enthusiastic, and wrote to Talleyrand that 'the affair . . . does not merit much attention. For a great length of time people have occupied themselves with means of propelling boats without men.' But he did refer the idea to the Académie des Sciences; they, too, were unimpressed and the question was dropped. However, there was one dissident voice, that of Etienne-Denis Pasquier, the Chancellor of France, who was to muse of Bonaparte's judgement, 'Never was he more badly served by his instinct. What might he not have been able to accomplish had he been the first to avail himself of this new means of reaching his most mortal enemy? Surprise will doubtless be felt that a genius, such as that of the First Consul, should not have at once grasped the range of the offer made him by Fulton.'[21]

These were not the only bizarre schemes presented to Bonaparte. It was suggested by a mining engineer named Mathieu that a tunnel should be dug under the Channel so that the Grande Armée could suddenly debouch into Kent. An inventor named Jean-Charles Thilorier proposed a gigantic balloon beneath which would be suspended a platform accommodating 3000 soldiers. This was to be launched on a southerly wind to waft across the sea to England but, asked to construct a quarter-size model of the *Thilorière*, he had to admit its impracticability. Another scheme was for a gigantic bridge to be built from Calais to Dover. Forfait himself suggested the building of 'floating forts', which were in fact to be one roofed battery on piles sunk in shallow water offshore, with rafts mounting more guns moored to it, which would command the mouth of the river Liane; on either flank a stone fort would be built on the rocky foreshore. The most ambitious undertaking was at Boulogne itself, where the Liane was dredged and widened, more than half a mile of quays built and a huge semicircular basin dug and lined with stone, capable of harbouring 100 gunboats and landing craft.

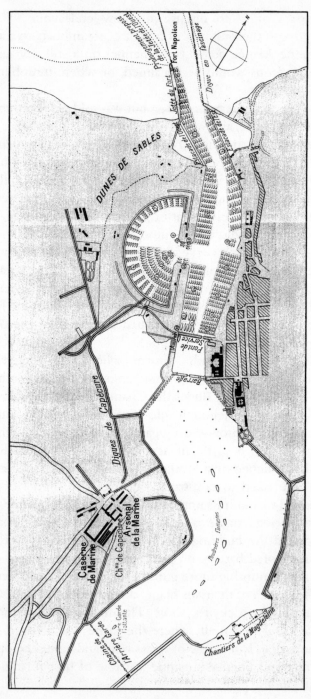

PLAN GÉNÉRAL DU PORT DE BOULOGNE

(D'après la Carte L. III ⁹⁄₇₉ des Archives de la guerre.)

LÉGENDE :

1. Pranes.
2. Bateaux de première espèce.
3. — de la garde impériale.
4. — de deuxième espèce.
5. Bombardes.
6. Péniches de l'amiral.
7. Péniches.
8. — de la garde impériale.
9. Caïques impériaux.
10. Caïques impériaux.
11. Corvettes de pêche.
12. Paquebot impériaux.
13. Paquebots de l'amiral.
14. Transports écuries.
15. — artillerie.
16. — bagages.
17. Bateaux du port.
18. Canots des états-majors.

Échelle approximative : $\frac{1}{10.000^e}$

A French plan of the port of Boulogne in 1804, showing the Bassin Napoléon

In September Bonaparte called for a complete order of battle. He was told that nearly 1400 vessels of all types were available, including fishing boats, each able to carry between 30 and 130 men, together with arms, equipment, ammunition and rations; artillery, wagons and horses would also have to be embarked. The total land forces available were 114,554 soldiers, including 76,798 infantry, 11,640 cavalry, 3780 gunners, 3780 waggoners and 17,467 non-combatants, including 1760 canteen women. Seven thousand horses were to cross with the cavalry and artillery. Now huge encampments stretched for miles to east and west of Boulogne. As planned, not all the invasion force would be held there, because Bonaparte always maintained that armies should disperse to feed and concentrate to fight; so other main concentrations were at Montreuil, St Omer and Bruges, with smaller camps near provincial towns, including Arras, Amiens, Tournai, Mayence, Meaux and Compiègne. For the diversionary attack on Ireland a holding area was established at Brest, while Irish volunteers waited to join it at Rochefort and Morlaix. In addition to troops committed to the assault, coastal defences accounted for another 60,000 men.

The diversion in Ireland depended on the landing being timed to coincide with an Irish insurrection, and in July this failed. Under the young Robert Emmet, a leader of the nationalist United Irishmen, a coup was attempted, Dublin Castle was attacked and the Lord Chief Justice murdered. But the rising did not spread and no reinforcements, let alone French troops, arrived from Brest. The rebels were routed by the British garrison and Emmet captured and executed. Yet in Paris this was seen as only a failed opportunity, not one that would affect the attack on England.

Admiral de Bruix published an order of the day declaring,

The First Consul, when he signified to me your destination, honoured me with the title of your Admiral . . . Brave seamen! The choice of Bonaparte renders me worthy to march at your head . . . Already you hear the cry of vengeance . . . Let those ships which insolently cruise along our shores . . . return and say to their Government, 'A fearful day is preparing; the winds of the sea, again favourable to the Conqueror of Egypt, may in a few hours bring him to our coasts and with him the innumerable companions of his glory' . . . The nation which oppresses the seas will be conquered by terror before it experiences the fate of arms and sinks beneath the blows of our heroes.[22]

But the British ships that cruised along French shores were not returning with such a message and not all who sailed in them were returning to England.

News that particularly disturbed the First Consul was the arrival in Brest of a British naval officer intent on studying the ships in the anchorage and dockyard. As his secretary, Louis de Bourrienne, put it, 'Having heard that a captain in the British navy had visited the dockyard of Brest, passing himself off as a merchant, whose passport he had borrowed, [Bonaparte] flew into a rage because no one had arrested him'; it is possible that he guessed the captain's name, although it was never revealed. At a meeting soon afterwards Bonaparte declared, 'If there had been a commissary of police at Brest, he would have arrested the English captain and sent him at once to Paris. As he was acting the part of a spy, I would have had him shot as a spy.'[23]

Many such stories circulated throughout France. Some were true and followed a long, evolving sequence of intrigue, planning and secret activity that had begun when the French Revolution had started to exceed the bounds of liberal ideals. The aim had been suggested in 1793, after the execution of King Louis XVI, in a letter from Edmund Burke, the philosophical politician, to his friend William Windham. 'France is strong at arm's length', he had written. 'She is, I am convinced, weakness itself if you can get to grapple with her internally.'[24]

There were soon to be more mysterious arrivals in France. On the night of 23 August 1803 a darkened sloop glided towards the cliffs of Normandy ten miles east of Dieppe. She was commanded by Captain Wright and engaged on 'a secret and delicate service'.[25] On a rising tide she closed the shore and a light gleamed from the cliffs 300 feet above the sea. A boat was lowered, seamen pulled on muffled oars and passengers scrambled ashore on sands below an unobtrusive fold in the cliffs. This place, half a mile from the farming village of Biville, was well known to smugglers for it was a deep cleft running inland, rising steeply to where they had cut a path through the sandy soil to the fields above, from which it was as obscured as from the sea. A rope had been lowered down the path, where it rose most steeply, to help one of the arrivals, a corpulent, powerfully built man, and at the top a horse was held ready for him so that he could ride, while the others walked with their guides, to a safe house, the remote farm of La Poterie. This was Georges Cadoudal, the conspirator of the *attentat* in the Rue Niçaise, on his way back to Paris.

During the months that followed the ship again materialized out of the night off Biville and more passengers were landed. Finally, on the night of 16 January 1804 eight men were put ashore at the same place, scrambled up the cliff path and were guided to La Poterie. There the leader of the party, Charles Pichegru, was welcomed by Cadoudal, who had travelled from Paris for the purpose. Together they set off for the capital, travelling by night. His mission accomplished, Captain Wright put his helm over and set a course to the Downs, he seeming as mysterious and elusive to his brother officers now as he had in the Levant. When his ship regained the shelter of the Downs, she did not anchor off Deal Castle and the adjacent naval yard but a mile to the south, off Walmer Castle. Captain Wright was pulled ashore and walked up the steep shingle beach and the short drive to the Tudor fort. Part country house, this squat, rounded building was the official residence of the Lord Warden of the Cinque Ports, the present holder of the ancient title being the former Prime Minister, William Pitt. He was not the sole resident, for some of the low-ceilinged rooms were occupied by a small secretariat, not all of whom attended to him and his correspondence. Captain Wright entered that occupied by an army officer, Pitt's cousin General Edward Smith, who enjoyed other, equally interesting, family connections: he was the uncle of Captain Sir Sidney Smith and his brothers Spencer Smith, the British minister in Stuttgart, and Colonel Charles Smith, who was currently stationed a few miles away at Dover. All of them were involved in the gathering of secret intelligence.

By reporting the successful conclusion of his mission, Wright ensured that news of the royalist conspirators' return to France would reach those who most needed to know in the shortest possible time. It was not Pitt who should be kept informed – although he was aware of subversion within France – so much as his successor as Prime Minister, Henry Addington, and the channel to him was through his brother Hiley Addington, a friend of General Smith. Although Henry Addington was even more anxious than Pitt to seem to be above any involvement with espionage, subversion, sabotage and even assassination, he needed to be kept informed and his brother became his link with secret intelligence. Like the others, Hiley led a double life. He and his associates all served as officers in the armed forces and as intelligence officers, or as liaison officers with those more deeply committed. This could lead to conflicts of interest, most notably in the case of Sir Sidney.

It was known that Lord Keith, who commanded the fleet based on the Downs, disliked and distrusted those involved with espionage and subversion and was well aware of the Smith brothers' dual roles. One of his subordinates, Rear-Admiral John Markham, was often distrustful and remarked that the French renegades were 'in strict intimacy . . . with all the Smiths and it is on their part alone that I consider any espionage can be expected'.[26] For his part, Sir Sidney valued his own intelligence work more highly than his naval and wrote to Hiley Addington that he was considering 'never again to [accept] . . . a captain's duty . . . in addition to occupation of a superior sort'.[27] But there were allies within the navy who deflected most intelligence requirements from Lord Keith; two of them were his second-in-command, Rear-Admiral Robert Montagu, who supplied small vessels for running agents to France when required, and the Secretary to the Admiralty, Sir Evan Nepean.

Difficulties with Lord Keith had been simmering for several months. In November Wright had written to him from Walmer Castle, enclosing a letter asking his assistance in 'executing a particular and delicate service of very high importance to the interests of this country. You would greatly contribute to the success of this service, if you would have the goodness to place the *Lively*, revenue cutter, at my disposal immediately to enable me to embark and proceed upon the service with the next ebb tide.'[28] Lord Keith was not accustomed to be addressed in such terms by a junior captain and wrote angrily to Lord St Vincent and Nepean, demanding an explanation because 'it is absolutely necessary that the whole of this dark business should be cleared up'.[29] Montagu, himself described by Markham to Lord Keith as 'that Prince of Intrigues', was therefore replaced by Rear-Admiral Philip Patton, whom he called 'a plain honest man'.[30]

Captain Wright made matters worse by complaining to Markham in December 1803 that he had been sailing 'some days off the enemy's coast and met their boats almost every night and never saw one of our cruisers'.[31] Lord Keith became even angrier, demanding to see the logs of the cutters *Hound*, *Griffin* and *Basilisk*, which were ostensibly under his command but had been used by Wright. His questions to the Admiralty seem to have been answered, for he wrote again that, 'Your expression respecting Captain Wright and others being intended as spies, surprises me. By whom are they sent?'[32] Keith was told that they were under the secret orders of the Foreign Secretary, Lord Hawkesbury, and he resented it as much as Lord Nelson had in the Mediterranean three years earlier, when another captain, Sir Sidney Smith, had seemed to act in a similarly self-important manner. Again he wrote to the Admiralty, 'On the subject of cutters employed by the Secretary of State, there is no reason why I should be let into the secrets they contain but it seems decent that I should be acquainted with the vessels so employed and not be told by my inferiors that such vessels are about.'[33] At Christmas his anger was unabated and he wrote again, 'Here is the *Griffin* cutter, Lieutenant Stuart, who went with Captain Wright; he says he understands the captain has been at Walmer since Tuesday last. I asked no questions, but he said it appeared to him something was not right and that he was sure that it was only when they [the French conspirators] liked that any communication took place.'[34]

Lord Keith distrusted the comings and goings at Walmer Castle and the small ships that lay at anchor offshore as much as he disliked the independence of Captain Wright. Again in December the latter had been in London without his knowledge and had then returned to Walmer with a French companion in his chaise. He also seemed to have his own aide-de-camp, also named John

Wright, described variously as his nephew or his illegitimate son, who was with him; the boy spoke fluent French and seemed to be used as a courier between agents within France and the British ships off the coast.

Walmer Castle was indeed a mysterious place. It was reported that huge amounts of gold coin had arrived there from London to be loaded aboard small craft bound for France. General Smith was privy to some of its secrets; he had not been responsible for mounting Captain Wright's operations in the Channel but for his communications and overland transport. He was similarly involved with his nephew Sir Sidney, who had given Wright the use of his own yacht for sorties to France during the summer and was currently cruising off the coast of the Low Countries in command of the frigate *Antelope* of fifty guns, together with a squadron of six sloops and two cutters – one named the *Lord Nelson* – with the temporary rank of commodore. The task given him by Lord Keith was to watch French preparations for invasion and intercept enemy gunboats and landing craft trying to creep down the coast from the Scheldt to the Channel ports. Another task had been given to him by his masters in the Aliens Office: to maintain contact with the network of agents covering that coast and based on Rotterdam.

Lord Keith was not alone among the admirals in his distrust of those involved with espionage. Indeed Sir Sidney Smith had appealed, in his usual high-handed way, directly to the Prime Minister about Wright's prospects as a naval officer:

> With regard to my friend Captain Wright, it is evident, notwithstanding Lord St Vincent's admission of his fair claim to promotion when (or, rather, if ever) he returned from his perilous mission to Paris, that it will not be granted by the Admiralty, for he has not been admitted to see Lord St Vincent for fear of creating a precedent for a crowd of other captains. You, who know little of my friend, and who know the delicate nature of the information he has to give, will say with me that he might fairly have been made an exception secretly.[35]

Another resident of Walmer Castle privy to much clandestine activity was a tall, thin, ungainly man of forty-two with a pointed nose and a receding chin and the complexion of a drinker. This was William Pitt, the former Prime Minister and promoter of secret operations, still privy to the twin approaches in the prosecution of the war: the broadsword of national defence and the stiletto of espionage, subversion and perhaps assassination. Just as Bonaparte's generals had used the year of peace to plan a direct attack on the British Isles, so Pitt had asked several of his former ministers to investigate the possibilities of destroying France from within by counter-revolution. The aggressive activity generated at Walmer Castle was known, perhaps, to a few officers and officials there and in London; the ships' companies involved would mostly have had the vaguest understanding of their tasks. Among the British, only the two Wrights, the Smiths and a few other officers and intelligence agents were aware of the scale and danger of their undertaking.

Pitt, as Prime Minister, had been aware of the plans to assassinate Bonaparte in 1800, which had so nearly succeeded, but had been careful to distance himself from direct involvement. Now Georges Cadoudal was, he knew, to attempt an even more ambitious *coup*: the assassination or abduction of the First Consul followed by the restoration of the Bourbon monarchy. A wide network of agents and conspirators was involved, but the key figures were Cadoudal, Pichegru and General Moreau, who had remained in France and in active commands throughout. Cadoudal was to make the *attentat* against Bonaparte, Moreau was to provide troops to secure strategic buildings and communications, and Pichegru was to provide the new Bourbon sovereign: a prince as yet unnamed and now in exile. All three principal conspirators were now in Paris, so there was nothing more to be instigated from Walmer Castle until news arrived from France. Wright was told to hold himself in readiness for any action that might become necessary.

6

Then to invasion be defiance given

THE BRITISH were accustomed to worrying about invasion. Five years earlier General Bonaparte had been on the Channel coast, hoping to cross, and, three years after that, it had been Latouche-Tréville, rebuffing Nelson himself. The elderly could remember the great war with France and Spain in the middle years of the previous century, when, despite the success of British arms in Canada, the Caribbean and India, every county had recruited its militia for defence against invasion. Every child was taught about successful invasions in the distant past by the Normans, Scandinavian and Germanic tribes and the Romans.

At first, not all those privy to reports from France were so concerned. Lord Grenville, the former Foreign Secretary, who had resigned with Pitt in 1801, wrote from his country house in August 1803, 'You will find me here very peacefully rolling my walks and watering my rhododendrons without any thought of the new possessor to whom Bonaparte may dispose them.'[1] In the same month Charles James Fox was not quite so sanguine, writing from his house at Chertsey to his brother General Fox in Ireland:

We just begun our harvest here, as some suppose for Bonaparte, but I am as stout as a lion. I believe he will not try, next that, if he does, he will be destroyed, or at least driven back at sea and lastly, even if he does land, he will frighten more than hurt us . . . At all events, an army in an enemy's country without any communication from their own, or any force at sea, is, in my judgement, in a very bad situation.[2]

However, Colonel Sir Henry Bunbury, on the quartermaster-general's staff in Kent and Sussex, and so preparing to face the brunt of an invasion, thought it would be 'madness in the British' to contemplate fighting an immediate defensive battle 'even in such tempting positions as the chalk hills offer'. British troops were not, he said, 'of a quality to meet and frustrate the manoeuvres' of an army such as Bonaparte now commanded. Instead, it was 'London itself, or rather along the skirts of Greenwich, Southwark and Lambeth,' that should be the chosen battlefield; there it would be 'our business to fight the great battle to the uttermost, day after day and night after night; bringing to the relief of every post fresh combatants from all parts of the Kingdom'.[3]

Now, once again, such contingency plans, old and new, were studied and discussed. The officer with principal responsibility for the defence of the realm was the King's second and most effective son, Frederick, Duke of York, the commander-in-chief of the army. A soldier since he was a boy, he had been a colonel at seventeen but had shown no aptitude for active service. Two expeditions to the Low Countries which he commanded were dismal failures, but he had a flair for administration and in 1798, at the age of thirty-three, he had been appointed Field Marshal of the Staff with an office at the Horse Guards in Whitehall. It had been an inspired appointment. The Duke reformed the army, introducing new regimental structures, training and equipment, reduced corruption and the abuse of patronage, founded the Royal Military Academy and the Staff College and became, as Lady Hester Stanhope considered, 'the best friend a soldier ever had'. She liked him too, and remarked, 'He is a blunt soldier, who pleases women because he is gallant and has some remains of beauty'.[4]

As the threat developed and he assessed priorities, he needed to know where the main danger lay. In October 1803 the Duke wrote to Admiral Lord Keith, then at anchor in the Downs, asking from which main continental ports the invasion armada would be likely to sail, whether such landing craft might try to pass the Goodwin Sands to reach the Downs and the flat beaches between

Ramsgate and Walmer, and what wind directions would be most favourable to the enemy. He then listed five stretches of coast from Land's End to the Firth of Forth, asking Keith's opinion on their comparative vulnerability.

Lord Keith replied at once with a long assessment. Matching possible landing sites with different wind directions, he explained which defences should be particularly alert when it blew from different points of the compass. Some he thought to be at little risk: there was not enough sheltered water on the Cornish coast and Plymouth was well defended; the Isle of Wight would prove a dead end for an invader, even if successful. However, Weymouth Bay was sheltered, the beach accessible and so vulnerable; all the beaches between Brighton and Folkestone were at risk; the west side of Dungeness would be vulnerable in an easterly wind and the east in a westerly. There were many suitable beaches along the east coast north of the Thames estuary, but there were sandbanks and other navigational hazards offshore and, once gained, the beaches were an increasingly long way from the main objective, London. However, Lord Keith was oddly dismissive of a threat to the Downs and the eastern shore of Kent, and wrote, 'I think the Downs are secure unless the enemy be superior at sea.'[5] He did not, of course, know that the Downs and those low, sheltered beaches were Bonaparte's chosen objective, as he intended to launch the invasion only when he was superior at sea.

The Duke of York knew that London must be the prime target for the invaders and planned his defences accordingly. The land forces were divided into three categories: the regular army, the militia and the volunteers. Much of the regular army had been abroad at the beginning of the year, the strategic reserve having been engaged in the final expulsion of the French from Egypt. Now they were returning and at Portsmouth in August 1803 Betsey, the wife of Nelson's friend Captain Thomas Fremantle, watched the Duke of York review troops on Southsea Common and noted in her diary, 'It was a very charming sight and I was particularly struck by a regiment of Dragoons only returned a few days ago from Egypt, every man being so extensively tanned that their complexion is really the same as that of the Egyptians.'[6]

Under the Duke's direction the army was improving fast. The

regular element numbered about 130,000 but of these some 50,000 still served abroad. These were augmented by the militia, a reserve of conscripts chosen by ballot and not expected to serve outside the United Kingdom. The Militia Act of 1802 had provided for the conscription of more than 50,00 men, who could be mobilized for full-time service, and this total was soon increased by 25,000. Together they formed a standing army of more than 150,000 men, of whom 50,000 were in Ireland. This force was divided between nine districts in England and one in Scotland, with nearly half the total concentrated in the south-east of England. For the balloted conscripts it was possible to avoid service by paying a substitute, buying exemption, or by joining the volunteers, which had been reconstituted after the year of peace.

The volunteers were a far larger force. They eventually came to number 410,000, of whom 70,000 were in Ireland; they, too, were not expected to serve overseas. Volunteers, who made up in enthusiasm what they lacked in military skills, were to be paid for eighty-five days' training a year, and some officers were in permanent cadres and so could draw salaries. So the grand total of land forces in the British Isles had – on paper, at least – amounted to more than 500,000 men, from trained riflemen to clumsy yokels.

The volunteers arose in an upsurge of popular patriotism. Uniforms, some of them splendiferous, were run up by jobbing tailors to local designs, but there was a shortage of weaponry, with priority given to arming Londoners and those defending coastal towns. At the end of 1803, 120,000 volunteers wore assorted uniforms but lacked muskets. Already they had changed the public conception of military service. Unlike the navy, the army had never been popular. Unfair as it often was, the officers were sometimes seen as rich dimwits who had bought their commissions as a social advantage, and the other ranks as country bumpkins or as those who found it a preferable alternative to prison. However, since the victory in Egypt, soldiers had acquired a new image, becoming subjects for admiring ballads and after-dinner toasts.

Recruiting campaigns were run on individual initiative, much as naval captains sought volunteers for their ships, using advertising slogans, posters, ballad sheets, newspaper editorials and personal persuasion. 'If you have qualities for a soldier . . . your country demands your exertions', declaimed a Somerset newspaper, 'Serve it then in the manner most constant to your station and to your feelings, and be – a VOLUNTEER!'[7] A typical recruiting ballad ran:

> Britons to arms! of apathy beware,
> And your Country be your dearest care:
> Protect your Altars! Guard your Monarch's Throne,
> The cause of George and Freedom is your own! . . .
> Then to invasion be defiance given,
> Your Cause is just, approv'd by Earth and Heaven! . . .
> The Tyrant never shall return to France;
> Fortune herself shall be no more his friend,
> And *here* the history of his crimes shall end –
> His slaughter'd Legions shall manure our Shore
> And England never know Invasion more!![8]

All agreed that their uniforms were dashing, and many a country squire or city merchant could see himself in a cocked hat, scarlet coat trimmed with gold and with a sabre at his side. Young blades would enlist in the cavalry, known as the yeomanry, to gallop to and fro on village greens and impress young women. There were church parades and inspections: in October 1803 church services were held throughout the country 'to invoke the God of Battles', followed, in London, by two inspections of the volunteers by the King in Hyde Park.[9] On one day more than 12,000 were on parade and on the next nearly 15,000, both parades watched by more than 200,000 cheering spectators. In Dorset, Betsey Fremantle noted, 'The Wimborne Volunteers have been ordered to march to Poole and their Captain, Doctor Pickford, a fat little man, was strutting up and down the town with a fussy step and important mien, which diverted us extremely but spread terror in the hearts of many of the inhabitants of Wimborne.'[10]

Within counties varieties of regiments were raised. The yeomanry was usually the most fashionable because recruits had to provide their own horses. Other crack regiments, such as the

Norwich Rifles, prided themselves on buying their own green uniforms, as did the Norfolk Rangers, whose colonel, Field Marshal Lord Townshend, aged eighty-two, had learned about skirmishing and sharpshooting in the forests of North America half a century earlier. Now, noted Lady Bessborough, he 'goes about everywhere in his uniform, saying he longs for the French to come and hopes to be in the thickest of the battle'.[11] More modest Norfolk regiments, such as the 134 men of the Swaffham Light Infantry, the 360 Blickling and Gunton Riflemen or the 180 Heydon Sharpshooters, were just as proud, commanded by local squires. Indeed, the county boasted sixty regiments named after towns and villages, varying in strength from 26 to 760. Keen volunteers frequently raised their own regiments, often on the most egalitarian pattern, such as the St Pancras Corps in London, which in August 1803 'elected three captains – viz.: Love, surveyor; Hughes, watch-maker; and Milner, plasterer'.[12]

The artist Robert Smirke – famous for painting scenes from Shakespeare plays – founded an Academy Corps of Artists but potential recruits seemed less enthusiastic than most 'from want of due exertion and attendance'.[13] After a dinner at Trinity House all fifty Elder Brothers – the administrators of shipping around the British Isles – volunteered: 'gallant and exceedingly good old men . . . now coming forward with the zeal and spirit of lads', noted a politician who was present.[14] There were even 'parochial corps': one London parson, fearing that a French landing 'would cause vast confusion and an entire stop to every employ . . . great numbers will be unemployed and likely enough to look for plunder. To the Parochial Corps, he looks for town defence against attempts of this kind.'[15] He was reassured that the Duke of York had already authorized the embodiment of three such detachments for the London parishes of St James, St George and Bloomsbury; this had the added advantage of providing exemption from conscription for the militia.

Volunteering could have social advantages through proximity with the famous in the ranks. The King himself had declared that he would fight if necessary but stopped his heir, the fat, dissolute Prince of Wales, from taking more than a nominal part in military affairs, although he could not be prevented from wearing elaborate uniforms. So reports of his loutish manners continued as before; one story that was widely told was of the Prince throwing a glass of wine into the face of the male guest seated next to him at dinner. With presence of mind the guest, 'without being disconcerted, immediately filled his glass and throwing the wine in the face of the person who sat next to him, bid him pass it round'. This was described as 'an admirable instance of mind and judgement upon an occasion of coarse rudeness'.[16] Dining with Captain Fremantle, the Prince himself drank six glasses of cherry brandy and a bottle of mulled port.

His brother the Duke of Clarence, who had been an unsuccessful naval officer and now lived with his mistress, the actress Dorothy Jordan, and their children at Bushey House, took command of the Teddington Corps, declaiming, 'My friends and neighbours! wherever our duty calls us, I will go with you; fight in your ranks; and never return home without you!'[17] They were not going anywhere but the parade ground, of course, but this kept enthusiasm high. 'As for this rascal Bonaparte,' he declared, 'I wish he was at the bottom of the sea. All naval officers think invasion impossible and this is clearly my opinion; yet what else can this Corsican scoundrel do against this country?'[18] Charles James Fox enlisted as a private soldier in the Chertsey Volunteers and William Pitt was appointed colonel of the Cinque Ports Volunteers and drilled his men every morning at Walmer Castle.

The timorous found the possibility of invasion a source of anxiety, even far inland. In Dorset, Betsey Fremantle visited a nervous woman friend, who, she reported, 'said very seriously that, as she had a horror of being what she call'd personally abused, she would put on men's clothes on the approach of the French'.[19] Invasion was a common subject of nightmares and the painter Joseph Farington recorded,

I had the last night the most distinct dream of Invasion that could possess the fancy. Of seeing French boats approach in the utmost order and myself surrounded by them after their landing. I thought they preserved great forbearance, not offering to plunder and that I was in the midst of them, conversing in broken English. It seemed to me that they came upon the

Country quite unprepared and met with no resistance . . . It seemed a perfect reality to me and I could scarcely believe it a dream for a little time after I awoke.[20]

The artists Hoppner and Opie were both said to be 'full of alarm of a French invasion', noted Farington.[21] Again children were being frightened by cautionary rhymes invoking an invader if they were disobedient:

> Baby, baby, naughty baby,
> Hush, you squalling thing, I say;
> Hush your squalling, or it may be,
> Bonaparte may pass this way.
>
> Baby, baby, he's a giant,
> Tall and black as Rouen steeple;
> And he dines and sups, rely on't,
> Every day on naughty people.
>
> Baby, baby, he will hear you
> As he passes by the house,
> And he, limb from limb will tear you,
> Just as pussy tears a mouse.[22]

Patriotic militarism swept the country. 'Every town was, in fact, a sort of garrison', remembered one young man in London, the future illustrator and caricaturist George Cruikshank.

In one place you might hear the 'tattoo' of some youth learning to beat the drum, at another place some march, or national air being practised upon the fife and, every morning at five o'clock, the bugle horn was sounded through the streets to call the Volunteers to a two hours' drill, from six to eight, and the same again in the evening and then you heard the pop, pop, pop of the single musket, or the heavy sound of the volley, the distant thunder of the artillery and then sometimes you heard the Park and the Tower guns firing to celebrate some advantage gained over the enemy.[23]

'Not only did the men form themselves into regiments of Volunteers but the boys did so likewise', he continued, 'My brother . . . formed one of these juvenile regiments and appointed himself the colonel. We had our drum and fife, our "colours" presented by our mammas and sisters . . . We also procured small gunstocks into which we fixed mop-sticks polished with a tinge of black lead to make 'em look like real barrels.'[24] The profusion of military bands was not to everybody's taste and when the painter Marie Vigée Lebrun was staying in Brighton she complained that 'The generals were perpetually reviewing the militia, who were for ever marching about with drums beating, making an infernal din'.[25] Most women seemed, however, to be caught up with the excitement, and the red of the infantry and the green of the rifle regiments became fashionable colours, with Lady Hester Stanhope, now out of mourning for Lord Camelford, dressing in scarlet, '*à l'Amazone*',[26] and another lady of fashion in 'a rifle dress of dark green velvet with a rifle hat to correspond'.[27]

The huge force of regulars and the militia were deployed in camps covering the principal ports and most likely landing sites. Even Lord Nelson's remote village of Burnham Thorpe, near the Norfolk coast, had its defences when a gun was mounted on a high sand dune – thereafter called Gun Hill – commanding the mouth of the little river Burn. South-eastern England was obviously most in danger and there defences were concentrated on Chelmsford north of the Thames and Chatham to the south. The former was to be defended by batteries on the highest ground to the east, and all but trunk roads were to be blocked or ploughed.

Should Chatham fall, a main line of defence for London was planned along the heights from Blackheath, Penge Common, Battersea and Wandsworth to the Thames west of the capital. To the south, a stand was envisaged along the Sussex Downs, a vulnerable point being the Dorking Gap, the deep valley of the river Mole between West Humble and Mickleham, where Fanny d'Arblay had lived.

Even as the generals planned their lines of defence, two artists, Farington and Hoppner, toured that same countryside, seeing the d'Arblays' former home at Camilla Cottage. Enraptured by this display of the 'picturesque', the former exulted over the view from 'a steep and richly wooded bank at the end of which is a peep of beautiful distance', then 'in a vale below passed through a wood which had an effect that enraptured Hoppner, who compared it to the inside of a fine old Gothic cathedral'.[28] Back in London, he found that sunshine and a beautiful view could quickly dull any sense of danger. 'I had a very agreeable walk through Chelsea', noted Farington in his diary that August. 'Crowds were in motion in every direction, availing themselves of the fine weather. The apprehension of Invasion has certainly at present very little effect on the public mind.'[29]

The principal warning of impending invasion and the calling to arms would be by the traditional lighting of beacons on hilltops, at least fifteen of them in Kent. These, it was suggested, should consist of at least eight waggon loads of wood ignited by three or four barrels of tar; in daylight, damp hay was to be thrown on the blaze to produce smoke. Inevitably hayrick fires were mistaken for the beacons, or these were accidentally lit, as was one in Berwickshire, where the poet Sir Walter Scott recorded that the yeomanry 'must have ridden forty, or fifty miles without drawing bridle'[30] to meet the imaginary enemy. In flat country, such as East Anglia, other means had to be devised. At Great Snoring in Norfolk the curate of the church was to hoist a large red flag on the tower, not only to alert the volunteers but also as a signal for the villagers to destroy anything of possible use to the enemy. Wherever the French landed, priority would be given to driving inland all horses and carts, sheep and cattle that they could use for transport, or for food. At Aldeburgh in Suffolk, the poet George Crabbe was woken by his son saying, 'Do not be alarmed but the French are landing and the drum on the quay is beating to arms.' Crabbe replied, 'Well, you and I can do no good, or we would be among them', turned over and went back to sleep.[31] It was, once again, a false alarm.

The Kentish seaside resorts of Margate, Broadstairs and Ramsgate had become fashionable; from the two latter, gunfire off Boulogne could be heard. Not only were the salons and assembly rooms crowded with smart young officers of the army and militia drafted to the coast from inland counties and looking for social diversion, but fleets of West Indiamen and East Indiamen, outward and inward bound, were constantly anchoring in the Downs and their well-to-do passengers coming ashore for entertainment, often by celebrated performers. 'In the evening', recorded the visiting Farington,

> we went to Ramsgate to the assembly room, where Madam Bianchi sang several songs at the pianoforte and Meyer played on the harp . . . A ball then commenced . . . There was much company and among them . . . Lady Hamilton with Mrs and Miss Nelson [Sarah and her daughter Charlotte Nelson, the admiral's niece], Lord Essex and many officers of the Hereford Militia, which he commands . . . Lady Hamilton is grown prodigiously large and exposed. Her fat shoulders and breast manifest, having the appearance of one of the Bacchantes of Rubens.[32]

News that she was staying with the William Nelsons at Canterbury reached Nelson off Toulon and he immediately wrote to her from the *Victory*, 'I am very uneasy at you and Horatia being on the coast for you cannot move if the French make the attempt; which, I am told, they have done and been repulsed. Pray God it may be true! I shall rejoice to hear you and Horatia are safe at Merton.'[34]

Nelson had been misinformed, but along the coast alarms had indeed begun. 'There are a thousand strange reports (but only reports) of all women, etc., being order'd from the coast (an end to sea bathing)', noted the usually phlegmatic Lady Bessborough, after a gale had brought a spate of rumours of the French fleet escaping from Brest during a storm. From the beach at Hastings she watched a flamboyant sunset over the sea, 'red as a glowing setting sun and bright streaks of light darting from every part of it . . . unlike anything I ever beheld – the people here are in the greatest alarm, thinking it portends the end of the world or – the invasion.'[35]

While in Portsmouth, Betsey Fremantle had been walking on the seaward ramparts one August evening, when, as she wrote in her diary,

> We were not a little surprised at seeing a great concourse of people on the beach, the yeomanry out, guns frequently fired,

signals made, the telegraphs at work and many sails in sight. I
was told it was supposed the French were effecting a landing as a
number of flat-bottomed boats were seen making towards the
shore. This created a very great alarm . . . as if really the French
were approaching. I felt much alarmed myself but, as everything
appeared quiet towards twelve o'clock, we went to bed in hopes
some mistake created this bustle.

Next morning, she added, 'I was very happy to hear this morning
that a fleet of coasters, who had been becalmed at the back of the
Isle of Wight, had occasioned our alarm and that no appearance of
an enemy remained today.'[36] At the same time, most of the inhabitants of Eastbourne, the seaside resort in Sussex, fled when a
French landing was rumoured to be imminent. To reassure the
coastal population, the Duke of York was told by the Admiralty
that he could count on the support of more than 450 warships of
all classes and some 800 small craft that could be armed and
manned by 25,000 of the Sea Fencibles, whom Nelson had found
so lacking in aggressive spirit two years earlier.

It was still the Royal Navy that summoned up national pride
with stirring ballads, particularly if they included the name of the
now far distant Nelson. One of them also coupled him with Sir
Sidney Smith and his defeat of Bonaparte at Acre:

> For hark! the thunder of the NAVY roars –
> Strong beats the pulse for WAR – loud sounds the drum,
> And our brave Sons invite the Foe to come;
> For they remember Acre's famous fight,
> When Britons put the vaunting Gaul to flight;
> Remember, too, the Battle of the Nile
> And at the threats of rash invasion smile.[37]

The British field commanders presented a confident front.
General Sir James Craig, who commanded in Essex, said in
September that

the French had twelve hundred gunboats at Boulogne and
might attempt to land sixty thousand men in England, which,

were they to do, the English force is now so arranged that in twenty-four hours an army of soldiers consisting of fifty-four thousand men, Regulars and Militia only, could be assembled in the county of Kent and, in addition, as many Volunteers could be brought together – so that nothing is to be apprehended.[38]

The fulcrum of defence against invasion was on the land and water within a twenty-mile radius of Dover, with Ramsgate to the north-east and Rye to the south-west. The Downs anchorage, running from Sandwich to Walmer, was the most active naval station on the British coast, and a tented camp at Shorncliffe on the chalk hills behind Sandgate was the sharpest point of the land defences. Keeping an eye on both from Walmer Castle was William Pitt, commanding the Cinque Ports Volunteers. He drilled his men daily and then made it his business to monitor the state of the country's defences at the point where defensive ideas could give way to the offensive. One of these had been the running of French royalists across the Channel; another was the training of a striking force at Shorncliffe camp, under the command of Major-General John Moore. An efficient Scot, a bachelor just past forty, with a quick intelligence, Moore had seen active service in America, the Mediterranean, the Netherlands, the Caribbean and, recently, in Egypt. In 1794 he had met Nelson in Corsica and been irritated by his interference in land operations. The two men were opposites in all but zeal; Moore later described Nelson as being 'covered with stars, ribbons and medals, more like the Prince of an Opera than the Conqueror of the Nile'.[39] Moore had proved a master of infantry tactics and was now regarded as the most innovative and promising officer in the army. His infantry brigade of nearly 4000 men was being retrained as light infantry, armed with the rifles, now under development, which, with their rifled barrels, were proving more accurate and had double the range of the standard, smooth-bore musket, the 'Brown Bess'. His favoured tactics were based on those developed in the forests of North America during the Seven Years War almost half a century earlier, notably by two young British generals, the Howe brothers. Designed to meet Indians and backwoods guerrillas on their own terms, their essence was speed and mobility, surprise and accurate shooting. To stress the need to merge with a landscape instead of standing in the open, dressed in red, white and gold, the riflemen's uniform was dark green and their buttons black; they marched at double the pace of line infantrymen.

Jack Moore as friends called him, became a regular visitor to Walmer Castle, not so much to discuss military matters with Pitt as to see the latter's niece Lady Hester Stanhope, who was there to act as his hostess, and the young general was much taken with her. Now aged twenty-six, handsome, sharp-tongued and impulsive, she was a stimulating companion to her uncle, advising him on the planting of the bleak grounds of the castle with fruit trees and, later, vines, shrubs, lime trees and transforming an abandoned chalk pit into a romantic, leafy glen.

She even involved herself with her uncle's military enthusiasms, attending 'parade after parade at fifteen, or twenty miles' distance from each other . . . The hard riding I do not mind but to remain almost still so many hours on horseback is an incomparable bore.'[40] It was as taxing on foot; she complained, 'I have been so drenched that, as I stood, my boots made two spouting fountains above my knees.'[41] She boasted of having redesigned the uniform of the Berkshire militia, who were camped near by, when, as she said,

somebody asked me . . . what I thought of them and I said they looked like so many tinned harlequins. One day, soon after, I was riding through Walmer village when who should pop out upon me but the colonel, dressed entirely in new regimentals . . . 'Pray, pardon me, Lady Hester,' said the colonel, 'but I wish to know if you approve of our new uniform.' Of course I made him turn about, till I inspected him round and round – pointed with my whip, as I sat on horseback, first here and then there – told him the waist was too short and wanted half a button more – the collar was a little too high – and so on; and, in a short time, the whole regiment turned out with new clothes.[42]

She watched an embarkation exercise when her uncle's regiment boarded thirty-five armed luggers from the beach at Walmer, and boasted, 'We are in almost daily expectation of the arrival of the

French and Mr Pitt's regiment is now nearly perfect enough to receive them.'

Lady Hester found Moore attractive and good company, a change from those she called 'vulgar sea-captains and ignorant Militia colonels'[43]; a friend described him as being 'above middle height, broad-shouldered and muscular, yet formed light and agile – his features fine and his keen, penetrating eye seemed to look through one's brain; the play of his countenance was very remarkable, expressing alike and without effort the open, familiar and bantering humour with which he greeted those he esteemed'.[44] 'I hear a great deal of General Moore', remarked Charles James Fox in London, 'and everything good.'[45] The friendship between Moore and Lady Hester blossomed to the point when it was rumoured that they might be secretly engaged to marry.

Moore himself had a low opinion of the volunteers' capabilities, but invited Colonel Pitt to visit Shorncliffe to watch the training. When, on arrival, the colonel eagerly announced, 'On the very first alarm, I shall march to aid you with my Cinque Ports regiments and you have never told me where you will place us', Moore, who had never considered the volunteers as part of his own battle plan replied, 'Do you see that hill? You and yours shall be drawn up on it, where you will make a most formidable appearance to the enemy while I, with the soldiers, shall be fighting on the beach.'[46] He was confident in his own light infantry and, as his brother Graham, a captain in the Royal Navy, said, 'Jack says his corps are not all what he would have them yet they will beat any of the French whom he leads them up to'.[47]

Moore was aware of the vulnerability of the coast he was to defend with a small, albeit effective, force. This cautious optimism was shared by many others concerned with coastal defence; one, Captain Francis Austen of the Royal Navy, brother of the aspiring young novelist Jane Austen, reporting on the danger to the beaches north of Deal, added that, 'in blowing weather, open flat boats filled with troops would, doubtless, many of them, be lost in the surf, while larger vessels could not, from the flatness of the coast approach sufficiently near.'[48] Deal, Walmer and Dover were well defended by fortresses and batteries, but Dungeness was another matter: patrolling its miles of beach was difficult because marching through shingle was exhausting and, once ashore, the enemy could spread out across Romney Marsh, where the only obstacles were narrow dikes. So it was here that the construction of the most formidable defences was ordered.

Along the south-eastern coast large-scale permanent defences began to be built. Redoubts and citadels were to protect the ports – notably Dover and Chatham – from landward attack. The shore was to be guarded by a chain of Martello towers, named after a fort that had held up a British attack in Corsica. These were drum-shaped, thirty-two feet high with walls thirteen feet thick, mounting a heavy gun and howitzers on the roof; seventy-four were to be built on the coast of Sussex and Kent, a further twenty-nine in Essex and Suffolk and more at other vulnerable points. The beaches of Dungeness around the expanse of Romney Marsh seemed particularly at risk – although marching across the shingle beaches and levels would be difficult, the only other obstacles were the hedges and dikes of Romney Marsh – so defences were planned just inland, beneath a low escarpment. Here a new water obstacle was dug, the Royal Military Canal, seven feet deep and running twenty-three miles from Rye to Shorncliffe; work began in September 1804.

The most remarkable project had been started a year before. This was an alternative seat of government in the centre of England, as far as possible from the sea, to which the King and the cabinet would move if London were threatened. At Weedon in Northamptonshire a vast military depot, including government offices, was built on the Grand Union Canal, linking it with London and Birmingham. There were barracks for a garrison of two infantry regiments, an arsenal, including twelve powder magazines, and three handsome brick and stone pavilions, one a modest palace for the monarch, the others for the government.★

After the British Isles had been on the defensive for almost a year, the invasion had yet to materialize. This was frustrating since the British heard reports of the defence of another island on the far side of the Atlantic to inspire them. This was Diamond Rock, a

---

★The Weedon depot was used by the Army until after the Second World War and most of it survives.

crag rearing from the sea off Martinique, which commanded the entrance to the most important French harbour in the Caribbean. Seized and held by a lieutenant and a hundred seamen of the Royal Navy, it had already defied all French attempts to recapture it for a year and was officially commissioned as HMS *Diamond Rock*; this was the sort of feat that the British imagined themselves performing on a far larger scale. But steadily the conviction grew that Henry Addington was not the man to lead them to such heights and that the national leader they required was Colonel Pitt of the Cinque Ports Volunteers.

7

To overthrow the tyrant

THERE WERE empty rooms in 12 Brompton Row – a house in the London suburb of Kensington rented by French tenants – at the end of 1803. Most of those who had been staying there over the past two years had gone but some of their friends, who had also expected to have left London by now, had not done so. These included the Duc de Bourbon, the Duc d'Orléans and the Comte d'Artois, all of whom had, as kinsmen of the dead king, been suggested as potential leaders of the monarchist movement in France. It was said that Addington had seen them all and had decided that the clandestine landing of leading dissidents might be permissible but that the introduction of a pretender was a risk too far. In any case, there was said to be a far more suitable candidate already on the Continent.

Small parties had been landed on the French coast throughout the summer and autumn by Captain Wright's brigs and cutters. They were to be the core of the conspiracy led by the three French generals. Bonaparte had always faced the rivalry of fellow generals, who had also fought for the Revolution, but all had been outmanoeuvred and one, General Kléber, his successor in Egypt, had been assassinated in Cairo; even the loyalty of Jean-Baptiste Bernadotte, due to be promoted to marshal, was being questioned. Of the present three, the two who had travelled from England were Charles Pichegru and Georges Cadoudal. The former, a sharp-featured soldier just past forty, had commanded the revolutionary armies on the Rhine and in Belgium in Robespierre's time and become president of the lower legislative chamber under the Directory; in 1797 he had become involved with royalist plotting and exiled to Guiana but had escaped to England. The latter, a heavily built, red-haired Breton aged thirty-two, had been a counter-revolutionary since 1793, commanding Chouan insurgents as a royalist general in north-western France; after escaping to England he had organized a training camp for guerrillas in Hampshire and planned the abortive attempt on the First Consul's life in December 1800.

The third general, who had remained in France, Jean Victor Moreau, was the most important by being the most popular. A man of intelligence, ambition and charm – as British visitors to Paris had discovered – his looks in youth had amounted to prettiness. After only two years as a soldier he had been promoted to brigadier in 1793 and two years later had followed Pichegru as commander of the Army of the North and the Army of the Rhine. Dismissed for suspected involvement with Pichegru in royalist plotting, he had later been given command of the Army of Italy and had joined Bonaparte's *coup d'état* of 1799, which had established the Consulate. In return he was again given the command in Germany when he defeated the Austrians at Hohenlinden, near Munich. Bonaparte still saw him as a rival but he was so popular that he kept his freedom, enabling him to dabble in conspiracies that might further his ambitions, which were, however, more personal than royalist. Bonaparte distrusted him and he was wary of others, including the sinister Fouché, feared as a potential Jacobin conspirator who might make use of any royalist plot. He was no longer Minister of Police, as the Department of Justice had been given greater powers in 1802; it was said that he was no longer trusted by the First Consul, who nevertheless found him indispensable and he remained at the centre of the regime's intelligence-gathering.

On cold, dark December nights small parties of men were still travelling from Biville towards Paris. On horseback, or occasionally in closed carriages, they moved from one *maison de confiance* to the next, usually isolated farmhouses or remote châteaux, their guides the royalist Chouan dissidents. Georges Cadoudal had made this journey twice and, after meeting Pichegru on the coast, had had to enter Paris again, which was difficult for one so recognizable as the burly Breton. General Pichegru and his servant Louis Picot travelled with him and several other conspirators, all of them armed. Outside Paris, Cadoudal and Pichegru together had boarded a gig and on 23 January 1804 successfully passed the Porte St Denis and made for the final safe house, a second-floor apartment near the Jardin des Plantes.

Two nights later Pichegru travelled through the dark streets to the Boulevard de la Madeleine, where Moreau and others were waiting. Among those at this meeting was a trusted conspirator named Joliclerc; but he was also in league with Fouché, to whom he would report later. According to Joliclerc, Pichegru had been unwise to introduce Cadoudal to Moreau, who regarded him as an assassin for his part in the attempt on the First Consul's life four years earlier. Both Pichegru and Cadoudal were worried by Moreau's attitude to the conspiracy. He was the key to gaining the support of other generals, and of the troops they commanded, so his co-operation was vital. But it now appeared that Moreau, while keen 'to overthrow the tyrant',[1] saw himself as his replacement, at least until a new constitution had been agreed and perhaps not even then; he even described himself as a future 'dictator'.[2] Certainly he was not interested in seating a Bourbon prince on the throne, for he now made it clear that he was a republican at heart. Pichegru and Cadoudal were aghast, and the latter declared that the conspiracy was finished. It was too late to retreat.

Although he did not yet know that the principal conspirators were in Paris, Bonaparte was aware of dangerous stirrings and that some of his generals were ambitious and restive. He also read reports from London and continental cities suggesting that something was afoot. Suspecting that British diplomats were involved, he instructed his own agents to infiltrate the intelligence networks he knew they had spun. A Captain Rosey, stationed at Strasbourg, was ordered to impersonate an aide-de-camp of a supposedly dissident French general; this he did with success, and among those who seemed to accept his story was Spencer Smith, Sir Sidney's brother, the British minister in Stuttgart. Although further incriminating reports arrived from other double agents, it was not until the end of January that Bonaparte was told that Cadoudal and Pichegru were in Paris and, indeed, that the former had been in the capital for nearly six months. He was told by Fouché that the latter had dined with a British minister in Kensington three days before landing in France. When his secretary, Louis de Bourrienne, reminded him that he had accepted Fox's insistence that the British government was innocent of plotting his assassination, Bonaparte exploded:

> Bah! you are a fool! *Parbleu!* I did not say that the English minister sent over an assassin and that he said to him, 'Here is gold and a poignard, go and kill the First Consul.' No, I did not believe that; but it cannot be denied that all those foreign conspirators against my government were serving England and receiving pay from that power . . . Is not Wright, who landed Georges [Cadoudal] and his accomplices at Dieppe, a captain in the British Navy?[3]

He was also told that both men were in touch with Moreau, who had, of course, unrivalled connections among senior officers. But the core of the conspiracy was still nebulous. The plot might explode into revolt at any moment, it seemed, and drastic steps had to be taken. Guards on the gates of Paris were strengthened, and all arrivals and departures checked as closely as during the Reign of Terror. Police agents were instructed to watch anyone known to have had links with the Chouans and other dissidents. A trawl through lists of suspects brought several arrests and vague charges of espionage but no firm evidence, so it was decided to try rougher tactics. Five prisoners were chosen and brought before a military court. Two were sentenced to death and shot the same day. Two more were acquitted. Then the fifth was brought forward, alone. This was a Dr Querelle, who had been landed at Biville by Captain Wright in August. He said nothing incriminating but was sentenced to death and taken to the condemned cell in the Abbaye prison. At dawn next day he watched from his window overlooking the prison courtyard as the soldiers of the firing squad paraded and a mounted escort arrived with the cab in which he would be taken to the execution ground. His courage broke; he called a gaoler and said that he had important information to give. Led before an interrogator, he confessed that he had landed with Cadoudal and named the *maisons de confiance* where they had stayed between there and Paris. He said that royalist conspirators from England had been in Paris for six months and that Cadoudal was still there, although he did not know exactly where. The First Consul was informed and General Savary was sent to Biville with fifty of his special gendarmes to make more arrests and to intercept another party of conspirators that Querelle had said were about to be landed by Captain Wright. Savary was told to expect the landing of a royalist pretender – a prince or duke – to lead a *coup d'état*. Some keepers of safe houses were arrested; others escaped. Among the couriers was a beautiful, fashionable girl of twenty, Nymphe Roussel de Préville, whose *nom de guerre* was *Prime-rose*, controlled by an agent known as *La Rose*. Warned of the danger, she changed into men's clothes and, despite her looks, passed as a youth named Dubuisson, riding into the Norman countryside and safety on a fast horse called La Blondine, which had been stabled at British expense for this purpose.

During the interrogation the name of a Parisian tavern, the Cloche d'Or, had been mentioned and it was raided by gendarmes. There they arrested Louis Picot, Cadoudal's servant, who was then identified by Querelle. At first he refused to speak or to accept a bribe, so he was tortured by thumbscrew and eventually confessed, giving two addresses where his master had been staying in the suburb of Chaillot, close to Passy. The houses were raided but Cadoudal was not there. However, the go-between who had hired the lodgings was discovered and forced to tell what he knew of the conspirators' whereabouts. More arrests and interrogation followed the same pattern and more addresses were discovered. It was obvious to the police that Moreau, Pichegru and Cadoudal knew that they were being hunted and that arrests, torture and interrogation would inevitably lead to each new *maison de confiance*, so were constantly on the move.

Finally they were captured. First, General Moreau was arrested on 13 February. Then, on the night of the 26th, Pichegru was surprised, asleep in bed; he reached for his pistol, failed to grasp it but wrestled furiously with the gendarmes. After fifteen minutes' struggle, lit by a candle held by a terrified servant girl, he was over-powered and, bound hand and foot, hustled to police headquarters on the Quai Voltaire.

Georges Cadoudal was still at large. Moving by night from safe house to safe house, he thought he had found a secure refuge in a hairdresser's shop in the Rue du Four on the evening of 9 March. However, a Chouan sympathizer who was being followed by police had been heard to order a cab for that night; a watch was kept on the coach house and it was noted that cab number 51 left, empty, at the appointed time. After dusk it was seen crossing the Place Maubert; it was followed and seen to stop in the Rue de la Montaigne Sainte-Géneviève. A large man wrapped in a cloak emerged from the shadows and climbed aboard. Shouting 'Georges!', the police ordered the cab driver to stop; he whipped up his horse and galloped away. More police lay in wait and in the narrow streets close to the Odéon two ran into the road and seized the horse's bridle. The door of the cab flew open and Cadoudal sprang out, a pistol in each hand. After shooting both policemen, and killing one, he ran into the gathering crowd, stopped and stood there calmly as if a spectator. After more police arrived, Cadoudal was recognized and arrested and, realizing further resistance was hopeless, allowed himself to be led away. At police headquarters he announced that he had come to Paris to do away with the First Consul. Taken to the Temple, he was locked in the cell next to Pichegru's. The principal conspirators had been caught but there was an even more important quarry: a Bourbon prince, who might pave the way to the throne of France for Louis XVIII, the exiled brother of the executed monarch. He was now aged forty-seven and wandering, fat and footloose, in exile through the European capitals, which he hoped were beyond the reach of Fouché's agents.

The prince's arrival – either by sea or across the eastern frontier – was rumoured to be imminent. There were a number of pos-sibilities but his identity was a mystery. A minor conspirator, Bouvet de l'Hozier, confessed under torture by garrotting that it was to be the Comte d'Artois. But the only one known to be close to the borders of France was the Duc d'Enghien. Aged thirty-one, handsome and charming, he was a direct descendant of King Louis XIII, grandson of the royalist commander the Prince de Condé, and the only son of the Duc de Bourbon, but had settled at Ettenheim in Baden to be near his German fiancée. There was little or no evidence to link him with the present conspiracy. It was known that he, like most prominent royalists, had once corresponded with William Wickham at the Aliens Office and, of course, Spencer Smith was now at Stuttgart, not far from Ettenheim. Otherwise suspicion rested on the report to Savary from a double agent that Cadoudal had been visited by an 'important personage . . . extremely well dressed . . . when he was in the room . . . everybody . . . rose and did not sit down until he had retired'.[4] His description did not match those other royal dukes. 'The description given of this mysterious person', wrote Fouché later, 'corresponded neither with the age of the Comte d'Artois, nor the person of the Duc de Berri . . . The Duc d'Angoulême was at Mittau . . . the Duc de Bourbon was known to be in London. Attention was therefore directed at the Duc d'Enghien.'[5]

In early March 1804 the three principal conspirators were in prison awaiting trial and the First Consul chose a trusted general for a secret mission. General Augustin de Caulaincourt had recently been his aide-de-camp, but was now commanding a brigade and was marked for further promotion. He was ordered to take fifty special gendarmes into Baden, kidnap the Duc d'Enghien and bring him back to France. On the night of the 15th the column rode into Ettenheim, surrounded the duke's house and ordered him out of bed and into a closed carriage. His dog jumped in after him and the prisoner and escort clattered into the darkness.

The cavalcade stopped at the fortress of Strasbourg and remained there for five days, awaiting further orders from Paris. When these arrived and the journey continued, other orders reached the commander of the fortress at Vincennes outside the capital. At seven o'clock on the evening of the 20th the Duc d'Enghien arrived there 'perishing with cold and hunger' and 'said he wanted something to eat and to go to bed afterwards', as an officer remembered.[6] He was told that his room had to be aired and so, still followed by his dog, he was taken to the officer's own room. Food was brought from the village and the duke invited the officer to eat with him. 'He spoke to me with great freedom and kindness', the latter continued, asking, 'What do they want with me?' and 'What do they mean to do with me?' But the officer had already guessed because during the day he had been ordered to have a deep hole dug in the castle courtyard; when he explained that the courtyard was paved, he was told to dig it in the dry moat outside.

After supper the duke retired to bed but before he could fall asleep he was ordered to dress and led to a room, where seven officers – a general and six colonels – sat behind a table: it was a court martial. He was asked details of his recent movements and replied easily and fully. Had he corresponded with other members of the Bourbon family? 'As might generally be supposed',[7] he had indeed corresponded with his father and grandfather. Did he know General Pichegru? 'I never saw him to my knowledge and I never had any connection with him. I know he wished to see me. I congratulate myself on never having known him, if it be true that he intended to employ the odious measures of which he is accused.'[8] Had he corresponded with anybody within France? Only with some friends with whom he had served as an officer, and only on private matters, he replied. With that, the interrogation ended and he was asked to sign the minutes. Bewildered and worried by the midnight trial, he wrote on the document, 'I earnestly request to have a private audience with the First Consul. My name, my rank, my manner of thinking and the horror of my situation induce me to hope that he will not refuse my request.'[9] The duke was then led back to his room, went to bed and fell deeply asleep.

Shortly before six o'clock on the morning of 21 March, less than ten hours after his arrival at Vincennes, the duke was woken by the officer with whom he had dined and told to dress. He was led out, his dog beside him, and down a dark stone staircase, with the officer leading the way. 'He asked where we were taking him', said the officer later. 'He received no answer. I went before the prince with a lantern. Feeling the cold air which came up the staircase, he pressed my arm and said, "Are they going to put me in a dungeon?" '

The staircase led to a door opening on to the dry moat. The sky was lightening and the duke could see officers, a quartermaster of the special gendarmerie, a file of six gendarmes with muskets and a freshly dug pit. Above, standing at the top of the steep bank, stood a watching figure; it was General Savary. Below, a captain stepped forward with a paper in his hand, took the lantern, and read the sentence of death. He stepped back. An order was given, the six soldiers presented their muskets and aimed at the Duc d'Enghien's chest. 'I gave the word to fire', said the quartermaster later. 'The man fell and, after the execution I learned that we had shot the Duc d'Enghien. Judge of my horror! I knew the prisoner only by the name of "the brigand of the Vendée"!'[10] The body was buried in the pit, which was filled in. The dog refused to leave and, when led away, kept returning to where his master had been killed, howling.★

As the news spread, Paris, all France and then the courts of Europe were shocked. One of the first to hear was Josephine Bonaparte, who cried, 'What barbarity!' She had known of her husband's decision to kill d'Enghien and had tried to dissuade him. 'How harshly he repelled my entreaties! I clung to him! I threw myself at his feet! "Meddle with what concerns you!" he exclaimed, "This is not women's business!" '[11] When Pitt heard the news he observed, 'Bonaparte has now done himself more mischief than we have done him since the last declaration of war.'[12] Even Fouché decided, 'It was worse than a crime – it was a blunder!'[13] Tsar Alexander of Russia was outraged because the duke had been kidnapped from the sovereign state of Baden, which was ruled by his father-in-law. Apologists for Bonaparte said that, whether or not there was incriminating evidence against d'Enghien, an example had had to be made to deter other royalists. The First Consul himself was sullen and defensive. When he eventually asked one of his generals for an opinion, he was told that he had 'acted well, but you and I are the only people to think so'.[14]

When the news of the arrests reached London on 5 March, a privy council was assembled for the following day. In consequence, the newly appointed Secretary to the Admiralty, Francis Marsden, passed requests to the Chouans on the coast of Normandy to make ready any available boats 'in order to favour

---

★The dog was acquired by King Gustavus IV of Sweden, who defied Napoleon. It wore a collar inscribed, '*J'appartenais au malheureux Duc d'Enghien*'.

the escape of General Pichegru, or other persons who have lately escaped from Paris'.[15] Meanwhile Captain Wright was commanding the brig *Vencejo*, manned by the Royal Navy and mounting sixteen short-range, 18-pounder carronades, and ordered to make for Quiberon Bay in the hope of picking up surviving conspirators, as several were known to have escaped and two had reached England. He sailed on 10 March, but preparations for the trials were progressing in Paris. Moreau, Pichegru and Cadoudal remained in their cells *en secret*. The first two had reasons for optimism, convinced that, such was their popularity, they would escape the usual penalty for treason. Then, on the morning of 6 April, a gaoler entered Pichegru's cell to open the shutters and saw him lying in bed, unusually still. Pulling back the sheet, he saw that he was dead, garrotted with his own neckcloth, which had been tightened to the point of strangulation by the twisting of a short stick. It was announced that he had committed suicide and that a volume of the works of Seneca describing a Roman suicide had been found in his cell. Rumour ran through Paris that he had been murdered by four Mamelukes, who then had themselves been silenced by firing squad.

In May the pace of events quickened. First, on the 7th, the crushing of the conspiracy against Bonaparte reached a climax. Captain Wright, accompanied by his nephew John, had been cruising in the *Vencejo* close inshore, among the shoals of Quiberon Bay off the rocky coast of Brittany for several weeks in the hope of sighting a sail, or a light, that might lead to the rescue of an escaped royalist. They were in company with the cutter *Fox*, and had chased and boarded a Spanish brig, on board which they found some American newspapers. They were months old but one included a verse addressed to the British, ending with the line 'Return victorious, or return no more'. These words came to obsess Wright – perhaps because of his long, dangerous vigil off the enemy coast – and his officers noticed that he would pace the deck muttering them 'in a kind of reverie'.[16]

That evening Wright had been ashore asking for news of any fugitives; there was none. Fog came down and his boat had trouble making a way through rocks and shoals to regain the ship. Then a gale blew out of the Atlantic and, as the *Vencejo* steered clear of the rocky hazards, the wind dropped and she lay becalmed. At first light it was seen that she was off Port Navalo and, through his telescope, Wright saw movement in the harbour. Then his worst fears were realized. Pulling towards them came one large French gunboat after another, under oars. They had no need of a wind, of course, and soon eighteen of them were counted. Wright, who again had been muttering 'Return victorious, or return no more', ordered his boats to tow the ship. At first they began to make way towards the open sea. Then the tide turned and the flood began to sweep her inshore again. The *Fox* carried oars as well as sails and Wright's officers suggested he transfer to her and escape, since he was most at risk if captured. She was some distance from the brig and, before he could decide, a gust of wind caught the cutter's sails and carried her out of earshot, out to sea and to safety. His ship's company stood to their guns but a flash and smoke from the leading gunboat, then about a mile distant, showed that the enemy was armed with long-barrelled, long-range 24-pounder guns; they could therefore fire with impunity while beyond the range of the British. Hope withered, but Wright decided to fight.

The French circled the becalmed brig, firing round shot and grape. A grapeshot slashed Wright's thigh but he had it bandaged and refused to leave the deck. He fought on, but the outcome was never in doubt unless a breeze came to the rescue of the brig. After four hours the ship wallowed, shattered; as her surgeon, John Lawmont, put it:

> Our firing almost ceased, three of the guns being dismounted and the rest encumbered with lumber from falling booms, the supporters having been shot away and the vessel nearly sinking, Captain Wright was forced to hail that he had struck [surrendered] just in time to save the lives of the few that could keep the deck, as the gunboats were rowing up alongside with numerous troops to board.[17]

The French scrambled aboard, took possession of the ship and then towed her through the rocks and shoals into the estuary of the river Loc.

After rowing up the river to the town of Auray, they landed the prisoners, taking the ratings to the prison and the officers to houses guarded by gendarmes. A few days later they were marched under escort to Vannes, the wounded Wright riding in a cart. On arrival he was taken to an inn and there interviewed by the provincial commander, General Julien, who remembered him; the general had been wounded in Egypt, captured and taken out to Sir Sidney Smith's ship, the *Tigre*, where Wright himself had given him his own cabin; so Julien ordered that his prisoner be made as comfortable as possible. He knew of Wright's subsequent career and the importance of his capture; he would certainly have to be sent to Paris forthwith. The captain travelled by coach under escort and, as he departed, his crew were allowed to say farewell. 'Captain Wright took an affectionate leave of them, many of whom shed tears', it was recalled. 'He said as he passed before them that in whatever situation he might be placed, he should never forget that he was a British officer.'[18]

Captain Wright did not know that the French officer accompanying him to Paris was carrying a letter from General Julien addressed to Fouché, who had been reappointed Minister of Police. He explained that, hearing a British ship had been captured, he had visited the prisoners to check whether they included 'any traitors like those who had lately been vomited on the coasts' and had 'recognized the celebrated Captain Wright, who had landed Pichegru, etc.', whom he had met in Egypt. He was sending Wright to Paris, together with his nephew, to act as his servant. He concluded, 'Captain Wright is a most artful and dangerous adventurer, who thought himself destined to act some high part – that he set all interrogatories at defiance as he acted on the orders of his Government and was accountable only to it – but, if he is properly questioned, he will make revelations of much importance to the Republic.'[19]

As Captain Wright reached Paris, important news reached the First Consul from London. Addington's administration had fallen and on 10 May 1804 William Pitt had again become Prime Minister. Details gradually filtered across the Channel. In England it had become increasingly clear that Addington was no war leader and was incapable of galvanizing the nation. Pitt knew himself to be the only man with the will and experience to take command

and in this belief he was supported by his rival Charles James Fox. In the House of Commons both had attacked the government on a range of issues, Pitt with his cutting sarcasm. Then, he came to the vital issue. 'We are come to a new era in the history of nations', he declared, 'We are called to struggle for the destiny, not of this country alone, but of the civilised world.'[20] Addington, decent as he was, could not rise to such heights and next day he resigned. Pitt returned to power but there was a price to pay: he had to abandon his championship of the Irish Catholics, for the time being, at least, and he was unable to choose the cabinet he had planned. Hoping to establish a broad-based, cross-party adminis-tration, he had wanted to include Fox. But the King, beginning to sink from eccentricity to insanity, forbade it; Pitt had to take office surrounded by lesser men from among his fellow Tories. Yet opti-mism had returned to the British; they had confidence in Pitt as the politician who could again forge the alliances that were the only imaginable means of defeating France. Napoleon was also aware of this.

The First Consul analysed his position. Aware that the killing of the Duc d'Enghien had outraged the governments of Austria, Prussia, Russia and, in particular, England, and that Pitt might well form them into a new coalition, he came to a decision. Realizing that they were, as monarchies, inspired and driven by the dynastic principle, which the conspirators had tried to restore to France, he would emulate them: the dynasty being his own. On 18 May 1804 the Senate, chosen by him for its compliance, announced that Napoleon Bonaparte was to be proclaimed Emperor of France; their decision was to be ratified by a national referendum later in the year, which would then be followed by his coronation.

Another ceremony had to come first: the trial of Moreau, Cadoudal and forty-seven others, including several women. This was due to open on 28 May, but it was not seen as a triumph for Bonaparte; indeed he, Fouché and Savary were worried. General Moreau was so popular within the army that they feared for the loyalty of the military escort that would accompany him from the Temple to the Palais de Justice. It would have to be strong enough to deter any rescue attempt but not so strong that it might itself mutiny and rescue him; all remembered the rescue of Sir Sidney

Smith from the Temple four years earlier by royalists disguised as republican officers. Cadoudal and the Chouans did not concern them because rural rebels would command little support in metropolitan Paris. In the event, Moreau did reach the court but, as his carriage passed the guard drawn up outside, the colonel in command clapped his hand on the hilt of his sword to indicate that, on an order from General Moreau, he would draw it in his defence. The mood in Paris was dangerous; as Fouché said, 'The air is full of poignards.'[21]

The streets through which the prisoners passed filled with silent spectators. Led into court, the entrance of Moreau produced a buzz of excitement and sympathy. As the indictments were read aloud, Cadoudal, who now expected no mercy, looked resigned but resolute, as did his fellow Chouans; only one looked shame-faced and he had taken Fouché's money to betray the others in the knowledge that, whatever his sentence, it would not be carried out. Intense interest was aroused by the questioning of Moreau, who, said one observer in court,

> was as calm as his conscience; and, as he sat on the bench, he had the appearance of one led by curiosity to be present at this interesting trial, rather than of an accused person, to whom the proceedings might end in condemnation and death . . . The result, clear as day to all present, was that Moreau was a total stranger to all their plots, all the intrigues, which had been set on foot in London.[22]

It was different with Cadoudal. There was little or no apparent sympathy for him in court, but while he had 'the manners and bearing of a rude soldier', according to the same spectator, 'under his coarse exterior he concealed the soul of a hero'.[23] He readily admitted the circumstances of his arrest, that he had fired on the police and had possessed two pistols and a dagger. Then he was asked, 'Where did you lodge in Paris?' 'I do not know.' 'What were you doing in Paris?' 'I was walking about.' 'Whom have you seen in Paris?' 'I shall name no one; I know no one.'[24] So he continued and, as questioning went on, 'he maintained the most obstinate silence'.[25] Later, outside the courtroom, an official suggested to

Cadoudal that, if he would renounce the plan to restore the Bourbons and his fellow conspirators, he could be pardoned and even offered some official employment, probably in a French colony. He replied, 'My comrades followed me to France and I shall follow them to death.'

On the sixth day of the trial a foreign witness was called: it was Captain Wright. He entered carrying a pair of manacles to demonstrate that he only attended under duress and in chains, which had only been removed on arrival at the Palais de Justice. 'He, however, refused to answer interrogatories put to him,' noted Bonaparte's secretary, Bourrienne, who was in court, 'declaring that, as a prisoner of war, he considered himself only amenable to his own government.' Thereupon the president of the court ordered that the transcripts of his interrogations be read aloud. When this had been done, Wright rose and said that, 'it was omitted to be stated that on these occasions the questions had been accompanied by the threat of transferring him to a military tribunal in order to be shot if he did not betray the secrets of his country'.[26] He was then led away.

On the day before verdicts were announced and sentences passed the prisoners had a last chance to speak in their own defence. Spectators were particularly moved by two of them, the de Polignac brothers, each of whom declared that he was ready to die if the other could be saved. On 8 June the courtroom and the streets surrounding the Palais de Justice were packed and tense. Then the sentences were declared. General Moreau and four others were only sentenced to two years' imprisonment. Georges Cadoudal and nineteen others – including one of the de Polignacs – were sentenced to death.

Within a fortnight the sentences had been reviewed. Moreau's was to be commuted to banishment; in the event, to the United States of America. Six death sentences were commuted, including, as arranged, that of the informer, and one of the de Polignacs, so that both brothers were spared. The rest, including Cadoudal's servant Picot, were to die.

The condemned showed great courage on 25 June, the day of their execution. On his way from prison to the scaffold in the Place de Grève, Cadoudal joked wryly, 'We have achieved more than we intended. We came to give France a king; we have given her an emperor.'[27] At the guillotine Cadoudal, realizing that the others might know that he had been offered a pardon under certain conditions, insisted that he die first so that, as Bourrienne recorded, 'his companions in their last moments might be assured that he had not survived them'.[28] His wish was granted.

8

Let us be masters of the world

'I DO not say that the French cannot come,' Lord St Vincent, the First Lord of the Admiralty, growled in the House of Lords, 'I only say they cannot come by sea!'[1] Such defiant confidence was the government's policy, yet Pitt was worried. While the initial French plan to cross under oars during a summer calm, or on a foggy winter night, had now been discounted, there was the risk that the enemy squadrons might be able to concentrate and dominate the Channel long enough to secure a landing of sufficient forces to occupy the south-east of England. As the newly proclaimed Emperor Napoleon remarked to Latouche-Tréville, 'Let us be masters of the world.'[2] This was wildly optimistic – command of the Channel would have to be seized and held for several days at least – but he was right in principle. That was why Nelson was in the Mediterranean with thirteen sail of the line blockading Latouche-Tréville's fleet in Toulon.

Other admirals had the same duty. Admiral Sir William Cornwallis and his Channel Fleet watched the French Atlantic ports with as many as thirty-three sail, divided into several squadrons, the two strongest waiting off Brest and Ushant. Admiral Lord Keith commanded the North Sea station, sometimes with twenty or more ships of the line, some thirty frigates and a swarm of smaller warships, based on the Downs to watch the coast from which the invasion might be launched. A subsidiary squadron commanded by Captain Sir Sidney Smith was patrolling the Dutch coast.

Meanwhile, the stalemate continued. Both sides could adjust their alliances: the Emperor Napoleon could consolidate his hold on the client states of central and southern Europe and Pitt could try to build another coalition against him. This would take time. Meanwhile it was important to take the offensive, if only for the sake of morale. But what could be done? The French were dominant on land, the British at sea. Early in 1804 it was estimated that the French armies ready to invade numbered 80,000 at Boulogne, 35,000 at St Omer, 14,000 at Dunkirk, 20,000 at Ostend and 10,000 at Bruges, a total of almost 160,000; in addition, 10,000 cavalry and artillery horses were waiting to be embarked. These were mostly 'fine, picked men, particularly the grenadiers', noted a British spy in Boulogne.[3] More than 1300 landing craft were ready and that number was to be doubled.

Before the French could sail, they must defeat or remove the Royal Navy, if only briefly. To achieve this, they would have to concentrate a fleet of fifty or more ships of the line from their Atlantic and Mediterranean ports. Little news arrived from the Mediterranean, so Nelson's name and activity could not be used to cheer the British people. He himself wrote of his boredom to his old friend Dr Benjamin Moseley. 'I have, by changing the cruising ground, not allowed the sameness of prospect to satiate the mind,' he began, 'sometimes by looking at Toulon, Villefranche, Barcelona and Rosas; then running round Minorca, Majorca, Sardinia and Corsica; and two or three times anchoring for a few days and sending a ship to the last place for onions, which I find the best thing that can be given to seamen . . . we seem forgotten by the great folks at home.'[4]

So, repeatedly, attention turned back to the principal threat to the British Isles: the Grande Armée and, in particular, the Emperor's headquarters at Boulogne; the urge to take direct action against this was a symptom of the frustration. After Nelson's failure there in August 1801 it was important that whatever was done was successful. There were French warships at sea off Boulogne, if only the familiar line of anchored brigs and gunboats guarding the harbour mouth and convoys creeping along the coast from Dunkirk and Calais. It was not enough for British frigates to snap up an occasional French coaster, or fire a few broadsides towards a shore battery. What was needed to demonstrate British resolution was to sink, or capture, a few of the Boulogne guardships, or perhaps to burn one of the forts built along the shoreline.

A major, albeit conventional, attack was launched against Boulogne at the end of August 1804, when sixty brigs and thirty luggers attacked the French line. A tremendous cannonade ensued; one British gunboat was sunk, and there were a few casualties. The exchange continued spasmodically for several days without having a noticeable effect on the French and the British sailed back to the Downs. Something more original was required.

For some new form of attack a naval officer of dash and imagination was needed. So, now that Nelson was beyond the farther shore of the Continent, two other, more junior, officers came to mind. One was Sir Sidney Smith and the other was Captain Home Popham. Both were clever mavericks and both had run foul of Lord St Vincent; however, the former was well connected in diplomatic and intelligence circles and the latter with the army, through the King's son the Duke of York, under whom he had served during the campaign in Flanders a decade earlier. But, other than repeating Nelson's attempt to cut out the guardships, what could they do?

Eclectic ideas circulated in the Admiralty. Blockships loaded with stone might be sunk in the mouths of French harbours. Details were sent to Lord Keith of a scheme for an aerial attack by balloons on the Flotille Impériale of landing craft. Thirty-two feet in diameter, the balloons could carry eight hundredweight of rockets and shells, to be released by clockwork. Their inventor, Charles Rogier, was confident of success, claiming that 'if the enemy should attempt to prevent the operation by striking the balloon with spiked rockets, it will fire the gas . . . [which would] communicate to the combustibles and bring them on their own heads. But if the balloons be sent in at night, the enemy will not perceive them till the moment of their operation.'[5]

Another possibility came through Robert Fulton. Once Fulton's difficulties with the French had become known in London, Addington had begun trying to entice him to England. During the Peace of Amiens a go-between named Smith – possibly one of Sir Sidney's family, if not Sir Sidney himself – had visited Fulton in Paris with handsome offers. There was haggling over terms, because the American's inventions – particularly his submarine – were regarded in London, as in Paris, as suspect. In April 1804, when Fulton had arrived in London, he at once applied, as a first step, for permission to work on the design for a steamship for export; he was granted permission to develop his invention but not, as yet, to export it.

Now that Pitt had returned to power, Fulton's ideas became more warlike, and he proposed 'a submarine expedition to destroy the fleets of Boulogne and Brest'.[6] There were several designs that Fulton had in mind; the most ambitious, a big boat, thirty-five feet long, with a crew of six, the ability to cruise for three weeks and to anchor when submerged. The idea was considered by a secret commission, which included Sir Joseph Banks, President of the Royal Society, the engineer John Rennie, the scientist Henry Cavendish, Captain Popham and William Congreve, the pioneer of rockets as artillery. Without consulting Fulton himself, the commission discussed his proposal and decided that the submarine might eventually prove a possibility but would be impracticable in operation.

Fulton was again disappointed. But just as he was about to abandon his efforts a series of chance meetings led to an introduction to Pitt, who invited him to breakfast at Walmer Castle. Fulton was a personable, persuasive man, whose stories about his life in Paris and experiences with the French fleet made him good company. He quickly persuaded Pitt and Popham that, even if they did not want his submarine, they would find his torpedo a decisive weapon. Two days later a contract for the development and production of torpedoes was agreed; Fulton was to be given the *nom de guerre* of 'Mr Francis'.

Torpedoes could be manufactured by competent ships' armourers, carpenters and gunners. There were several types, all also known as 'carcasses': the two-ton 'coffer' was the largest, twenty-one feet long, boat-shaped, with wedge-like bow and stern; wooden, but caulked, lead-lined and covered with tarred canvas, it was packed with forty barrels of gunpowder. The coffer was ballasted so that its deck was flush with the surface and fitted with a buoyed grappling hook to catch the mooring cable of an enemy ship, so that the current would carry it alongside. Before launching, a wooden plug would be removed to start the clockwork fuse which would fire a pistol and detonate the charge.

The smaller versions were designed to be used in pairs, linked by a rope; they would also be launched up-current of a moored enemy so that the torpedoes would be carried against either side of the ship. These were the 'hogsheads', which, fitted with primitive slow-burning or clockwork fuses, were described by Lord Keith, who distrusted such newfangled weaponry: 'We have tried an experiment with a tin lantern . . . having a tube fixed to the lower part and that tube fitted with a slow-fire composition and put in a cask charged with gunpowder and combustible balls; the cask has ballast boxes below it to keep it steady . . . They are about the size of a forty-gallon cask.'[7] Torpedoes, not being self-propelled, could be delivered by submarines, or launched from ships' boats, ballasted to lie low in the water and manned by a crew dressed in black with blackened faces so that, as was reported to Whitehall, 'the boats . . . are rowed under water, each by two men whose head and shoulders only are above water . . . the experiment has been tried in the basin at Portsmouth by night.'[8] Other trials were held off Lymington in Hampshire, and the weapon was shown to senior officers from the Admiralty on the Thames at Putney, west of London.

The hogshead was described by Lieutenant Abraham Crawford of the *Immortalité*, a frigate captured from the French in 1793, as

a newly-invented engine of murderous contrivance and most destructive force. These engines were made of copper and . . . spherical in form; hollow to receive their charge of powder, which, by means of machinery that worked interiorly, and so secured to be perfectly watertight, exploded at the precise moment that you chose to set it to. The mode of managing them was in this wise: two, attached together by means of a line coiled carefully clear, were placed in the boat ready to be roped overboard. The line was buoyed by corks, like the roping of a seine [net], so as to allow the carcasses to sink to a certain depth and no further. When you had approached near enough to the vessel against which you meant to direct the carcass and saw clearly that you were in a position that the line could not fail to strike her cable, one carcass was dropped overboard and, when that had extended the full length of the line from the boat, then the other, both having been carefully primed and set to the time, which would allow of their floating to their destined object before they exploded. Of course, it is presumed that wind and tide set in the direction, so as to ensure their not deviating from their course . . . The carcasses drifted until the line, which attached them together, struck the cable of the vessel, when it was presumed that the carcasses, one on either side, would swing under her bilge and, at the fated moment, explode and shatter her to pieces.[9]

Like St Vincent and most of his own naval contemporaries, Crawford hated the idea: 'This species of warfare, unmanly and, I may say, assassin-like, I always abhorred.' He went on:

Under cover of the night to glide with muffled oars beneath the bows of a vessel and, when her crew is least suspicious of impending danger, to affix such an infernal machine beneath her bottom and in a moment hurl them to destruction, in what does it differ from the midnight attack of the burglar, who steals into your house and robs his sleeping victim of money and life?[10]

Other naval officers, who could imagine a future for submarine warfare, had mixed feelings. One typical view was that 'battles in future may be fought under water: our invincible ships of the line may give place to horrible and unknown structures, our frigates to catamarans, our pilots to divers, our hardy, dauntless tars to submarine assassins, coffers, rockets, catamarans, infernals . . . How honourable!'[11]

Some thought otherwise. Among those fascinated by Fulton's ideas was Captain Johnstone, the smuggler. On his return to England from America in the summer of 1804, he was granted the promised pardon, engaged as a pilot by the Admiralty and put to work with Fulton. If the American sometimes felt ill at ease with conventional naval officers, he liked the tough, roguish Kentish seaman. Even when the Admiralty abandoned any thought of developing submarines, Johnstone remained enthusiastic, perhaps because of their potential for smuggling: to the navy his knowledge of the tides and shoals of the narrow seas would remain invaluable.

Torpedoes – let alone submarines – took time to build, so the conventional surface ships of the Royal Navy continued their harassing of the enemy coast and coastal shipping. One squadron of frigates and brigs, commanded by Captain Smith, patrolled the shores of the Low Countries, while another, under Captain Popham, operated down-Channel from Dunkirk, mostly off Boulogne. The latter consisted of the *Immortalité*, three brigs and a cutter, and Crawford recorded brief bombardments, the occasional minor capture and other 'sharp bouts with the batteries and flotilla'.[12]

There were other missions, too. Although the Pichegru-Cadoudal plot had collapsed, with its leaders dead and Captain Wright imprisoned in Paris, there were still strange civilians to be taken on unspecified missions emanating from Walmer Castle. In August 1804 Crawford's frigate 'again proceeded off Boulogne,' he noted,

> taking with us a gentleman, whom, as his name never transpired, I must still designate by the appellation of 'Mr Nobody' . . . During the fortnight this gentleman passed on board, the *Immortalité* was kept constantly close inshore, whenever the state of tide and weather would permit, in order to give him an opportunity of pursuing certain researches upon which he seemed intent and which, to give him his due praise, he did with the greatest earnestness and coolness, unruffled and undisturbed by the showers of shot and shells that fell around the ship, splashing the water about her at every instant. The objects of this scrutiny seem to be to ascertain . . . the fortifications around Boulogne and the position and bearings of the different batteries, which faced the sea, and also the exact distance at which the flotilla in the roads was anchored from the shore.[13]

'Mr Nobody' was not a welcome passenger because his presence on board was making the ship 'a target for our friends to amuse themselves by practising at'.[14] Yet there was something unusual in the air that may have accounted for his presence. For three days in the middle of August the French gun brigs lying under the protection of their shore batteries responded to the British presence with unusual vigour, hitting three of the squadron's ships. Through telescopes it could be seen that, close inshore, boats were passing up and down the moored lines of guardships as if inspecting them, and on board could be seen the blue and gold uniforms of senior officers. This, thought Crawford, suggested 'that Bonaparte was present at the time and that, under the eye of their newly-elected Emperor, they fought with resolution and boldness unknown to them before'.[15]

This was indeed so, as was to be demonstrated on 16 August. 'Mr Nobody's' telescope had often scanned the heights to the east of Boulogne, where, near the pavilions of the Emperor and his senior commanders and between the great hutted encampment and the sea, lay a wide, shallow, grassy bowl that was sometimes used as a parade ground, or for exercising cavalry. On this particular morning it presented an extraordinary spectacle. Across the clifftop stretched a glitter of sunlit steel: helmets, breastplates, sabres and bayonets. The Grande Armée was on parade. It was the day after the Emperor's thirty-fifth birthday and had been chosen to mark the third anniversary of Nelson's defeat off Boulogne by Latouche-Tréville. But the parade was not only to celebrate those dates, and for Napoleon to inspect the army he intended to lead across the Channel. It was to inaugurate a new order in the rebuilding of France as the heart of a global empire with the Emperor, the royal family and an aristocracy, as an addition to the system of honours to strengthen the foundation of the army. Napoleon was to decorate more than 2000 soldiers with the Légion d'Honneur. The ideas for such a military and civil order – its design was based on the old royalist Croix de St Louis – had been conceived two years before and the first decorations had been presented on 15 July that year in the chapel of the Invalides in Paris, at a ceremony which the Emperor had opened by reciting the oath of allegiance, which those present were to repeat.

He had then left for Boulogne, accompanied by his brothers Joseph and Louis – both now princes – together with his ministers and marshals. The parade was staged with high theatricality. The natural arena was shaped like a scallop shell, fanning out from the clifftop and with a hillock at its apex. On this had been built a dais decorated with 200 captured banners, some short-torn and blood-stained, weapons and armour. Also on the dais and approached by twelve steps was an ancient throne said to have been made in the seventh century for the Frankish king Dagobert, and now for the use of the Emperor Napoleon.

It was a bright, breezy day, with cumulus clouds floating in a blue sky and the chalk cliffs of England gleaming across the horizon. However, also out at sea could be seen the sails of British frigates and brigs, just beyond the range of the guns along the shore. Throughout the morning the troops assembled, having marched from as far as Arras. The Imperial Guard formed around the saluting base with massed bands to one side and 2000 drum-mers to the other. Facing them, drawn up on the slopes were the soldiers who were to be decorated by the Emperor and behind them, massed in twenty columns and in battle order, were 80,000 men from sixty regiments and twenty squadrons of cavalry. On the highest ground beyond stood some 20,000 spectators.

At noon the Emperor and his entourage left their pavilions, and it began. As the shore batteries fired royal salutes and 2000 drums rolled, a cloud rolled back and the sun shone. Napoleon mounted the dais, the drums beat the charge and the whole parade marched forward, closing tightly around the throne. 'Everyone was thrilled with martial ardour at this splendid moment', a spectator remem-bered. Now the ceremony of allegiance followed, ending with a roar of '*Vive 'l'Empéreur!*' and the brandishing of sabres and muskets by the assembled thousands.

The distribution of medals began. They had been heaped in the shield and helmet of the fifteenth-century hero Bayard, and throughout the afternoon the Emperor presented them to soldiers of all ranks. He had prepared himself efficiently. As his secretary Bourrienne remembered:

He would say to one of his aides-de-camp, 'Ascertain from the colonel of such a regiment whether he has in his corps a man who has served in the campaigns of Italy, or the campaigns of Egypt. Ascertain his name, where he was born, the particulars of his family and what he has done. Learn his number in the ranks and to what company he belongs and furnish me with the information.' On the day of the review, Bonaparte, at a single glance, could perceive the man, who had been described to him. He would go up to him as if he recognized him, address him by name and say, 'Oh, so you are here! You are a brave fellow – I saw you at Aboukir – how is your old father? What! you have not got the Cross? Stay, I will give it to you.' Then the delighted soldiers would say to each other, 'You see, the Emperor knows us all; he knows our families; he knows where we have served.' What a stimulus this was to soldiers, whom he succeeded in persuading that they would all, some time or other, become Marshals of the Empire![16]

Later in the afternoon the wind freshened into a gale, blowing the watching British warships away from the coast and towards England. The Emperor's staff had been anxiously looking out to sea through telescopes, while Decrès, the Minister of Marine, Berthier, his Minister of War, and General Junot looked worried, and soon Napoleon himself became agitated. Then, as Madame Junot put it,

At length the Minister of Marine received a message, which he immediately communicated to the Emperor; and the latter snatched the glass from the hand of M. Decrès with such violence that it fell and rolled down the steps of the throne. All eyes were now directed to the point to which I had observed the Emperor watching and soon we discerned a flotilla, consisting of between 1000, or 1200 boats, advancing in the direction of Boulogne from the different ports and from Holland.

Saved from the British by the providential gale, the convoys had arrived on time as planned.

'But the satisfaction of the Emperor was not of long duration', continued Madame Junot.

An emphatic oath uttered by M. Decrès warned the Emperor that some accident had occurred. It was soon ascertained that the officer who commanded the first division of the flotilla had run foul of some works newly erected along the coast. The shock swamped some of the boats and several of the men jumped overboard . . . The accident was exceedingly mortifying, happening as it did, in the full gaze of our enemies, whose telescopes were pointed towards us and it threw the Emperor into a violent rage. He descended from the throne and proceeded with Berthier to a sort of terrace, which was formed along the water's edge. He paced to and fro very rapidly and we could occasionally hear him utter some energetic expression indicative of his vexation. In the evening a grand dinner took place . . . About six o'clock, just as dinner was served for the soldiers under tents, a heavy fall of rain came on. This augmented the Emperor's ill-humour and formed a gloomy termination to a day which had commenced so brilliantly.[17]

Because of the rain, the planned firework display was postponed and held the following evening. Then, as Napoleon watched from his clifftop pavilion, 'the sky was lit up with thousands of luminous bombs and innumerable rockets, while fifteen thousand Roman candles shot up their stars in a ceaseless stream . . . Subsequently, the town, ramparts and triumphal arches were all illuminated and a brilliant ball closed the fête.'[19] Next day the Emperor watched another sort of pyrotechnic display when the wind allowed British ships to return inshore for two hours of exchanging round shot with the shore batteries.

Napoleon's mood would have been further depressed had he heard the news from Toulon that, two days after his distribution of the Légion d'Honneur, the naval officer most deserving of such recognition, Latouche-Tréville, had died. He had never recovered from a tropical infection caught at Santo Domingo and, although Nelson was to joke that he had ruined his health climbing to a mountain top to look for the blockading British, the two admirals had been well matched and respected one another. His successor was to be a lesser man, the Comte Pierre de Villeneuve. He had made his mark by commanding the rear of the French line at the Battle of the Nile, when he had cut his cables and escaped capture, or destruction. It was not a good omen for the Emperor's grand design against England.

Now was the moment for the invasion to begin, it was thought, for what else could follow such an overture? But, instead, the Emperor left Boulogne, heading east to meet his Empress in Belgium. Yet this might be an example of Napoleon's trickery, feints and disinformation, because the summer would soon end, autumn weather would be less predictable and the Grand Armée could not wait in its camps indefinitely. So the operations planned by the British against Boulogne would go ahead, probably towards the end of September. Popham would be in immediate command and his superior, Lord Keith, had no option but to accept orders to give all help to what the former called Fulton's 'new curiosities' and assume overall command.[19] But then not only did the admiral postpone the attack until October; he also decided that surprise was unnecessary and anchored his squadron within sight of Boulogne several days in advance, counting 150 French ships moored in the defensive line offshore. Keith flew his flag in the *Monarch* and was accompanied by five other ships of the line, five frigates, a swarm of sloops, bomb ketches, the usual variety of gun vessels and, most importantly, the 'infernals'. These consisted of four explosion vessels – brigs packed with gunpowder, shells and inflammables, in effect, huge floating bombs – and a variety of torpedoes, Fulton listing 'five large coffers, five small and ten hogsheads'.[20] This was, indeed, something new. The aim would be to sink or burn as many of the enemy as possible.

On 2 October wind, weather and tide were right for the attack and Lord Keith ordered that it begin soon after nine o'clock that night. The boats of the fleet advanced in three divisions, with the larger ones carrying carronades to protect the others, which towed the explosion ships or carried torpedoes. One young officer, John Allison, who commanded the *Leopard*'s cutter, carrying a pair of torpedoes, sighted anchored enemy ships ahead and, as he put it,

> driving directly for them by the tide, at the distance about half a cable [about 100 yards], I took the pin out of the aftermost cask . . . I put my ear to the machinery and heard it going, then ordered it to be thrown overboard and told Mr Gilbert . . . to

take the pin out of the case in the bow . . . then ordered the cask to be thrown overboard . . . I think they must have heard the splashing of the casks from the shore as they commenced firing musketry immediately, the balls coming over the boats.[21]

At the same time the other torpedoes were being launched, while in the explosion vessels the crews were lighting the fuses or starting the clockwork and scrambling into boats towed astern. Flashes, explosions, shots and shouts filled the night but nobody could see what was happening. The British, having launched their torpedoes or cast the explosion ships adrift, pulled back against the tide towards the ships of the line.

The French could see no better. As Crawford wrote, a French pinnace with crew of thirty-six and commanded by an ensign,

more enterprising than his companions, saw a cutter-rigged vessel approaching and advancing steadily for the French line, pulled for her resolutely with the intention of boarding and, should she prove a fire-vessel, which previous explosions led him to suspect, tow her clear of the line and then try to extinguish the fire. The English officer and crew had already left the vessel, so the first part of his intention was easily performed. A few of [the French ensign's] crew jumped into a punt, which was towing astern of the abandoned craft, whilst he and the remainder ascended her side. But scarcely had the poor fellow ascertained that she was indeed a *brûlot* [fireship] and was trying to find out whether any trace of fire was to be discovered, than she blew up and launched him and his devoted crew to instant destruction: the only men, out of thirty-six, that escaped death were the few, who had been ordered into the punt to assist in towing the vessel's head around.[22]

Other than that, no significant damage was done to either side and the stalemate continued. Surprisingly, Lord Keith was encouraged, telling the Admiralty that a similar attack on a larger scale might 'hold forth a reasonable prospect of a successful result'.[23] The new weapons were mocked in a British sailors' song,

See fireships, my frog-toasters, to entertain John Bull;
Of brimstone and of bottles, they, like some heads, are full.
See here my casks and coffers with triggers pulled by clocks!
But to the Frenchman's rigging, who first will lash these blocks?
Catamarans are ready (Jack turns his quid and grins)
Where snugly you may paddle in water to your chins . . .
Your project new, Jack mutters, avast! 'tis very stale:
'Tis catching birds, land-lubbers! by salt upon the tail.[24]

The French naval command was equally disdainful of the weaponry as 'a horrible attempt against the laws of war by seeking to
destroy an enemy without exposing themselves to any dangers'.[25]

Two months later Popham tried to destroy a wooden offshore
fort with a fireship and two pairs of torpedoes and Sir Sidney
Smith made another attack; both operations failed. Although Lord
Melville, the First Lord of the Admiralty, was satisfied that, as a
result of the attacks on Boulogne, 'panic has laid hold of the army
intended for the invasion',[26] Fulton's 'infernals' fell out of favour.
So something more would have to be tried. Congreve suggested
that his rockets, combined with torpedoes, would be effective: the
enemy, looking up at the fiery missiles descending on their inflam-
mable ships, would fail to notice the torpedoes being launched in
the darkness below. Sir Sidney Smith, who in May had left his
command of a squadron off the Low Countries, was also applying
himself to the problem. He realized that, even if a few more
French ships could be destroyed off Boulogne, the heavy shore
batteries would prevent any attempt to bombard the harbour from
the sea and now the French had laid floating booms moored to the
sea-bed in front of their line to ward off torpedoes. There was one
possible alternative: an assault landing at Boulogne such as he had
led in Aboukir Bay.

But while infantry could scramble ashore from ships' boats, they
could do so only in small parties; also the landing of artillery was a
problem. So he set about designing a new type of landing craft, far
in advance of anything devised by the French. This was to be a
large catamaran, its twin hulls joined by a platform with a ramp,
which could be lowered for landing. The Admiralty was impressed
and authorized the building of a prototype on the Thames. Smith's

sketches were developed into a catamaran with a platform twenty feet square, which underwent trials on the river between Greenwich and Chelsea, rowed by six men and rigged for sails. This proved a success and two larger versions were ordered, one forty-eight feet long and able to carry a field gun and fifty soldiers; the other, double that length and powered by eight oars on each side, sixteen paddles between the two hulls and gaff-rigged sails on either beam. Both were lined with cork for buoyancy and, when loaded, only drew eighteen inches of water. While these were under construction, the British frigates and brigs continued their patrols, cutting-out raids and reconnaissance along the enemy coast.

The frustrated British studied any means of getting to grips with the French, who themselves were self-absorbed. On 2 December 1804 Paris shook to the thunder of guns and the peeling of bells while huge crowds filled the streets. It was the coronation of the Emperor Napoleon I, the foundation of the new imperial dynasty and of the French empire. The royal status of General Bonaparte had been proclaimed earlier that year and a submissive Senate had endorsed all the requirements of the self-invented heir to the Emperor Charlemagne, King of the Franks and ruler of Christian Europe. The only trouble had been within the Bonaparte family, as to their own royal precedence, but this the Emperor had silenced with bullying and bribery: threatening to quash their titles, or offering crowns of lesser European kingdoms.* Now the climax was reached with a spectacle equal to that on the clifftop at Boulogne. What Bourrienne described as 'the glitter of gold, the waving plumes and richly-caparisoned horses of the imperial process'[27] left the Tuileries for the cathedral of Notre-Dame, passing the gloomy turrets of the Conciergerie prison, through streets decorated with wooden Gothic arches festooned with flags and laurel. The Emperor was dressed in crimson velvet, embroidered with gold and silver, in lace, white silk stockings, white velvet slippers embroidered in gold; he wore a diamond-encrusted sword and carried the sceptre of Charlemagne and the Bourbons'

---

*Three of Napoleon's brothers became kings: Joseph of Naples, then Spain; Louis of the Netherlands; and Jerome of Westphalia.

symbolic Hand of Justice. He had become a glittering pantomime figure, hardly matched by the flamboyant Prince of Wales on the other side of the Channel, his dress a far cry from the simple artillery officer's uniform and revolutionary cockade he had worn a decade before. The Emperor was accompanied by the Empress Josephine, also aglitter with diamonds and emeralds on white silk and satin beneath a train of crimson velvet lined with Russian ermine.

The couple entered the cathedral, a choir of 400 sang the *Te Deum* and, as they approached the altar, a priest rose to greet them. It was the Pope, Pius VII. Napoleon had recognized that the formal approval of the Vatican was essential in Catholic Europe and this, too, he had ensured by bullying and bribery. But even here he sprung another surprise. After receiving the blessing from the Pope, Napoleon turned to the golden crown, which lay ready on a velvet cushion, raised it himself and, turning his back upon the Pope, placed it on his own head. Josephine approached and curtseyed to her husband and he thereupon crowned her, too. The heralds then shouted, 'The most glorious and most august Napoleon, Emperor of the French people, is anointed, crowned and enthroned. *Vive l'Empéreur!*' Again the guns thundered along the Seine, echoed by batteries across France to Boulogne and heard by soldiers on the cliffs of Kent. That night Paris exploded with festivities and fireworks, and crowds danced in the Place de la Concorde, where the guillotine had stood but where wine now flowed instead of blood.

The Emperor himself now prepared to leave for Boulogne and the expected invasion of England. First, there was further ceremony to attend and a letter to write. The ceremony was a massive military parade on the Champs de Mars, when regimental standards were replaced by carved and gilded imperial eagles. The letter was to King George III of England, suggesting a return to negotiations for a peace that the Emperor did not want and knew had no chance of beginning because of the terms he proposed. It was, however, an excuse to begin a letter to his principal enemy with the familiar and vaguely insulting terms of an equal: 'Monsieur mon frère . . .'[28]

The sound of the guns and the bells of Paris carried across the rooftops and the river to the village of Passy to be heard by Fanny d'Arblay and her little family in exile. Despite the amnesty granted to her husband and a junior position allowed him in a government office, she kept very quiet indeed. Fearful lest she be thought disloyal to France, or to be passing secret messages to London, she had ceased her lively correspondence with her friends at home. When she did write, she was careful to use the French revolutionary calendar and to avoid anything that might be construed as criticism of the regime. In the only letter she is known to have written to her father in 1804 she merely wrote, 'We live in the most quiet and, I think, enviable retirement . . . Our view is extremely pretty . . . and always cheerful; we rarely go out, yet always pleased to return. We have our books, our prate and our boy – how, with all this, can we complain of our narrow and narrowing income?' Her only complaint was 'my deprivation of the society of my friends'.[29]

Even after the extravaganza of Napoleon's coronation and the presentation of the eagle standards on the Champs de Mars within view of their windows, she only wrote to her father that Alexandre had to trudge daily, for at least an hour each way, to his office in the buildings department of the Ministère de l'Intérieur as he could not afford any form of transport. Otherwise, she wrote, 'we continue steady to our little cell at Passy, which is retired, quiet and quite to ourselves with a magnificent view of Paris from one side and a beautiful one of the country to the other.'[30] From her window she could see across the city to the conical turrets of the Temple prison, where the sound of jubilation reached another lonely expatriate, Captain John Wright, imprisoned and still demanding to be treated as a prisoner of war rather than as a spy. He was aware that the French knew exactly who he was and what he had been doing. Despite his silence in the witness box at the trial of Moreau, Pichegru and Cadoudal, he had been interrogated privately by the presiding judge, Jacques Thuriot, who had voted for the execution of King Louis eleven years earlier. Again he refused to answer questions, but witnesses were produced and their evidence was damning.

Two were particularly hurtful. One was an old friend, François de Tromelin, who had taken part in Sir Sidney's rescue in 1798, driving a coach that had carried him and Wright from the gates of the Temple through the dark streets of Paris. Later Sir Sidney had taken him to the Middle East as a staff officer but at the Peace of Amiens he had publicly assumed his true identity. He had then been granted a pardon, the restoration of his family estate in Brittany and a commission as major in the republican army. Now, when Thuriot asked him, of Wright, 'Have you not known him before? Have you not been conducted with him to the tower of the Temple in the year IV [1796]?', de Tromelin replied, 'Yes'. There was no need to say more. When Wright was asked whether he remembered de Tromelin, he said that 'he would not give any answer'.[31]

More damaging was the appearance in court of Wright's own nephew John, who was also identified by de Tromelin. The boy tried to be careful. When asked if he knew 'in England, of a con-spiracy against France', he replied only, 'I have heard it talked of in the province of Kent, at Greenwich, about six months ago.' But he lowered his guard and when Thuriot asked, 'How often have you seen men disembarked upon the coast of France from the corvette, which you sailed in?' he replied, 'I have not seen any disembarked since within two months, or thereabouts.'[32] Afterwards the boy wept and told another English lad, who was said to be Sir Sidney Smith's nephew, 'I shall never see my uncle again. Bonaparte is going to kill him.'[33]

Although Wright had been threatened with execution during his first interrogation, the terms of his confinement were now relaxed. A week after the execution of the principal conspirators, he was joined at the Temple by two officers – one of them his first lieutenant, Lieutenant James Wallis – and twenty-two sailors from his ship, together with his nephew and another boy. Captain Wright was able to treat them to wine and beer, while he himself was allowed to enjoy presents of 'wine, rum, brandy, pastry, etc.', he could read French newspapers and was 'allowed his books, pens, ink and paper'. He supervised some education for the two boys, who 'visited the door of Captain Wright twice a day in order to repeat their lessons of French grammar, mathematics, etc.'[34] Despite this, he was worried; not because of his involvement with the conspirators but because of his links with Sir Sidney Smith in the Middle East, when the latter had waged effective psychological warfare against Napoleon. 'Bonaparte will destroy me,' he told a friend, 'he has not forgotten our proclamations in Egypt, nor what we have written to him, nor the reproaches which we have addressed to him on the subject of his crimes at Jaffa, these being the massacres of Turkish prisoners of war.'[35] The outlook suddenly darkened when, after two months, his former shipmates were suddenly sent to a prisoner of war camp, leaving him to face imprisonment alone. He only had time to ask Wallis to look after the two boys as 'a sort of foster-father to my little admirals in embryo'.[36]

Left alone with his reading and writing, Wright was, however, able to make contact with other prisoners by passing notes and tapping messages on the floor and ceiling for, like Smith, he was skilled at clandestine communication, an essential preliminary to escape. Then, one morning, a party of police, including the inspector-general of the Ministry of Police officers, burst into his room and 'surprised him in the act of writing a note', whereupon he 'put into his mouth the note . . . The agent of police threw himself upon the neck of Captain Wright, who nevertheless persevered in masticating the note, which the officer wished to get possession of. A scuffle took place and blows were given and received; the inspector interfered and terminated it; and all the papers of Captain Wright were taken away.'[37]; in future, he would only be allowed to receive the official French newspaper *Le Moniteur*. He was now a prisoner in solitary confinement, *en secret*, hoping for rescue, or exchange, but aware that he might remain a lonely prisoner for the rest of the war. He had two comforts: one, that he heard before his communications were cut that the Admiralty had confirmed him in the rank of post-captain, so that he would now move up the Navy List automatically and, if he survived, would eventually become an admiral; the other, 'a little amiable cat that has just taken the caprice of laying her whole length on my paper and purrs to me.'[38]

In view of his escape from the same prison with Sir Sidney Smith nine years earlier, the French were aware that another escape might be attempted. But the network of royalist agents that had succeeded then had been broken and dispersed on the collapse of the Cadoudal conspiracy. Other networks were being slowly assembled but the British had to concentrate on more direct action in the Channel and against the ports from which the invasion might be launched. In England, Sir Sidney was devoting himself to the planning of more small-scale actions against the enemy in the narrow seas. Captain Wright would have to wait.

9

A sweet kiss will be ample reward

THE MAIN defence against invasion was not, however, the frigates and brigs sailing to and fro a few miles off the enemy coast
between the Texel and Brest. It was far more distant, in the deep
stormy waters of the Gulf of Lyons, in the anchorage among the
scatter of the barren Maddalena Islands off the northern cape of
Sardinia, where Nelson and his ten sail of the line awaited the
French fleet, upon which depended the invasion of England.
Here, off Toulon, or in the calm of Agincourt Sound, the anchorage off the Maddalenas, with a high sun baking the decks and
melting the caulking in their seams, the wind heated by the Sahara
and scented by the mountain herbs of Provence, Corsica and
Sardinia, it was difficult to imagine that this was the main defensive
bulwark of the chalk cliffs of Kent and the levels of Dungeness and,
indeed, of London.

Also watching and waiting in the Atlantic, off Brest and the
ferocious rocks and shoals of Ushant, was Admiral Cornwallis and
his Channel Fleet. Squadrons had to be detached from time to
time – he also had to watch Rochefort and the other Bay of Biscay
ports and the coast of Ireland – but he tried to keep a dozen sail of
the line within striking distance of Brest, except when the heaviest
gales drove them to shelter in Torbay or Cawsand Bay.

These were the big ships: the first-rates of 2500 tons, with more
than 800 men handling their vast spread of sail and 100 guns or more;
the workhorse 'seventy-fours'; and frigates for reconnaissance

and hunting prizes but not for lying in a line of battle. The British were nearly always at sea, attuned to wind and weather, but the French were usually blockaded in their ports and unaccustomed to heaving decks.

The successful invasion of England had always hinged on the ability of the French squadrons to escape from port and through the British blockade, then to concentrate and dominate the Channel and southern North Sea. Napoleon, Decrès and their admirals had drawn up a variety of plans. One was for landings in the south-east of England to be preceded by an invasion of Ireland, mounted from Brest, to entice the British squadrons away from their principal objectives. The essence of Napoleon's strategy was that two or more squadrons should break out, join forces and take action that would draw their heavy ships away from the Channel. The admirals chosen to carry this out were the most experienced available: at Brest, Vice-Admiral Honoré Ganteaume; at Rochefort, Rear-Admiral Edouard-Thomas Burgues Missiessy; and at Toulon, Latouche-Tréville's successor, Admiral Villeneuve. The first plan was that the main Toulon squadron should break out, run through the Straits of Gibraltar, join the squadron from Rochefort, cross the Atlantic to capture the British islands of St Lucia and Dominica and reinforce French possessions there, while smaller squadrons would attack British trading posts on the African coast and the remote Atlantic island of St Helena; meanwhile, Ganteaume would sail from Brest with 18,000 troops to land in Ireland. 'These successive shocks at the main points of their commerce will make them realize at long last just how vulnerable they really are', decided Napoleon, adding that the British 'will certainly not expect anything else'. Villeneuve would then return across the Atlantic with his combined fleet to the Channel, where he would be joined by Ganteaume, who would have sailed around the north of Scotland and south down the east coast of England. 'It will be easy to surprise them', Napoleon continued, 'the Grand Armée . . . will then enter the county of Kent.'[1]

There was still some hesitancy and the grand design had been modified to what amounted to a dress rehearsal. Missiessy was to sail from Rochefort and Villeneuve from Toulon, the former to attack British Islands in the Caribbean and the latter to raid the northern coast of South America; then they were to combine and steer for the Channel. But Missiessy's six sail of the line and Villeneuve's eleven would clearly not be enough to cover the invasion of England. Nevertheless, Missiessy's squadron – including several frigates and brigs and with 3500 troops embarked – escaped from Rochefort in a snow squall on 11 January 1804 and sailed west through a violent Atlantic storm, which blew the British blockading squadron off-station. A week later Villeneuve left Toulon while most of Nelson's ships were anchored in Agincourt Sound in the hope that their absence from the horizon would tempt the French to sea and a battle. When a frigate was sighted by Nelson's flagship, the *Victory*, off the Maddalenas, flying the signal that the French were out, he had at once ordered his squadron to make sail. His plan misfired for he did not know where they were bound and such clues as he had gathered hinted at Sicily or Egypt. So, cleared for immediate action and with crews sleeping between their guns, the British had run south through the Straits of Messina, then east to Alexandria.

Short of frigates, Nelson had not enough fast ships to search for the enemy and wrote in his frustration, 'What would I give to know where they are bound to, or to see them! The result of a meeting I should be a wretch to doubt.'[2] There was no sign of the enemy, so he headed west again and off Malta, a month after he had begun his hunt, he learned the truth: Villeneuve was back in Toulon. He had, on leaving Toulon, encountered gales so strong that he had put about and run for shelter. Despairingly Nelson wrote to Emma, while he was anchored off Majorca, sheltering from more gales, 'I do assure you, my dearest Emma, that nothing can be more miserable, or unhappy, than your poor Nelson . . . My reports from off Toulon state the French fleet as still in port; but I shall ever be uneasy at not having fallen in with them. I know, my dear Emma, that it is in vain to repine; but my feelings are alive to meeting those fellows after near two years' hard service. What a time!'[3]

So it was only Missiessy's squadron that sailed into the calm, blue water of the Caribbean. After reaching the French island of Martinique on 20 February, he landed his troops and there planned attacks on British islands and shipping. High among his priorities was the capture of Diamond Rock, the outcrop, a mile off the coast of the island, officially listed by the Royal Navy as 'His Majesty's Sloop *Diamond Rock*'.[4] Its summit almost inaccessible above sheer precipices, the rock commanded the main sea routes to and from the port, Fort de France, and, since the British had seized it nearly eighteen months earlier, it had proved its worth. Heavy guns had been mounted on its heights; as one eyewitness remembered, 'Were you to see now along . . . a perpendicular acclivity, the sailors are hanging in clusters, hauling up a four-and-twenty-pounder by hawsers, you would wonder! They appear like mice hauling a little sausage.'[5] Still camped in caves and on ledges high above the sea, a hundred British seamen under James Maurice (now promoted to commander) manned heavy guns and long guns with a range of near two miles, so forcing any ships bound for Fort de France to run the gauntlet of their fire. This was, of course, seen by the French garrison as a strategic triumph for their enemy and an affront to their honour.

Missiessy began to fulfil his orders to 'really ravage British trade', although his expected reinforcements had not arrived.[6] But he captured thirty-three British merchant ships and, although he had not the military force to occupy British islands, he could threaten them and demand large ransoms and this he did at Dominica, St Kitts, Nevis and Monserrat. However, he did not attack Barbados or St Lucia, and he left Diamond Rock unmolested. This particularly rankled when news eventually reached Paris, Napoleon declaring, 'I choked with indignation when I read he had not taken the Diamond Rock'.[7]

A British squadron sent in pursuit of Missiessy was still wallowing across the Atlantic when, on 12 March, the French admiral received orders to return to France. He sailed a fortnight later and, a week after that, his pursuers finally reached the Caribbean; he was then nearing Rochefort, where he anchored on 20 May. During his cruise Missiessy had been told of the Emperor's pleasure at his success but, on arrival, was dismayed to hear that this was no longer so. He learned that, three months before, the Emperor had ordered that his squadron should remain in the Caribbean to await the eventual arrival of Villeneuve. The orders had never reached him and now the grand strategic design was in ruins. The Emperor was furious and Missiessy wrote to Decrès, 'I find it extremely painful to learn that he is not satisfied . . . after I had acted most vigorously and used all my experience, all my intellectual facilities and the last ounce of my strength.'[8] A new plan would now be needed.

It was obvious that Napoleon would try again and that he would launch a naval offensive on an overwhelming scale. In London, and in the blockading squadrons tossing in the Atlantic, they could only wait, knowing that the result would depend upon the duel of wits, seamanship and command between two admirals, Nelson and Villeneuve, in the Mediterranean. His attention focused on the number of masts visible in the deep, almost land-locked harbours of Toulon, Nelson had fallen into a routine of cruising or lying in familiar anchorages, instantly ready to make sail and give chase. He himself never went ashore; even in Agincourt Sound, when he sent a present of silver candlesticks to a priest ashore in gratitude for his kindness, the gift was delivered by an officer. In fine weather life could be pleasant, particularly for the officers. The admiral was called before dawn and after 'breakfast on tea, hot rolls, toast, cold tongue, etc. . . . we repair upon deck to enjoy the majestic sight of the rising sun (scarcely ever obscured in this fine climate) surmounting the smooth and placid waves of the Mediterranean, which supports the lofty and tremendous bulwarks of Britain, following in regular train their Admiral in the *Victory*', recorded a young surgeon in the flagship.

Between the hours of seven and two, there is plenty of time for business, study, writing and exercise. At two o'clock, a band of music plays till within a quarter of three, when the drum beats the tune called *The Roast Beef of Old England* to announce the Admiral's dinner, which is served up exactly at three o'clock and which generally consists of three courses and a dessert of the choicest fruit, together with three or four of the best wines, champagne and claret not excepted. If a person does not feel himself perfectly at ease, it must be his fault . . . Coffee and liqueurs close the dinner at about half-past four, or five o'clock, after which the company generally walk the deck, where the band of music plays for nearly an hour. At six o'clock, tea is announced, when the company again assemble in the Admiral's cabin, where tea is served up before seven o'clock and . . . the party continue to converse with his Lordship, who at this time generally unbends himself, though he is at all times free from stiffness and pomp . . . At eight o'clock, a rummer of punch with cake, or biscuit is served up, soon after which we wish the Admiral a good night (who is generally in bed before nine o'clock).[9]

Over British strategic thinking hovered another threat: that of Spain. For a decade the Spaniards had been in thrall to France for fear of invasion. When war had resumed in 1803, Napoleon demanded that Spain either provide him with a fleet and troops, or pay a large subsidy, the latter being preferable as it would leave Spain nominally neutral, although allowing French warships to use Spanish ports. Madrid had agreed but was told by London that this would be seen as an act of war. To pay the subsidy, Spain had to await the arrival of treasure ships from South America.

A squadron was detached from both Nelson's and Cornwallis's fleets to intercept these, now known to be four frigates bound from Montevideo for Cadiz. This would be a pre-emptive strike without benefit of formal declaration of war; the intention was to capture the frigates and impound the bullion so as to prevent Spain from paying the subsidy. Nelson planned the intercepting force to be overwhelming in the hope that the Spanish would surrender without a fight. But the ship of the line, intended to overawe the Spanish captains, failed to arrive and only four British frigates intercepted the four Spaniards on 5 October 1804. Fighting began and one of the Spanish ships blew up, killing a hundred, including the family of the Captain-General of Peru, who had been passengers. The other three surrendered. Spanish pride was outraged and on 12 December 1804 Spain declared war on Britain.

There was another insult to follow. A week later Spanish lookouts on the cliffs near the port of Ferrol had reported two British ships of the line close inshore; then a boat had pulled ashore and landed what appeared to be a shooting party: men with fowling-pieces and gundogs. Patrols were ordered to intercept them. The men with sporting guns were, in fact, the newly knighted Major-General Sir John Moore and his brother Commodore Graham Moore with Rear-Admiral the Hon. Alexander Cochrane, uncle of the dashing Captain Lord Cochrane. They were less interested in shooting than in studying the terrain with a view to landing an expeditionary force to capture Ferrol, for Moore was to command what was only known as a 'secret expedition' against France and Spain. Their reconnaissance was soon over and, sighting approaching patrols, they had to run for the beach and their boat. When news of this reached Madrid, their purpose was understood.

On his return, General Moore advised against an amphibious assault on Ferrol. Even so, Pitt, with his grasp of global strategy, planned to take the offensive as well as defending the British Isles. Moore was still to command an expeditionary force of something between 10,000 and 20,000 men. No destination had been decided but, if not Ferrol, it might be India, the West Indies or the Mediterranean.*

Spain's entry into the war had loaded the balance of power against Britain. Not only did the two major Spanish naval ports, Cadiz and Cartagena, lie to either side of the Straits of Gibraltar, but there were innumerable secure anchorages – notably Ferrol, Corunna and Vigo. Even more dangerous were more than thirty Spanish ships of the line, divided between the Atlantic and Mediterranean. At this time the French force available for immediate action against Britain was twenty-one sail of the line at Brest, six at Rochefort and eleven at Toulon, together with frigates and enough landing craft to embark more than 150,000 troops.

But even the alliance of France and Spain did not isolate the Mediterranean Fleet from home as drastically as might have been feared. Mail was regular, taking four to six weeks each way, and, when fresh ships joined the fleet, there was always news from home. When the battleship *Canopus* arrived and Captain Francis Austen came on board the *Victory* with a letter from a mutual friend in England, he would also have brought the latest gossip from Bath, where his family lived, including his sister Jane, who was about to make her name as a novelist.†

---

*It eventually sailed in June 1806 to the Mediterranean to resume the late Lord Nelson's support of the Kingdom of the Two Sicilies.
†Jane Austen had already drafted her first three books, which were later published as *Sense and Sensibility*, *Pride and Prejudice* and *Northanger Abbey*.

Napoleon's new plan – his fifth – was ready in March and this time it would make full use of his new ally, Spain. Again Villeneuve was to evade Nelson and break into the Atlantic. He would call at Cadiz to collect a Spanish squadron under the command of Admiral Federico Gravina and together they would cross the Atlantic to Martinique. There they would wait for forty days to be joined by Admiral Ganteaume's squadron from Brest, finding time, while waiting, to attack Diamond Rock. Then, having lured the main British fleet in pursuit, they would sweep back across the Atlantic to the Channel. There, in overwhelming strength, the combined Franco-Spanish fleet would cover the crossing of the Grande Armée.

On the evening of 29 March 1805 the moment came. A brisk breeze was blowing from the north-east ready to carry the French from Toulon to the Straits of Gibraltar. Nelson was thought to be off Barcelona – although he was, in fact, off Majorca – leaving only two frigates to watch for the enemy. It was to be a repeat of the last escape. Villeneuve's eleven sail of the line, with 3000 troops embarked as reinforcements for Martinique, sailed, steering south-west under full press of canvas.

The Admiralty had disposed its ships to meet as many contingencies as possible. With Nelson and his twelve ships of the line in the Mediterranean, Vice-Admiral Sir John Orde was off Cadiz with six of the line; Vice-Admiral Sir Robert Calder with eight off Ferrol; off Ushant and covering the French Atlantic ports lay the Channel Fleet, now seventeen strong, commanded first by Vice-Admiral Sir William Cornwallis, then, when he went on leave, by the veteran Lord Gardner; based on the Downs and covering the southern North Sea and the Channel was Admiral Lord Keith with his eleven battleships, the strengths of the fleets and squadrons constantly varying as ships left for replenishment, or reinforcements arrived. All available ships were ordered to sea, causing domestic confusion and upheaval after the relatively uneventful years of stalemate. When Captain Fremantle's ship, the *Neptune*, was ordered to sea in May, to join Lord Gardner, his wife, Betsey, wrote in her diary, 'I heard today from Fremantle from Portsmouth, where he made every arrangement about his wine and cabin furniture and expected to get to Plymouth tomorrow. His ship is quite ready for sea, so that he will sail immediately. We all stayed at home, I feel low and not quite well.'[10] She may have been consoled by reading a letter written by her husband off Ushant at the end of the month, saying, 'my low spirits are excessive and I do nothing but take snuff and read Shakespeare when I am off the deck'.[11]

The news of Villeneuve's second escape from Toulon had reached Nelson on 4 April, and again he had no evidence as to his destination. So, while awaiting news, he steered south-east to wait north of Palermo, well positioned in the central Mediterranean to pursue the enemy eastward or westward when further news arrived. It came on the 18th and it was that Villeneuve with his eleven big ships had passed Gibraltar ten days earlier and was now somewhere in the Atlantic. But now the wind that had helped the French changed and hindered the British, and it was not until the beginning of May that Nelson passed the Straits, there to be faced with a familiar question: where had Villeneuve gone? Probably northward to collect the squadrons from Spanish and French ports and head for the Channel to cover an attempt at invasion. So, leaving a ship of the line and several frigates to watch the Mediterranean in case Villeneuve doubled back, he headed for the chops of the Channel between Ushant and the Scilly Isles to await further news. This came sooner than expected. Between the capes of Trafalgar and St Vincent he hailed a Portuguese warship and the news was shouted from her deck that the French fleet had been sighted sailing west; that could only mean an attack on the sources of British wealth in the Caribbean. Nelson sailed in pursuit.

Despite knowing that he was a week behind his quarry, Nelson was still able to control his impatience. When the *Superb*, commanded by his friend Captain Richard Keats, proved a slow sailer and reduced the fleet's speed to five knots, Nelson told him, 'If we all went ten knots, I should not think it fast enough, yet I would have you assured that I know the *Superb* does all that which is possible for a ship to accomplish and I desire that you will not fret upon the occasion.'[12] Such understanding had always endeared him to his captains and now he trusted them with simple instructions for action on meeting the enemy: 'Take you a Frenchman apiece and leave me the Spaniards.'[13]

There was still the overwhelming problem: exactly where had the French gone? Had they headed straight for their own base at Martinique or gone to attack a British island, which might be any in the chain from Jamaica to the north-west to Trinidad, 1500 miles to the south-east?

Still shaken by Missiessy's marauding, the British merchants and sugar planters had hoped that the Admiralty would prevent a repetition. At first all that reached Nelson were rumours until he anchored in Carlisle Bay, off Barbados. There he heard conflicting reports. The theatre commander, Rear-Admiral Alexander Cochrane, expected the French to attack Jamaica and four of his squadron had been sent there, leaving only two to reinforce Nelson. Ashore the British generals – Sir William Meyers on Barbados and Robert Brereton on St Lucia – were certain that the French had gone south to attack Trinidad, the latter repeating a specific report that twenty-eight of their sail of the line had been sighted heading south. This second report seemed reliable and, although Nelson himself expected the enemy to lie at Martinique, he felt bound to make for Trinidad. As he steered south he wrote to Emma, 'I find myself within six days of the enemy and I have every reason to hope that the 6th of June will immortalise your own Nelson . . . Pray for my success and my laurels I shall lay with pleasure at your feet and a sweet kiss will be ample reward for all your faithful Nelson's hard fag.' But when he arrived, the calm, blue-green bays of Trinidad and Tobago were empty and, as he ordered his fleet to put about, he wrote to her again, 'Ah, my Emma, June 6th would have been a great day for me . . . I have ever found that if I was left and acted as my poor noddle told me was right I should seldom err.'[14]

As he had thought, Villeneuve had indeed gone to Martinique. Reinforced by one more French and six Spanish sail of the line from Cadiz, his force now numbered eighteen to Nelson's ten. As he had approached, a Spanish ship steered too close to Diamond Rock and was battered by the British 24-pounders. So this would be his first priority and he sent a squadron and a strong detachment of troops to take it. The French had no difficulty in getting ashore on the narrow beach, but there their troubles began. Commander Maurice and his men had retired to their upper batteries, above sheer cliffs and reached only by rope ladder. From there they shattered the French landing craft with round shot and the soldiers, without supplies or even scaling ladders, found themselves marooned and subjected to what was, in effect, aerial bombardment. After four days British ammunition was running low when an earth tremor cracked the rainwater cistern – their only source of drinking water – which then ran dry. There was no alternative, and on 2 June Maurice surrendered what became known as 'His Majesty's late sloop *Diamond Rock*'[15] after a successful commission of seventeen months.

Villeneuve's orders were to wait forty days to be joined by Admiral Ganteaume and twenty-one ships of the line from Brest. During that time he was to capture Dominica, St Lucia, Trinidad, Tobago and then, perhaps, St Vincent, Antigua, Grenada and Barbados. If Ganteaume had not arrived by 22 June, Villeneuve was to return across the Atlantic and make for Ferrol, where he would be joined by the rest of the huge fleet that would then sweep north to command the Channel for the invasion of England. He felt no threat from the British because the last he had heard of Nelson was that he was looking for him off Egypt.

With so many choices Villeneuve dithered, satisfied that his ships had taken not only Diamond Rock but also a British convoy of fifteen ships from Antigua laden with sugar, rum and coffee. It was then that he heard Nelson had arrived at Barbados, albeit with a fleet about half the size of his own. Fearing that any delay to capture a British island might result in a repeat of the Battle of the Nile, Villeneuve decided to ignore the Emperor's order to await Ganteaume until 22 June and to run for home at once. On 10 June the French and Spanish fleet sailed for Europe.

Nelson, sailing north-west, passed the islands that had sighted the French, but where had they gone? To attack Jamaica or, having achieved their aim of luring his own fleet away from Europe, were they already on their way back across the Atlantic to cover the invasion? Jamaica was the richest prize of all and there tension rose. Lady Nugent, the Governor's wife, wrote in her diary on 18 June,

Another day of uncertainty and anxiety. An express . . . to say that Lord Nelson, not having found the French fleet at

Trinidad, had come on to Martinique as quick as possible; but we are still uncertain whether the enemy remains there, or has come this way . . . Whichever may be the true report, our suspense must soon be at an end; but it is a painful state for us all, and a horseman does not come to the door, day or night, but I tremble all over and almost lose my breath from anxiety.[16]

One Englishwoman had actually seen the enemy; Mrs Jane Kerby, living on Antigua, wrote home:

You will have heard, no doubt, how the combined fleet escaped by magic; how in reality (for I counted them myself) they rode triumphant on our element for some weeks; how the gallant hero of the Nile followed them; how he, misled, could not catch them; and how they, afraid of him, gave up the attack on the little England of the archipelago [Antigua], whose bulwarks are rock instead of oak; how they tried to look warlike and form a line of battle but they could not; but how, alas!, they scampered after our sugar, took fourteen ships full of that and various good things going to our friends; and how to our great joy they burnt this treasure . . . by the manoeuvres of a [British] sloop of war, who, afraid of being taken, threw out signals as for approaching friends and they, *toujours Nelson en tête*, saw his ghost and destroyed their prizes in the most premature and shameful hurry. I cannot attempt to describe our terrors, movings, removings, packings and unpackings. I consider myself now quite as a heroine, having commanded myself . . . Since Lord Nelson left us, which was on the 12th or 14th June (the French fleet having been with us on the 8th), we have been quiet.[17]

Now Nelson was relying on his own instinct. He reckoned that he was only four or five days behind the French and, when leaving Antigua on 13 June, felt certain that they were on their way back to Europe. This was the greatest risk of all and he wrote to the Admiralty, 'Every line of battle ship that can be spared from hence may be wanted in the Channel' and he, too, steered east, laying course for the Azores and Gibraltar. On 21 June he came the closest to sighting his quarry, and noted 'Saw three planks, which I think came from the French fleet. Very miserable, which is very foolish.'[18] On 20 July the *Victory* anchored off Gibraltar, Nelson landed and recorded, 'Went on shore for the first time since June 16th, 1803, and from having my foot out of the *Victory*, two years wanting ten days.'[19]

Two days later Villeneuve, now leading twenty ships of the line through fog 100 miles west of Cape Finisterre, ran into an ambush. Suspecting the French would act as they had, Nelson had sent a fast brig to warn the Admiralty of his belief. Acting on this, reinforcements were sent to Vice-Admiral Sir Robert Calder, who with fifteen of the line watched the approaches to the Channel and Brest, where Ganteaume still lay, unable to escape. Villeneuve could not avoid action and the fleets fought all afternoon until the fog thickened at dusk, Calder taking two Spanish ships of the line and inflicting far greater damage than he received. Next morning the opposing fleets were becalmed, seventeen miles apart, and there they lay all that day. Next morning the wind freshened but Calder, content with his success, made no effort to follow the enemy and by dark the French had made their escape to the south.

Villeneuve ran for the safety of a Spanish port and entered Vigo on 28 July; he sailed round the headlands into Ferrol four days later. Now the strategic scene was stark: the Mediterranean was no longer of consequence and the bulk of the French and Spanish fleets were in Atlantic ports from Cadiz to Brest. There they could be blockaded by the main British squadrons but they could also break out and make for the Channel, where the Grande Armée was waiting to embark. As Nelson knew to his cost, no blockade could be total. The stalemate was resumed.

After more than two years protecting the English coast from far distant waters, Nelson was allowed home on leave. An old friend, Hercules Ross, a retired sugar planter, expressed the national mood when he wrote to him, 'I have both by night and day accompanied your Lordship across the Atlantic . . . and imagination has often carried me aloft to look for the flying enemy. Though disappointed, thank God my noble friend has returned in health. But there still remains some great action to be achieved by him worthy of his fame.'[20]

10

Lose not a moment ... England is ours

A T THE beginning of August 1805 tension had reached a height when, on the 3rd, Napoleon returned to Boulogne: the Grande Armée was ready to embark and his fleets and squadrons were ready to challenge the British fleet guarding the approaches to the Channel, either in battle or by luring it away. Nelson's Mediterranean command was to be extended to include the western seaboard of Spain and Portugal.

The *Victory* anchored at Spithead on 18 August, and Nelson immediately wrote a note to Emma Hamilton at Merton: 'I am, my dearest Emma, this moment anchored and . . . I have ordered a Post Office express to tell you of my arrival. I hope we shall be out of quarantine tomorrow, when I shall fly to dear Merton . . . The boat is waiting, I must finish. This day two years and three months I left you.'[1]

Next day he was ashore at Portsmouth, sitting in the parlour of The George inn drinking tea, while awaiting the chaise he had ordered to carry him through the night to his home in Surrey. It was a wet evening and at nine its wheels were rattling over the cobbles of the High Street, through the arched gateway in the fortifications and into the English countryside. Beyond, it was a changed scene. At Hilsea and on Portsdown he passed ranks of tents where the militia were encamped and, as the chaise bowled through inland villages on the London road, the tavern forecourts were busy with men in uniform and yeomanry horses. The nation was geared for war as never before.

Nelson's choice of a house at Merton, just off the road between Portsmouth and London, proved the value of its position and at six o'clock next morning the chaise swung into the drive, crunching over the gravel to the front door before the household had stirred. When they did, joy exploded. 'What a day of rejoicing at Merton!' declared an ecstatic Emma, 'How happy he is to see us all!'[2] She dashed off notes to his relations – all, of course, except his wife, Fanny – inviting them to visit. 'Thanks, my dear Lady, for your scrap,' replied his sister Susannah Bolton from Norfolk. 'It was indeed short and sweet and sweet was the intelligence that my dearest brother was arrived in England. What a paradise he must think Merton, to say nothing of the Eve it contains.'[3]

Next day they drove in their carriage to London. While Emma went to a house she rented in Clarges Street, her lover was, for propriety's sake, to stay at a nearby hotel; at Merton they could ostensibly be chaperoned by her mother, who used the name 'Mrs Cadogan'. Nelson made his official calls. First he reported to the new First Lord of the Admiralty, Lord Barham, aged nearly eighty, who had replaced Lord Melville after the latter's resignation following a financial scandal. Then he saw the Prime Minister, Pitt. As they discussed strategic contingencies, the renewed stalemate was clear. Although a new alliance with Austria, Russia and Sweden against Napoleon had been created, their huge armies on the far side of the Continent seemed unable to relieve the immediate threat of French invasion.

Nelson was now the most famous man in the country, embodying its spirit far more potently than King George, or even Pitt. Crowds followed him through the streets of London, noting that he had 'the balancing gait of a sailor' and that 'his skin is now very much burnt by having been so long at sea'.[4] Those who met him at Merton were surprised to find a quiet, polite man of forty-six in sober civilian clothes, but noted that 'the penetration of his eye threw a light upon his countenance, which tempered its severity and rendered his harsh features in some measure agreeable . . . Lord Nelson has not the least pride of rank; he combined with that degree of dignity, which a man of quality should have, the most engaging address in his air and appearance.'[5]

On one of his visits to London he called on Lord Castlereagh, the Secretary of State for War and the Colonies, at his office in Downing Street. There in a waiting-room★ he saw a young major-general with a high-bridged nose and an air of command, whom he did not recognize. Major-General Sir Arthur Wellesley, who immediately recognized the other man, was lately returned from his brilliant actions against allies of the French in India. Later, he remembered:

> He could not know who I was but he entered at once into con-versation with me, if I can call it conversation, for it was almost all on his side and all about himself and, in reality, a style so vain and so silly as to surprise and almost disgust me.
>
> I suppose something that I happened to say may have made him guess that I was somebody and he went out of the room for a moment, I have no doubt to ask the office-keeper who I was, for when he came back he was altogether a different man both in manner and matter. All that I had thought a charlatan style had vanished and he talked of the state of the country and of the aspect and probabilities of affairs on the Continent with a good sense and knowledge of subjects both at home and abroad that surprised me equally and more agreeably than the first part of our interview had done; in fact, he talked like an officer and a statesman.[6]

Also in Castlereagh's office Nelson met Captain Sir Sidney Smith, vibrant with activity. The two had so much in common that they could be seen as rivals, although the former had a marked advantage in rank, fame and achievement. Indeed, a few years earlier Sir William Hamilton had told Colonel Hiley Addington, who had watched, if not controlled, Smith's activities from Walmer Castle, that, despite the widespread belief that Nelson heartily disliked Smith, 'Be assured that Lord Nelson now under-stands Sir Sidney well and really loves and esteems him; and . . . will give him every proof of it, if ever they should meet on service together . . . They are certainly the two greatest heroes of the age.'[7]

★The room survives at 12 Downing Street.

Since his spectacular defence of Acre, which had sealed Nelson's own triumph in Aboukir Bay, the latter had come to admire Smith, probably without real affection. Their similarities had been compounded by the scandal of Smith's own love affair with a celebrity; in his case the Princess Caroline, the estranged wife of the Prince of Wales. Smith could carry some influence over his cousin William Pitt and, perhaps as a result, the Prime Minister now presided over a meeting with Castlereagh, Nelson and Smith, who brought with him Robert Fulton and William Congreve. Like Nelson, Smith was enthusiastically aggressive but he proposed that the only way to attack Boulogne was unconventional. Fulton's torpedoes could sink the French ships anchored offshore, while Congreve's rockets could burn the landing craft in the harbour.

On 9 August Fulton had written to Pitt, using his *nom de guerre*, Robert Francis, proposing the large-scale use of his weaponry. Suggesting the formation of a squadron of frigates and cutters adapted to carry his torpedoes, he urged that it should be 'under the command of an active, enterprising officer, who should have an independent cruising commission to run along the whole line of the enemy's coast and attack any vessels of the enemy'.[8] Nelson, like Lord Keith and other senior naval officers, instinctively disliked and, perhaps, feared the potential of the new weapons but warmed to Smith's vitality and originality and gave his ideas cautious support. In any case, Nelson was in a magnanimous mood; he was so far ahead of Smith in fame that he could afford to be so. So that August he invited him to dine at Merton, where he was entertaining a succession of naval friends, mostly his own captains but including the Duke of Clarence, who, on the King's command, had not been allowed to resume his naval career but had remained the admiral's friend.

The house and garden at Merton were happy places. The extravagant, sometimes ostentatious, even vulgar, entertaining of the year of the Peace of Amiens was in the past; now it was domestic contentment and hospitality for family and friends. At dinner there would often be two large tables: one for the adults – the Nelsons and the Boltons, neighbours and naval friends – and the other for children, including Horatia, now described as Lord

Nelson's adopted daughter. Sir Sidney would have seen, as did another friend from Mediterranean days, Lord Minto, Nelson dining with

> Lady Hamilton at the head of the table and Mother Cadogan at the bottom . . . He looks remarkably well and full of spirits. His conversation is cordial in these low times . . . Lady Hamilton had added to the house and the place extremely well without his knowing she was about it. She is a clever being after all: the passion is as hot as ever.[9]

Two dreamlike weeks passed and then the spell was broken soon after sunrise on 2 September, when the household was again woken by horses' hoofs and wheels grinding on gravel. It was a chaise carrying Nelson's friend Captain Henry Blackwood from Portsmouth with dispatches from Admiral Collingwood to the Admiralty. As the two met, Nelson said, 'I am sure that you bring me news of the French and Spanish fleets and that I shall have to beat them yet.'[10] Blackwood replied that that was so. On 13 August Villeneuve had left the neighbouring harbours of Ferrol and Corunna with a combined Franco-Spanish fleet of twenty-nine sail of the line. But, instead of sailing north to join Ganteaume and his twenty-one off Brest, he had run south and taken refuge in Cadiz, where he arrived on the 21st.

This came as a surprise in Paris as much as in London, for Villeneuve was expected to steer for Brest and the Channel. The day after his arrival in Cadiz, Napoleon had written to him and to Ganteaume, ordering, 'We are all ready, everything is embarked. Show yourself for twenty-four hours and all is over.'[11] The British did not, of course, know this, but the immediacy of the threat seemed confirmed by a signal from their frigate the *Immortalité*, cruising off the Channel coast of France; as she passed Ambleteuse her look-outs had sighted 'a large body of men, amounting, as we judged, to eight thousand or ten thousand, reviewing on the beach'.[12] There had been reports of a bungled embarkation exercise but the Emperor was known to have arrived at Boulogne, so was this inspection the immediate prelude to the invasion? Could the scattered British squadrons concentrate in time to face what might be a combination of more than fifty French and Spanish battleships?

Nelson followed Blackwood to Whitehall that morning. There Lord Barham and then Pitt himself told him what he had expected to hear. This time the enemy must be not just contained but destroyed. The Mediterranean and its Atlantic approaches would come under the command of one admiral. Modestly, Nelson proposed Collingwood. 'No, that won't do, you must take command', said Pitt, adding that he should be ready to sail in a few days. 'I am ready now', replied Nelson.[13] When Barham invited him to choose the captains for his fleet, Nelson waved the offer aside: 'Choose yourself, my lord. The same spirit actuates the whole profession. You cannot choose wrong.'[14]

On returning to Merton, Nelson began to put his affairs in order and to say farewell to family and friends. Many of the latter were naval officers and it was his custom after dinner to take them for a walk in the garden to discuss the strategy and tactics he planned to use. He told Captain Richard Keats, who had been so embarrassed by delaying the fleet with his slow ship in the long chase across the Atlantic, what he proposed should the enemy emerge from port. 'No day can be long enough to arrange a couple of fleets and fight a battle according to the old system', Nelson began. He then explained that to reach a quick decision he would divide his own fleet into three divisions: one, composed of the fastest ships, would be held in reserve; the other two would steer for the enemy line at right angles and in line ahead, although that would render them vulnerable in the final approach. 'I would go at them at once, if I can, about one-third of their line from their leading ship', he went on. 'What do you think of it? I think it will surprise and confound the enemy. They won't know what I am about. I will bring forward a pell-mell battle and that is what I want.'[15]

For Sir Sidney Smith he had a surprising question: would Sir Sidney join his fleet in command of the inshore squadron? Nelson had been impressed by the tenacity with which Smith was worrying the enemy along their northern coast and that was exactly the sort of aggressive attitude he would need off Cadiz. Nelson added that he already had the Prime Minister's agreement to this. Later

Smith wrote to his old friend William Windham, saying that he had been 'called upon by Lord Nelson (in consequence, he told me, of his suggestion to Mr Pitt, in which he agreed) and offer'd command of the Inshore Squadron in the Mediterranean with full powers to act as circumstances might render practicable in attacking the enemy'.[16] First, however, he would have time to bring his plans for an attack on Boulogne to a head. The command of such a squadron would require appropriate rank and Sir Sidney was delighted to hear that, in November, he would hoist his flag as a rear-admiral.

It was clear from the beginning what form Smith's inshore squadron would take if he had his way: there would be a rehearsal off Boulogne. So with Pitt's support Castlereagh overrode Admiralty doubters, ordering the fitting of 'armed defence ships' and launches to embark torpedoes. These were loaded, sent to Dover and put under Smith's command. At the same time the Admiralty was required to build 'ten double canoes . . . to be fitted with frames for the use of Mr Congreve's rockets', 500 of which were ordered.[17] Castlereagh was caught up in the excitement, not only of ordering newfangled weaponry but also, almost as if he was to take command himself, in choosing the men to take them into action. Only the most 'intelligent and enterprising of the seamen' could be picked for 'Mr Francis's mode of warfare', he declared, and they must qualify as specialists in torpedoes 'except upon being found deficient in enterprise, courage or exertion'.[18]

Castlereagh impressed on Smith, who was notorious as a compulsive talker, 'the necessity of perfect secrecy and every despatch . . . as the enemy are likely, at the slightest alarm, to move their most valuable vessels from Boulogne'.[19] The purpose of the plan was to achieve what Nelson had not managed and to do so by these unconventional means. There would be no boarding of enemy ships; they would be sunk by torpedoes. There would be no long-range bombardment with cannon-balls; incendiary rockets would be launched at a range of two miles to burn the landing craft in the Bassin Napoléon within the harbour of Boulogne. Nor would this be all. Once the new weapons had proved themselves, they would be used elsewhere: off Cadiz.

While British eyes were on the Atlantic and the Channel, the

French now looked east. The day after the Emperor had sent his sailing orders to Villeneuve and Ganteaume, worrying news arrived from Italy. King Ferdinand IV, the hitherto timorous ruler of the Kingdom of the Two Sicilies, had demanded that the French military occupation of Naples should end. Such impertinence must have been prompted by more than the recent arrival of a small British force at Malta. It could only mean an Austrian guarantee of support and, perhaps, that they were planning to actively join forces with Russia and Britain in the alliance against France which they had agreed in April.

On 22 August Napoleon ordered Villeneuve, 'Sail; do not lose a moment; enter the Channel with my assembled squadrons; England is ours'.[20] On the same day news reached him that the French fleets had not combined and were not sweeping towards the Channel. Villeneuve had gone south to Cadiz, where his ships were already short of supplies. 'It is out and out betrayal', stormed the Emperor. 'That Villeneuve is the worst possible sort of wretch . . . He would sacrifice anyone and anything to save his own hide!'[21]

On 24 August Napoleon dispatched an ultimatum to Austria, insisting that it reduce its troops in the Veneto, which Napoleon had made over to it a few months after he himself had overthrown the Venetian Republic in 1797. War in central Europe had always been a possibility for which the Grande Armée had been ready as an alternative to the invasion of England, as that could always have been postponed. If a massed assault on France by the huge Austrian and Russian armies was threatened, counter-action against them would take priority.

Napolean realized that the Austrians and Russians would not be able to mount a major westward offensive until the spring, whereas he had a large and superbly trained army as ready to march east as to attempt a Channel crossing. The Grande Armée could launch a pre-emptive strike against these new enemies and be back in France, ready to invade England, in perhaps six months.

I shall invade Germany with two hundred thousand men and shall not halt until I have reached Vienna, taken Venice and everything Austria has in Italy and driven the Bourbons from Naples. I shall stop the Austrians and Russians from uniting. I

shall beat them before they can meet. Then, the Continent pac-
ified, I shall come back to the camp on the ocean and start work
all over again.[22]

He then ordered five armies to march south-east; three from the
Channel coast, one from the Netherlands and another from
Hanover. On 29 August they began to break camp and take to the
road. Four days later the Emperor left Boulogne for Paris. At St
Cloud he heard that the Austrians had already entered Bavaria,
heading west, so there was more urgency than anticipated. Fresh
orders were sent to Villeneuve; he was now to leave Cadiz and
head south, return to the Mediterranean, collect troops from
Cartagena and secure Naples, cutting off the Austrians from any
seaborne help sent by the British or the Russians. Then, because
he had lost confidence in the admiral, he decided that he must be
replaced forthwith by Admiral François-Etienne Rosily, who
would have to travel from Paris, via Madrid, but should reach
Cadiz before Villeneuve had sailed.

The news was quick to reach London and on 24 August Lord
Keith, in his flagship off Ramsgate, noted, 'It appears that the
enemy may be contemplating movements to the eastward. I desire
that . . . the whole squadron, as well off Boulogne as in the Downs,
is kept in constant readiness for making any movement that
circumstances may render necessary.'[23] Where exactly the French
might be was a matter for intense speculation.

Whatever transpired, the British looked to Lord Nelson for sal-
vation. No other naval or military commander, or political leader,
had ever inspired such confidence. Before Nelson admirals and
generals, however successful, had been seen as remote and
shadowy figures, rarely recognizable in the formal, heroic poses of
the engravings that celebrated their victories. Nelson was different.
The empty sleeve, pinned across the blue uniform coat embroidered with orders of chivalry, proved that he had accepted as much
danger as those he commanded; the rude caricatures of him – the
parson's son – cavorting with his friend's wife, once a *demi-
mondaine*, showed that he had human failings; stories of his kindness and humanity had come ashore and spread. He was seen as a
saviour.

In these final days before returning to sea Nelson divided his time between Whitehall and Merton. He had several meetings with Pitt and their talks went beyond naval strategy. Nelson had abandoned the political aspirations that Emma had encouraged during the Peace of Amiens. Then he had supported Addington and been willing to speak generously on his behalf in the House of Lords but was resentful that this loyalty had brought only mockery and the ruin of any prospects in politics. So he had transferred his allegiance to Pitt and wanted to make his political position clear before he faced his greatest challenge; there was also the possibility, on his return, of further employment, perhaps as First Lord of the Admiralty.

'In my interview with Mr Pitt', he said later, 'I gave some specimen of a sailor's politics by frankly telling him that, not having been bred in courts, I could not pretend to a nice discrimination between the use and abuse of parties; and therefore must not be expected to range myself under the political banners of any man in or out of place. That England's welfare was the sole object of my pursuit.' He added, 'Mr Pitt listened to me with patience and good humour; indeed paid me some compliments and observed that he wished every officer in the service would entertain similar sentiments.'[24]

During the second week of September there was a final meeting with the Prime Minister and – in the absence of the King, who was on holiday at Weymouth – an audience with the Prince of Wales, whom Nelson had long despised and feared as a possible rival for the favours of Emma Hamilton. He returned from this latter meeting at Carlton House to Merton to dine with friends and neighbours on the eve of his departure for Portsmouth. Lord Minto, his worldly friend from the Mediterranean, was there and glad to meet an old acquaintance, James Perry, editor of the *Morning Chronicle*, whom he had once had imprisoned for libel; the two men shook hands in reconciliation. The evening was charged with emotion. 'Lady Hamilton could not eat and hardly drink and near swooning at table', reported Minto, 'It is a strange picture.' He added what could be seen as a final verdict on Nelson: 'He is in many points a great man, in others a baby.'[25] Privately, Nelson and Emma went through a form of marriage that was not binding in the eyes of the law or the church. This was the receiving of Holy Communion, followed by a blessing and an exchange of rings.

As usual before an expected battle, Nelson veered between optimism and pessimism, religious faith and fatalism. This time he was cast down by the memory of a West Indian fortune-teller, who had once told him that she could see no future for him beyond the year 1805; dreams of a happy return to Emma and Horatia and then, perhaps, high office or a blissful retirement to Sicily seemed in doubt. On the evening of 13 September he tiptoed into the night nursery to say farewell to his daughter. He knelt by the side of Horatia's cot, rose and left the room, only to return four times for another look at the sleeping child. He then climbed aboard the chaise waiting in the drive and his last words at Merton were to the stable lad, who held open the door: 'Be a good boy till I come back again.'[26]

Nelson's life had often veered between the sublime and the ridiculous in recent years, but now he seemed to have found confidence and serenity. At a coaching-inn on the Portsmouth road, while the horses were being changed, he wrote in his pocket-book: 'Friday night at half-past ten, drive from dear, dear Merton, where I left all which I hold dear in this world, to go to serve my King and Country. May the great God, whom I adore, enable me to fulfil the expectations of my country.'[27]

On arriving at The George inn at Portsmouth at six o'clock the next morning he immediately wrote a note reporting this to 'my dearest and most beloved of women, Nelson's Emma'[28] before leaving to board a boat on the shingle beach and join the *Victory*, lying off the Isle of Wight. A crowd had gathered to see him leave, among them a young clergyman, the Reverend Thomas Socket, tutor to the two sons of Lord Egremont, who, recognizing the historic importance of the occasion, had brought a party over from Petworth to see Nelson depart. The day before, they had sailed to Spithead in a hired cutter to see the flagship and perhaps go on board, only to find that the admiral had not arrived and the *Victory* was working her way out to St Helen's Bay prior to sailing; so they had returned disappointed. But at seven that morning the tutor heard that Nelson had arrived at the coaching-inn in the High Street and, as he wrote:

I got up and dressed myself immediately and went to the inn, where I found so great a crowd in the gateway that it was not without some exertion that I could gain admittance. Just as I got to the foot of the stairs, I met Lord Nelson fully dressed with three or four stars on his breast; he seemed very anxious to get on board. Soon after Lord Nelson went out into the street . . . when he was followed by a number of people, who crowded after him in all directions to gain a sight of him. I was amused by the eagerness of a common sailor I met, who was running with all his might and who, on being asked by another if he had seen him, replied, 'No, but, d--n the old b----r, I should like to see him once more' and away he posted at full speed. This I suppose to be the ultimate expression of nautical affection.[29]

I I

A great and glorious victory

O N 19 September 1805, four days after Nelson had sailed from
Spithead in the *Victory*, bound for Cadiz, Lord Castlereagh
wrote to Sir Sidney Smith, 'I recommend your seeing Lord
Barham without delay. He is prepared to see you and to arrange
the transfer from Boulogne to Cadiz without there being any time
lost.'[1] He was referring to the unconventional force with which
Smith was planning to attack Boulogne and then Cadiz, thus pre-
empting the conventional battle that Nelson was preparing to fight
in the Atlantic. What might be expected to be achieved by stately
ships of the line and their thundering broadsides might also be
won by the rockets and torpedoes of William Congreve and
Robert Fulton under the direction of the equally original Sir
Sidney.

Smith was now aware that some, at least, of the Grande Armée
had struck camp around Boulogne, even if only temporarily, and
this suggested an even more ambitious plan to take advantage of
their absence: the assault should be military as well as naval. He
persuaded Castlereagh that an attack on Boulogne to destroy the
port as well as burn the landing craft was feasible and that Sir John
Moore's light infantry brigade at Shorncliffe was ideal for the task;
the Duke of York, the commander-in-chief of the army, was also
persuaded.* Castlereagh thereupon wrote to Moore:

---

*A comparable plan in 1942 led to the raid on Dieppe.

The Duke of York will have expressed to you the desire His Majesty's Government feel to have your opinion of the practicability of making an attempt against the Boulogne flotilla under the protection of a land force. I have desired Sir Sidney Smith to confer with you upon this subject . . . The point to be considered is the possibility of landing to the westward of Boulogne a force sufficient to turn the sea defences, which, being silenced, would admit of our naval force communicating immediately with the troops on shore, who might then possibly occupy a position from whence the flotilla in the basin might be destroyed without the necessity of attacking, or reducing, the town.[2]

Exciting rumours began to circulate of secret expeditions involving Nelson, Smith and Moore, although the newspaper read at Shorncliffe, the *Hythe Gazette*, was already proclaiming, 'All idea of invasion is now at an end. We learn that the Camp at Boulogne has been broken up.'[3]

Plans went ahead. A hundred torpedoes were ordered and Smith also decided to include fireships and 'explosion vessels', packed with gunpowder and combustibles, to blast a way through the booms and nets that the French were believed to have rigged across the harbour mouth. The Admiralty agreed that Captain Johnstone, 'our friend the smuggler',[4] should be engaged as a pilot for the attack, which he would lead in the cutter *Nile*, manned by fellow smugglers. Both Lord Barham and Lord Keith were wary of Smith's enthusiasm, particularly because Nelson had already sailed for Cadiz, which was a far more important objective than Boulogne. Indeed, Barham wrote to Castlereagh:

If you do not immediately send Sir Sidney off to Cadiz, without thinking of Boulogne, that part of the project that bids the fairest for success will be lost. The combined squadrons now lie in a huddled, disorderly state at Cadiz. If the rockets can be of use, a better opportunity cannot be desired. Nothing here depends upon Johnstone, nor reconnoitring boats. The object lies fair and has a fleet to support it.[5]

Nelson, now assumed to be near Cadiz, was informed and on 3 October he replied courteously but without enthusiasm,

The way is open to Mr Francis. But I have little faith; however, that is for His Majesty's Ministers: he shall have every assistance from me. The rockets, if the account of them is true, must annoy their fleet very much; but I depend more upon hunger for driving them out and upon the gallant officers and men under my command for their destruction than any other invention. But rely, these gentlemen shall have every justice done their plans.[6]

But Smith was far too intensely focused on his plan for Boulogne to be diverted from it. He knew that a spy in France had reported that, the Grande Armée was 'immediately to be withdrawn from the coast and part to rendezvous at Strasbourg and Coblenz. If such an event takes place, the chief Ministers of your King might easily land a body of men between Ambleteuse and Boulogne, or Etaples and Boulogne, while light vessels attack and burn the flotilla at Boulogne.'[7] Sir John Moore was less enthusiastic but agreed to a reconnaissance and joined Smith in the frigate *Antelope* at the end of September for a cruise off the French coast.

'General Moore and I have every advantage that weather and good light can give us to see all that can be seen', wrote an enthusiastic Smith to Castlereagh, while still off Boulogne. 'The flotilla is . . . hauling up the harbour in a dismantled state: thirty-two sail came out . . . on our approach yesterday evening and now lie off the pier, where they shall not lie long if the weather allows of the coffers being sent in.' He reported that five or six thousand French troops had emerged from their huts on the cliffs to the east of the town, 'firing a *feu de joie*' and that flags were flying, perhaps in celebration of some reported victory. 'I cannot take my eyes off this moving scene for long', he continued, but he had noticed Moore's lack of comparable enthusiasm, adding, 'General Moore, I am persuaded, would do his utmost to realize any plan laid down for him . . . but he is too wary to undertake such a task voluntarily, though, of course, foremost when ordered to go to work. We go on, as usual, pleasantly and well together.'[8]

Next day Smith landed Sir John Moore at Dover and the general at once wrote to the Duke of York, saying, 'I have no hesitation to say that no attempt should be made on Boulogne but with a considerable force'; more tellingly, he pointed out the problems of the open anchorage there and the difficult winds and tides off the beach, which meant that 'troops cannot be re-embarked from it in bad weather'.[9] He then rode over to Walmer Castle to put his views even more forcefully to Pitt; indeed he was so convincing that plans for an amphibious attack were cancelled.

Even so, knowing that a line of French ships was again moored off Boulogne, Smith could not resist the temptation to plan another attack to prove the worth of the new underwater weapons combined with Congreve's rockets; it would be another rehearsal for the attack on Cadiz. He would use ten large, strongly built Dutch coasters fitted with watertight magazines for Congreve's rockets, which would be launched from twin-hulled catamarans because craft with rounded bottoms would roll too heavily for accurate aim; each craft armed with forty-eight rockets. Muskets, pikes and pistols were ordered for the seamen, although boarding was not intended, as Smith had heard that the French would adopt new tactics: instead of fighting on deck, they would go below after hoisting a signal light so their neighbours in the line could rake their empty decks with musketry and grapeshot. In the hope of confusing the enemy's defences several of the large landing craft that he had designed were to take part; each could carry an infantry company and several field guns and had ramps to be lowered for landing. Fulton was delighted at the prospect of what he described as 'an experiment on a small scale to try the effect of my submarine bombs, or torpedoes'.[10] After collecting his ships from the Downs and the torpedoes, rockets and landing craft from Dover, Smith returned to Boulogne on 1 October. That evening the *Antelope* and her consorts anchored just beyond the range of the French shore batteries. Furious activity was seen on board the thirty ships offshore, with boats bringing more men out from Boulogne.

Shortly after midnight, when all was quiet, the French reported the approach of what they took to be fireships about to be ignited and opened fire. Smith had dispatched eight galleys, each carrying two linked torpedoes to be attached to the enemy's mooring cables, but held back his rocket ships because the enemy line occupied the most distant position from which rockets could be fired into the Bassin Napoléon. Yet he did order Congreve to fire four rockets at the French ships 'horizontally to ricochet on and from under the water'; all missed and the catamarans pitched so violently that two shot into the sea and, reported Smith, 'as we could see by the fire . . . they burst under water'.[11] Only one torpedo galley reached the enemy line and as she approached a brig, Fulton reported that the French 'exclaimed that the infernal machines were coming and fired a volley of musketry', then 'fearing the effect of the explosions, they all ran aft and were in the greatest confusion'.[12] The linking rope was set across her mooring cable and, as hoped, the tide carried the two torpedoes against either side of the ship, their clockwork fuses ticking. The explosions lit the scene like lightning but the French commander, Admiral La Crosse, described how the brig was 'thrown up and covered with water and had no other damage than her windows broken'.[13] Smith later reported that the torpedoes had filled with water and, kept only half afloat by their cork casings, had sunk too deep to damage the hull. Another torpedo, which had broken adrift, was found by a French boat and was being towed ashore when it blew up, killing four French seamen. Others were washed up on the beach and La Crosse reported the discovery of a clockwork fuse, 'a lock like that of the fire-machines, which the English used last year with as much ridicule and as little success'. When the attack was reported to Napoleon, he described it as 'breaking the windows of the good citizens of Boulogne with English guineas'.[14] Not even Sir Sidney Smith could describe his attack as a success.

Castlereagh wrote to the Earl of Chatham, the Master of the Ordnance, that 'one of the objections to experimental warfare is its tendency to break in upon the established forms of office . . . In the present instance, the Admiralty was not acting upon any wish of its own but rather yielding to an arrangement which was pressed upon them by me in consequence of Sir Sidney Smith and Mr Congreve.'[15] Smith's superior, Lord Keith, and the Admiralty itself had had enough of his hyper-activity. On 3 October Keith wrote to Smith, 'Experience has convinced me that any attempt to dislodge a few brigs from the roads will be attended with no good consequences, even although it succeeded, as they would resume their station the next tide . . . whilst the risk on our part is considerable and the expense great and certain'.[16] On the same day he wrote to Lord Barham complaining that Smith had 'told me nothing we did not know these two last years; and, as far as attempting to burn a few vessels . . . it is nonsense: we shall get our ships crippled, fail of success and be at a great expense.'[17] Next day the First Lord wrote to the Secretary for War complaining, 'To support this kind of warfare . . . will bring our judgement into disrepute and end in nothing but disgrace. The vessels employed upon it might be used to much more advantage in an attempt on the enemy's fleet at Cadiz.'[18] Lord Barham also complained to Smith's patron, Lord Castlereagh, 'There seems to me such a want of judgement in our friend Sir Sidney that it is much safer to employ him under command than in command.'[19]

Finally, the Prime Minister suggested that the debate be resolved by formal trials to be held at sea off Walmer Castle, although he himself could not be present. Fulton had modified his torpedoes with additional cork for buoyancy and fuses set for fifteen minutes. The trial was set for 15 October and would be close inshore so that it could be watched from the ramparts of the castle; the target ship, the brig *Dorothea*, would be anchored in the road used by ships engaged in clandestine operations, well away from curious crowds on the beach at Deal. As well as Smith and Fulton, many naval officers assembled, some ready to scoff; Captain Owen, a dashing frigate captain, offered to stay on board the brig during the attack and a Captain Kingston remarked that, if a torpedo exploded under his cabin while he was at his dinner table, 'he should feel no concern for the consequence'.[20]

Two boats, each manned by eight men under the command of a lieutenant, who had taken part in the last attack on Boulogne, pulled out to the brig. The linking rope was slung across the mooring cable and the two torpedoes were swept down either side of the ship. There was a pause. Then, said Fulton, 'the awful explosion took place: it lifted the whole body of the vessel out of the water and broke her completely in two in the middle. The main mast and pumps were blown out of her and in one minute nothing of her was to be seen but floating fragments.'[21]

The new technology had triumphed at last. 'The news will, of course, get over to Boulogne',[22] Sir Sidney told Castlereagh, and hopes for a successful attack on Cadiz were raised high. Smith's plan was that showers of incendiary rockets fired at a range of two miles at the enemy fleet from outside the harbour would so occupy the French and Spanish in fire-fighting that they would not see the galleys creeping into the anchorage to sink them with torpedoes; after this there would be no combined fleet left for Nelson to fight out at sea. Even the most conventional of his naval critics grudgingly acknowledged the success of Smith's trial. But Lord St Vincent, the First Lord of the Admiralty under the previous administration, remained hostile and his comment to Fulton was shrewd, that 'Pitt was the greatest fool that ever existed to encourage a mode of war, which they who commanded the seas did not want and which, if successful, would deprive them of it.'[23]

A thousand miles away, in the admiral's cabin of the *Victory*, lifting to the slow Atlantic swell, Nelson's thoughts were far from bizarre weaponry, amphibious raids and clandestine operations. All his experience now came together in composing the climactic confrontation for which he longed. As in his seafaring youth, a ship's timbers, ropes and canvas combined with the muscle and skill of her crew and his own qualities of command to make it almost a part of his own mind and body; now this was extended to all the great ships of the line that lay, heaving to the sea, beyond his cabin windows. His arrival had been eagerly awaited. At the end of August Fremantle had written home, 'I hope Lord Nelson will come out as he is the life and soul of the squadron he serves with'[24]; then on 2 October he had written again, 'The arrival of Lord Nelson has given us fresh life . . . the confidence we place in Nelson gives us all animation.'[25] The admiral had arrived on 27 September, preceded by a frigate with orders for Collingwood not to mark his arrival with saluting guns and signals, which, although the fleet was out of sight of land, might be picked up by a passing fishing boat. So the *Victory* quietly joined the twenty-seven other battleships, and their captains were pulled over to the flagship in their barges, together with Admiral Collingwood.

'The reception I met with on joining the fleet caused the sweetest sensation in my life', Nelson wrote to a friend. 'The officers, who came on board to welcome my return forgot my rank as Commander-in-Chief in the enthusiasm with which they greeted me. As soon as these emotions were past, I laid before them the plan I had previously arranged for attacking the enemy.'[26] His briefings were generally after dinner in the *Victory*, and all his captains had dined with him during the first three days after his arrival, several of them more than once; fifteen were at table to celebrate his forty-seventh birthday on 28 September the day after he had joined the fleet. The briefings were simple and confined mostly to the calculated risk of the planned approach in two or three columns in line ahead; after that, it would be ship-to-ship fighting. He knew that, by throwing his entire fleet at the enemy's centre and rear, the van – the remaining third of their strength – would take so long to work round and form line of battle that, when they did, there would be few French or Spanish ships left for them to support. He explained this in a letter to Emma:

> When I came to explain to them the Nelson touch it was like an electric shock. Some shed tears, all approved – 'It was new – it was singular – it was simple!'; and, from the admiral downwards, it was repeated – 'It must succeed, if ever they will allow us to get at them! You are, my Lord, surrounded by friends, whom you inspire with confidence.'[27]

In the hope of enticing Villeneuve to sea Nelson held his fleet out of sight of land, with a chain of frigates relaying the signals of others close inshore from which movements of the enemy could be watched. As always he was short of frigates: 'I am most exceedingly anxious for more eyes and hope the Admiralty are hastening them to me. The last fleet was lost to me for want of frigates; God forbid this should.'[28] But while there were enough to watch the thirty-three ships of the line in their Cadiz anchorage, there would not be enough to track them should they escape. But would they try to do so? He knew they were short of supplies and that might eventually force them out. But mostly it would be because they were achieving nothing in Cadiz and, knowing Napoleon's impatience and imaginative switches in strategy, he could not believe that they would be allowed to swing round their anchors indefinitely. He did not, of course, know that Napoleon had decided to replace Villeneuve, nor guess that this in itself might be enough to force the French admiral to sea.

But first Nelson performed a characteristic act of kindness. Admiral Calder had expected praise for his brush with the French fleet, which had indeed deflected them south into Spanish waters and away from Brest and the Channel. So he was shocked to hear that he was being criticized for failing to follow the enemy as relentlessly as Nelson would have done and that he had been ordered home to face a court martial. With a battle probable, it would have been appropriate to send him home in a frigate, or an even smaller ship, but to spare him this humiliation Nelson allowed him to return in his own flagship, a battleship of ninety-eight guns, one of only eight ships of that force in his fleet.

As the days passed, there were other tasks. 'We are all busy scraping our ships' sides to paint them in the way Lord Nelson paints the *Victory*', which was yellow with wide black stripes so that they appeared chequered when the gun ports were open, wrote Captain Fremantle of the *Neptune* to his wife, Betsey. He also told her that he had dined with Nelson twice in the flagship and, on the last occasion, had 'sat with him until eight o'clock when he detained me to see a play that was performed by seamen on board the *Victory*; I assure you it was very well conducted and the voice of the seaman, who was dressed in great form and performed the female part, was entertaining to a degree.'[29]

On 14 October the watching frigates signalled that the enemy were moving closer to the harbour mouth. This would have been the moment for Sir Sidney Smith to attack with his 'infernals', but he of course was still intent on a rehearsal off Boulogne. Nelson busied himself in his cabin writing letters – sometimes for six hours or more – to the Admiralty, to friends and, of course, to Emma Hamilton. She was writing to him with the encouragement that he had always relished. In one letter, giving news of Horatia, she wrote, 'Oh, Nelson, how I love her but how do I idolize you – the dearest husband of my heart, you are all this world to your Emma. May God send you victory and home to your Emma,

Horatia and Paradise Merton, for when you are there it will be paradise.'[30]

Four days later came the signal he awaited and he wrote to Emma:

My dearest, beloved Emma, dear friend of my bosom, the signal has been made that the enemy's combined fleet are coming out of port. We have very little wind, so that I have no hopes of seeing them before tomorrow. May the God of Battles crown my endeavours with success . . . I hope in God that I shall live to finish my letter after the battle . . . May God Almighty give us success over these fellows and enable us to get a peace.[31]

Nelson's serenity was compounded of confidence and fatalism and in the *Victory* it was noted that 'Lord Nelson had made up his mind to the loss of a limb – and before he sailed he went to inspect a coffin, which was given him . . . and was made out of the wood of *l'Orient* (in the Battle of the Nile), saying he should most probably want it'.[32] Nelson's calm was manifest in his concentration on daily routine and writing letters not only to friends but on the detailed business of the fleet. On the 19th he wrote to the victualling office complaining that they had sent his ships rice, which seamen did not like, instead of cheese, which they did; and he ordered a large quantity of cocoa, saying it was popular.

In Cadiz, Villeneuve was leading his fleet to sea with foreboding. He had received his orders for the Mediterranean and he knew that he was to be superseded, but he realized that if he was able to pass Gibraltar and reach Toulon, his reputation and career might be saved. On 19 October a breeze was blowing from the north-east, ready to carry him south; this was the time to make sail. Recognizing Nelson's tactical cunning, he was expecting an attack on his rear division, so he planned to hold a third of his fleet in reserve under Admiral Gravina, sailing to windward of the main force, ready to come to their aid. On that day twelve of Villeneuve's big ships left Cadiz, to be followed by the remaining twenty-one next morning. All he could see were a few British frigates cruising to and fro out in the Atlantic; but he knew what waited beyond the horizon.

The combined fleet numbered thirty-three ships of the line – eighteen French and fifteen Spanish – mostly 'seventy-fours', although some with sixty-four or eighty guns, and four with more than a hundred. The Spanish *Santísima Trinidad*, mounting a hundred and thirty, was by far the most powerful ship at sea that day. The French and Spanish formed mixed squadrons and their quality was variable, the most effective ship being a 'seventy-four', the *Redoutable*, whose ship's company had been trained by Captain Jean-Jacques Lucas in close-quarter fighting, sniping, grappling and boarding; her guns' crews were trained to rush to the upper deck, grabbing cutlasses and tomahawks, to leap on to the deck of an enemy ship alongside; like Latouche-Tréville, Lucas employed soldiers, and infantry sharpshooters were ready to fire at officers on an enemy's deck. On paper, the twenty-seven British sail of the line were out-gunned: the enemy mounted over 400 more guns than they and outnumbered them not only in ships but also in men, with almost double their numbers. However, despite the long chase across the Atlantic and back earlier in the year, the French and Spanish seamen often suffered from having been too long in port over recent years, so were unable to match their opponents in working and fighting their pitching and rolling ships.

On 20 October Nelson had not himself seen the enemy, only signals relayed by his chain of frigates. However, expecting Villeneuve to be heading for the Mediterranean and realizing that only he could bar the way south – Cornwallis would be waiting with the Channel Fleet off Brest should the French move north – he sailed slowly for the Straits of Gibraltar. Another signal then reported that Villeneuve was still to the north, having had to stand out to sea when the wind shifted to the south-west, so Nelson put about to resume his earlier station off Cadiz. The wind changed again to a westerly, which would enable Villeneuve to run for the Straits, hoping to avoid Nelson, so the French admiral ordered his fleet into battle formation, with Gravina commanding the detached reserve. This change of orders and course threw the French and Spanish into confusion and after three hours they headed south in a loose, ragged armada nine miles long.

As the sun rose above the hills of Spain on Monday 21 October, Villeneuve saw the British stretched across the horizon to the north-west; not the eighteen ships of the line that he had expected, but twenty-seven. Should he crowd sail and head for the Straits in the hope of out-running Nelson and then making for the safety of Cartagena, or Toulon, or even fulfil his orders from Napoleon and head for Naples? Deep in depression he weighed the alternatives and the chances for an hour. Then he reached his decision and ordered his fleet to put about, reversing its course and heading north towards the safety of Cadiz. Then, abandoning his original tactical plan, he ordered his captains to maintain the single line of battle and steer out to sea, keeping Cadiz to windward. But Nelson was to windward of him, so there was no avoiding action now. Hampered by veering wind, the French and Spanish captains struggled to take up some viable formation in which to fight but by ten o'clock that morning the combined fleet lay in a long, straggling crescent, the former rear in the van – this now commanded by Admiral Pierre Dumanoir Le Pelley★ – and the van in the rear – now commanded by Admiral Gravina. Some ships were bunched together, while others lagged astern of the next ahead. At eleven Villeneuve saw the British fleet sailing towards him in two columns. They would be in range of his heavy guns in an hour, and he comforted himself with the thought that his line would then be able to concentrate its fire on the two leading ships.

At first light Nelson had estimated that they should be in action at about midday, so there was plenty of time to prepare. There was no need for further orders because he had already arranged that his fleet should approach in two columns, each led by three of the heaviest ships, to smash their way through the enemy line. The weather column was to be led by himself in the *Victory*, the lee column by Collingwood in the *Royal Sovereign*. Once the planned mêlée had begun there would be no need for signals, which in any case could not be seen through the smoke. By mid-morning the

---

★A distant kinsman of Lieutenant Charles Pelly, who had been wounded in Nelson's attack on Boulogne four years earlier.

columns took shape, although the *Africa*,★ having missed a signal and become separated from the fleet in the night, was far to the north.

The ships' companies were given a meal and changed their clothes. The officers put on clean underwear to minimize the risk of infection if they were wounded; the seamen tied cloths around their heads to stop sweat running into their eyes and as a little protection for their ears from the noise of gunfire. Nelson himself toured the gundecks, talking and joking with the guns' crews, who had laid out their shot, powder charges, rammers and spongers and the restraining ropes on the gun carriages and sanded the decks so that they would not slip in the blood that would soon be swilling across them. Later his flag-captain, Thomas Hardy, was called into the admiral's cabin to witness his will, which left Emma Hamilton

> a legacy to my King and Country, that they will give her ample provision to maintain. I also leave to the beneficence of my Country, my adopted daughter Horatia Nelson Thompson and I desire she will use in future the name of Nelson only. These are the only favours I ask of my King and Country at this moment when I am going to fight their battle.[33]

Alone in his cabin, Nelson began to write. Brought up in a parsonage and steeped in Biblical language, later taking inspiration from the oratory of Henry V in Shakespeare's play, from which he liked to quote, his prose now matched the moment. It was not so much a personal prayer that he wrote but one that was intended to be read by others, should he not survive the day:

★Nelson's great-great-great-granddaughter Mrs Anna Tribe recalls a senior Australian naval officer who told her of a strange dream he had had when young. He had then read no naval history but dreamed that he was on the quarterdeck of ship of the line in action and could smell the burnt powder and hear the guns. A group of officers stood near by and he heard one say, 'What of Africa, my Lord?' It was so vivid that he remembered the dream, remaining puzzled that, at such a time, the officers should ask about Africa. Many years later, reading about Trafalgar for the first time, he realized that it might have been the ship rather than the continent.

May the great God, whom I worship, grant to my Country and for the benefit of Europe in general a great and glorious victory, and may no misconduct in anyone tarnish it, and may humanity after victory be the predominant feature in the British Fleet. For myself individually, I commit my life to Him who made me and may his blessing light upon my endeavours for serving my Country faithfully. To Him I resign myself and the just cause which is entrusted me to defend. Amen, amen, amen.[34]

When his signal officer, Lieutenant Pasco, entered, he saw Nelson on his knees and withdrew to the quarterdeck, where the admiral followed him to say that he wished to make signal to the fleet. This was to be, 'England confides that every man will do his duty.' When Pasco explained that the word 'confides' would be difficult to spell in signal flags and could he substitute 'expects', Nelson replied, 'That will do. Make it directly.' Across on the quarterdeck of the *Royal Sovereign* Collingwood, seeing the flags fly up the flagship's halyards, grumbled, 'What is Nelson signalling about? We all know what we have to do.'[35]

Villeneuve was now only about twenty miles from Cadiz and safety, but the British were swooping towards him over the long swell, driven by a light breeze. In both fleets gun ports were open, guns run out, cocked and primed. The British lee column had drawn ahead of Nelson's, although his ships had set all sails. Nelson's final signal was to Collingwood: 'I intend to push or go through the end of the enemy's line to prevent them from getting into Cadiz.'[36]

At midday a French 'seventy-four', the *Fougueux*, fired the first shots at Collingwood's van and then broadsides began flashing along the French and Spanish line. The British, unable to reply, sailed on as roundshot howled overhead, threw up water spouts, tore their sails and splintered their timbers. Twenty minutes later Collingwood took his revenge as he burst through their line, raking the bows of the *Fougueux* and the stern of the colossal Spanish *Santa Ana* with double-shotted broadsides. 'See how that noble fellow Collingwood takes his ship into action! How I envy him!' exclaimed Nelson on the quarterdeck of the *Victory*, while Collingwood was saying, 'What would Nelson give to be here!'[37]

Forty minutes later Nelson, too, was in action, for most of that time under fire but unable to respond. At first, he did not know where Villeneuve's flagship, the *Bucentaure*, lay in the line; then, after being told that she was eleventh from the van, he altered course to bring the *Victory* under her stem. As he did so, the *Redoubtable* closed with the French flagship to block the *Victory's* way and the *Bucentaure* loosed a raking broadside into her bows; unable to reply, the *Victory* was raked and shot through by both ships. On the quarterdeck Nelson's secretary, John Scott, standing by the admiral, was cut in two by a roundshot and, close by, a double-headed shot slashed through a file of marines. The fore-topmast was shot away, sails shredded and the wheel splintered, so that the ship had to be steered from below. A splinter ricocheted off the buckle of Captain Hardy's shoe and Nelson was heard to say, 'This is too warm work, Hardy, to last long.'[38] But it did.

After forty minutes' suffering the *Victory* could at last reply. As she closed the stern of Villeneuve's flagship, Hardy shouted an order and one of the two heavy carronades mounted on the fore-castle fired a 68-pound shot and a canister of 500 musket balls through her stern windows, followed by a rolling broadside from all her port-side guns, double- or treble-shotted. The French flag-ship shook and lay stunned in a cloud of smoke and wood dust. As the *Victory* turned to face the *Redoutable*, the ships collided, locking their rigging and yardarms, each loosing broadsides, gun muzzle to gun muzzle. Fremantle's ship, the 98-gun *Neptune*, also raked the *Bucentaure* and, passing the *Victory* to burst through the French line, ran alongside the most powerful enemy ship, the *Santísima Trinidad*, to fight her until she surrendered. Smoke billowed across their upper decks, parting to expose brief tableaux of battle. Those who saw the horrors at close quarters, or the distant panorama of sea, smoke and shattered ships, would never be able to describe it except in practical prose. Occasionally, one would try, such as Midshipman Henry Walker, who put it into doggerel:

> The bodies lay all on our decks,
> Scuppers ran with blood;
> It made the seas around us
> Look like a purple flood.[39]

On the quarterdeck of the *Victory* Nelson paced to and fro. He was wearing a blue coat decorated with gold epaulettes and his four orders of chivalry embroidered on the left breast. Although advised before the action to change into a plain coat to avoid identification, he had refused, saying there was not time. Probably he was sighted by one of Captain Lucas's snipers in the mizzen-top of the *Redoutable* or perhaps it was a random shot, but at twenty-five minutes past one Nelson jerked, dropped to his knees and rolled on to his side, shot through the shoulder. Hardy ordered him to be carried below, the admiral spreading his handkerchief over his face so that he should not be recognized. He was laid in the cockpit on the orlop deck below the waterline, where the surgeon and his mates worked on the wounded, bandaging, tying tourniquets and amputating arms and legs. As Hardy leaned over him, Nelson said, 'Hardy, I believe they have done it at last, my backbone is shot through'[40] and when William Beatty, the surgeon, began to cut away his clothing, said, 'You can be of no use to me, Beatty, go and attend those whose lives can be preserved.'[41] Nelson lay dying in the dim light of horn lanterns; as the concussion of broadsides shook the ship and those about him strained to hear his whispers against the thunder of the guns and the screams of the wounded, his words were remembered.

For more than two and a half hours friends came to kneel beside him: from the upper deck Hardy and Midshipman Bulkeley, whose father he had known twenty-five years earlier, in the Caribbean; Alexander Scott, the chaplain; Burke, the purser. Constantly by him were his steward, Chevalier, and the surgeon, Dr Beatty; Pasco, the signals lieutenant, had been wounded and was lying near by. Beatty had probed the wound and found that the musket ball had penetrated his left shoulder at a steep angle, cut through an artery and a lung and lodged in the spine; there was nothing the surgeon could do but try to ease his pain. As familiar faces peered down at him, Nelson muttered, 'Remember me to Lady Hamilton. Remember me to Horatia . . . I have left a will and left Lady Hamilton and Horatia to my country . . . My sufferings are great but they will soon be over . . . yet one would like to live a little longer, too . . . How dear is life to all men . . . God be praised, I have done my duty.'

As the great 36-pounder guns on the deck above crashed in recoil, the shock of discharge, setting the lanterns jumping and guttering, the smoke eddying down the hatchway, Nelson groaned, 'Oh! *Victory, Victory!* How you distract my poor brain!' He kept asking for news of the battle above: 'I hope none of our ships have struck?' After an hour Hardy returned from the deck to report 'a brilliant victory' with at least fourteen or fifteen enemy ships captured. 'That is well,' he replied, 'but I had bargained for twenty.'[42] It was time for farewells. He asked Hardy to kiss him, and the tall captain knelt and kissed his cheek and forehead. Then, to the chaplain, 'Doctor, I have not been a great sinner.' His voice weakened and became difficult to hear against the gunfire. 'Remember that I leave Lady Hamilton and my daughter Horatia as a legacy to my country . . . never forget Horatia. Thank God I have done my duty.' Finally, 'Drink, drink. Fan, fan. Rub, rub . . .' Nelson opened his eyes and closed them. At half-past four his steward called the surgeon. Shortly afterwards Captain Hardy wrote in the logbook of the *Victory*, 'Partial firing continued until 4.30 p.m., when, a victory having been reported to the Right Hon. Lord Nelson, K.B. and Commander-in-Chief, he died of his wounds.'[43]

12

Why, 'tis I, little Johnny Bull

ON THE day that Nelson died victorious off Cape Trafalgar,
Lord Castlereagh wrote to Captain (soon to be Rear-
Admiral) Sir Sidney Smith from Downing Street: 'The success of
Mr Francis's experiment gives me great confidence in our means
of annoying the enemy in their ports with little comparative risk to
ourselves. I am anxious to hear of the destruction of the Boulogne
flotilla, if it was only for the purpose of liberating you for more
important enterprises.'[1] By this he meant the attack by torpedoes
and rockets on the French and Spanish fleets he assumed still to be
lying at Cadiz.

Five days later he wrote to Lord Nelson, whom he assumed still
to be waiting in the Atlantic, hoping for Villeneuve to put to sea.
It was a long report on the trials of Fulton's – or Francis's – torpedoes off Walmer Castle, pointing out that if these were successful
at Cadiz the damage to the enemy would be lethal, whereas fire
ignited by Congreve's rockets could be extinguished.

With respect to the enemy's fleet in Cadiz, I hope your Lordship
will either have the glory of destroying it at sea, or that we shall
find the means, sooner or later, of getting them in port. I have
not thought it desirable to send either Mr Congreve, or Mr
Francis to your Lordship till they have provided themselves with
all the necessary means of giving effect to the respective modes
of attack.

He still had confidence in them, and added that soon, 'I hope to forward both these weapons to your Lordship and I am sure your Lordship will facilitate their application.'[2]

Soon afterwards Castlereagh wrote another letter to Nelson, doubtless inspired by Sir Sidney Smith. This expanded on the plan to burn the enemy fleet in port by actually 'laying hold of Cadiz', following the rockets and torpedoes with an assault landing by troops such as Smith had put ashore in Aboukir Bay. The suggested time would be March or early April 1806 so that the force would be available for other operations by the end of that month. 'If an attempt is to be made on Cadiz,' he wrote, 'I am inclined to believe (on which point I should be naturally desirous of receiving your Lordship's opinion) that 40,000 British troops would have little to fear from any, or all, the force Spain could assemble and that such an army might, in a week's time, do everything at Cadiz that we should have any motive for attempting.'[3]

As he wrote this, Lord Nelson's corpse was floating head-down in a large barrel of brandy lashed upright on the main deck of the *Victory* as she wallowed, under tow, towards Gibraltar. Like many of his ships, she was badly damaged, having lost her mizzen mast and her main- and fore-topmasts. She was no longer a flagship for on the evening of the battle Collingwood had hoisted his flag as acting commander-in-chief. As the battle ended and the shattered ships of both fleets heaved on a rising swell, a gale blew out of the Atlantic. Nelson had forecast this as he lay dying and passed an order for Collingwood to anchor as soon as the fighting ended. But the latter decided against anchoring, partly because he wanted to take his ships out to sea and away from the dangerous shore and partly because many ships had had their anchors, cables and cat-heads shot away and could not anchor even if ordered to do so. If this seemed the safer option, the consequence was catastrophic. The storm that struck that night blew for three days and eight of the prizes foundered, including both the *Bucentaure* and the *Redoutable*, taking with them hundreds of their survivors and most of the wounded. No British ship had been lost in the battle, or was lost in the storm. It had been as decisive a victory as Nelson could have wanted.

Not until 26 October was Collingwood able to give his dispatch to the lieutenant commanding the schooner *Pickle* for passage to England and the Admiralty. Seventeen French and Spanish ships had been captured, one had caught fire and blown up – the flash of the explosion had been seen from the rooftops of Cadiz – and fifteen had escaped. The French had lost nearly 3400 men killed or drowned, and some 1200 wounded; the Spanish, more than 1000 killed or drowned, and 1400 wounded; between 3000 and 4000 prisoners had been taken from the combined fleet. The British losses had been about 450 killed and 1700 wounded. Of the French and Spanish ships that had escaped, four, commanded by Dumanoir Le Pelley, were to be intercepted on 4 November off Cape Ortegal by a British squadron under Captain Richard Strachan and, after a fierce action, were all captured. Of those that reached Cadiz, five, led by Commodore Julien de Cosmao-Kerjulien, who had captured Diamond Rock earlier in the year, were to make a sortie on 23 October and recapture two Spanish prizes from the British, only to lose three of their own number to another storm. The commodore's own ship, the *Pluton*, and the two prizes managed to return to Cadiz. It had been a gallant gesture.

Two of Nelson's captains had been killed in the action and the others now veered between elation and grief. Fremantle, whose powerful *Neptune*, of ninety-eight guns, had been one of three heavy ships that had led Nelson's line into battle, had felt his loss 'very severely indeed'[4] but also celebrated his own capture of the huge Spanish *Santísima Trinidad*, of 130 guns. His prize had later sunk but he noted that among the 450 prisoners he had taken from her 'I have found also an excellent French cook and a true Spanish pug dog'.[5] He was sorry, too, that the command of the fleet had reverted to Collingwood, who lacked his old friend's charisma; although he could show a whimsical wit in the company of women, with his officers he was, Fremantle found, 'a cold sort of animal'.[6] He mourned over the only reminders he had – a lock of Nelson's hair and 'his best spying-glass . . . a precious relict of a very sincere friend'[7] – and, their shared professional interests apart, missed the convivial dinner parties and unpredictable flashes of humour and insight.

So, as the ship rolled between Cadiz and Gibraltar, he, sad and lonely, wrote to his wife, 'I do little more than play with my pug dog'. He named 'my companion' Nympha and wrote that she 'always receives me with greetings and congratulations'. The pug 'sleeps in the bed with me and is solaced every morning from the warm blankets into a large tub of cold salt water, this keeps her clear of fleas'. He bought her a kitten as a companion but, a few days later, was writing that 'she is at this instant worrying an unfortunate kitten that is her companion. I mean to buy myself a parrot at Gibraltar and perhaps a monkey to amuse myself with.'[8]

After the battle and the storm, gloom had descended on the fleet but a thousand miles to the north-east all was activity and anticipation of a battle that had, in fact, already been fought. On the night of 28 October, the day Lord Castlereagh had written to Lord Nelson about Smith's plan to destroy the enemy fleet in Cadiz, Fulton's torpedoes were again in action off Boulogne. The target was one of the twenty-seven French brigs moored off the harbour mouth, and a four-oared gig put off from a British frigate to lay the linking rope across her mooring cable. 'It exploded and made a similar crash as the brig [the *Dorothea*] lately exploded in the Downs', reported the lieutenant in command and his captain, watching from the frigate, told Smith that, 'there seems no doubt of this brig being destroyed.'[9] Yet he had to admit that, as the sun came up, 'We this morning find the same number of brigs (27) in the roads.'[10] However, Smith's report, as quoted in *The Times*, claimed that he had 'destroyed a large gunboat, which lay at anchor under the protection of the batteries, by means of a carcass, which, soon after midnight, was sent in and blew the gunboat to atoms'.[11]

The frigate that had launched the torpedoes, the *Immortalité*, was still anchored off Boulogne but out of range of the shore batteries when a pinnace was seen approaching from the harbour, towing a small punt. This was then cut adrift and the pinnace returned to Boulogne. This 'excited so much curiosity' on board the frigate that a boat was sent to investigate and, as a midshipman recorded,

In half an hour, the boat returned, having the punt in tow, in which had been found a note from Admiral La Crosse, who then commanded the flotilla, addressed to the English commodore, and which contained the following words, 'The Austrian army of one hundred thousand men is no more. General Mack is a prisoner at Ulm and Prince Ferdinand is put to flight.' That an army, which had only quitted the vicinity of Boulogne in the early part of September, should have traversed such an extent of country . . . and, after annihilating an army of one hundred thousand men . . . have established itself in Ulm, the key of all Austrian movements and positions . . . seemed so far to exceed all that one had ever heard, or read of in ancient or modern warfare, that the account was considered a fabrication and wholly disbelieved.[12]

The news was true; Napoleon's victory had been won on 21 October. As confirmation followed, the sea between the cliffs of England and France no longer seemed dangerous.

As the sky darkened over Paris on the night of 27 October 1805, the sound of a flute drifted over the rooftops. It came from behind the shutters of a barred window high in a medieval keep, its grey stone bulk capped by conical turrets, standing within the high walls of the Temple prison. The light of a candle in a stone-walled room would have shown the flute-player to be an Englishman aged thirty-six; a good-looking, strongly built man with a high-bridged nose and brown hair brushed back from thoughtful eyes and high forehead. On the table before him lay a copy of the *Moniteur* newspaper and a chart of the river Danube. The former reported the Emperor Napoleon's crushing defeat of the Austrians at Ulm; the latter covered the territory across which he was now marching to face another Austrian army and the Russians. On the mantelpiece stood a teapot and a coffee-pot, a case of geometrical instruments, a paint box, a silver watch and a tin lantern. Beyond, in the shadows, were fifty or more books on shelves and rolls of charts lay on a desk; there was a looking-glass and, in an alcove, a narrow bed made up with sheets, a counterpane and two pillows. The only clues to the man's identity were a small spyglass, a cocked hat and a blue uniform coat with gilded brass buttons. This was Captain Wright, who, were he not imprisoned, might now have been with Sir Sidney Smith, preparing for the attack on Cadiz. But he was said to be in good spirits, hoping to be exchanged for a captured French officer but prepared for continued captivity, having just ordered two new shirts and a book about the French language.

The faint notes of the flute continued until after midnight; some said for one hour beyond, others for two. At dawn the next day a gaoler named Savard arrived at the Temple gates for the day shift and, soon afterwards, his duties took him to Captain Wright's door. This he unlocked and, entering, crossed to the window and threw open the shutters. He turned and looked at the figure on the bed. Wright, wearing a cotton nightcap, was lying on his back with the sheet drawn up to his chin. Savard noticed that he seemed curiously still but that his eyes were open and that his face seemed, as he put it, contorted. He pulled back the sheet and saw that Captain Wright's throat had been cut and that he was dead. There was little blood on the bed but a trail of it across the floor. In his right hand, which lay beside his thigh, was a white-handled razor. The razor was closed.

Later that day the prison authorities announced that Captain John Wesley Wright, apparently depressed by reading news of the Emperor's victory at Ulm, had committed suicide. But some in the Temple itself later swore that he had heard other news – the first report of Nelson's victory off Cape Trafalgar – and was elated. The battles at Ulm and off Cape Trafalgar had been fought on the same day and Wright had died a week later. The news of Ulm had certainly reached Paris but could news of Trafalgar have arrived there in that time? Had Captain Wright – and others – known of Trafalgar and could he have been murdered in revenge? If so, on whose orders?

The news of the victory off Cape Trafalgar reached London in the early hours of 6 November by the hand of a young naval officer riding in a light chaise drawn by fast horses from Falmouth, where the schooner *Pickle* had arrived thirty-seven hours earlier. A special *Gazette Extraordinary* was instantly prepared, but it was twenty-four hours before it could appear in the morning newspapers. So that morning *The Times* was reporting the news from Dover that 'a great bustle has prevailed today in getting on board all the apparatus, stores and combustibles, which have been so long preparing here and there is no doubt but an attack on some of the enemy's ports . . . will take place in a few days'. It added that Sir Sidney's two twin-hulled landing craft had been on trials under additional sails, 'preparatory to their sailing with the expedition'.

On the same day, the 6th, the newspaper also reported the aftermath of Napeoleon's victory at Ulm and speculated as to the next strategic moves. On the same page was another report under the heading, 'CAPT. WRIGHT', quoting two Paris papers, the *Gazette de France* and the *Journal de Paris*. One report read: 'Capt. Wright of the English Navy, a prisoner in the Temple, who had disembarked on the French coast Georges and his accomplices, has put an end to his existence in prison, after having read in the *Moniteur* the account of the destruction of the Austrian army.' The other report read: 'The day before yesterday, Mr Wright, the English officer who last year disembarked the assassins of England on the coast of Brittany and was imprisoned in the Temple, after having read the bulletins in the *Moniteur*, and uttered much abuse against the Austrians, and particularly against General Mack, cut his throat with a razor.'

The Times commented:

> We fear there is no doubt of the fact of Captain Wright's decease but we cannot believe that a gallant officer, who has so often looked death in the face and was proverbial for courting danger, fell in the manner mentioned. Those, who ordered and perpetrated the midnight murders of Pichegru and the Duke d'Enghien, can, no doubt, explain the nature of Captain Wright's death.[13]

But now news from the Atlantic spread across most of England by mail coach. At Swanbourne in Buckinghamshire, Betsey Fremantle heard it the morning after it had reached London, from a housemaid. 'I was much alarmed by Nelly's ghastly appearance immediately after breakfast', when she entered with the news that 'a most dreadful action had been fought off Cadiz, Nelson and several captains killed'. She felt 'indescribable misery' until the post arrived with news that her husband was safe and that

Poor Nelson was no more, he lived . . . to know he was victorious. In the midst of my delight to hear Fremantle had been preserved in this severe action, I could not help feeling greatly distressed for the fate of poor Nelson, whose loss is irreparable . . . Poor Nelson! had he survived, it would have been glorious indeed. Regret at his death is more severely felt than joy at the destruction of the combined fleets.[14]

Her sister Eugenia declared on the same day, 'This day brought us most glorious news but our joy was damped by the loss of poor Nelson . . . we all gave him our tears.'[15]

The news made the same impact in the most languid reaches of the aristocracy as in the streets of London, where faces were shocked and tear-stained. On the 6th, before the publication of the newspaper reports, Lady Harriet Cavendish, daughter of the Duke of Devonshire and his celebrated wife, Georgiana, wrote to her sister from Chiswick:

> I am safe in supposing you have heard all the details of the great events that have roused even me from my usual apathy upon those subjects. Poor Lord Nelson. The universal gloom that I hear of from those who have been in Town is the strongest proof of the regret he so justly deserved to occasion as otherwise I suppose such a victory at such a moment is everything, both for our honour and safety, and could have driven us half wild.[16]

Her aunt Lady Bessborough, pertinent as ever, put Nelson's death into historical context. 'He could not have picked a finer close to such a life', she wrote, 'Do you know, it makes me feel almost as much envy as compassion . . . I think I should like to die so.'[17]

Joseph Farington was staying in a remote country house in Norfolk. The day after the news reached London he noted, 'At one o'clock, the postmaster at Rougham sent his post-boy with orders to stop while an extraordinary *Gazette* was read.' Next day the county newspapers printed Collingwood's dispatch and, four days after that, Farington showed he was aware of its historical importance by making a pilgrimage to Nelson's birthplace, near by at Burnham Thorpe. The rector, the Reverend Daniel Everitt, the successor to the admiral's father, showed them the recently rebuilt rectory. 'I expressed a wish that an obelisk, or something of the kind, should be placed there by subscription,' Farington continued, 'but Everitt did not seem to encourage it, observing that it would bring people to see it.'[18]

On the same evening that the news was published, the Theatre Royal, Covent Garden, added to its production of *Venice Preserv'd*, in which Sarah Siddons was performing, 'A Loyal Musical Impromptu called *Nelson's Glory*, a representation of the late Triumphant Naval Engagement'.[19] Within days, print shops displayed hastily engraved, inaccurate illustrations of the event and hawkers sold broadsheet ballads praising Nelson. There seemed to be almost religious undertones: the lost hero as the martyred saviour of his people, whose death had redeemed not so much their sins as his own; little thought was now given to the scandalous Lady Hamilton. As commemorative engravings became more elaborate, some illustrated Lord Nelson's apotheosis with the hero borne aloft by angels, tritons and assorted allegorical figures, including Fame, Neptune and Britannia.

On 6 November, the day on which the *Gazette* announced Nelson's victory, a copy reached Dover and Sir Sidney Smith realized that his services would not, after all, be required at Cadiz. He thereupon sent a *Gazette* across the Channel by a cutter to be floated ashore in an unmanned skiff. The news reached Paris by overland courier at about the same time; usually rumours preceded confirmation by several days. Two dispatches had been sent by the French ambassador in Madrid: the first on 22 October, reported an inconclusive battle; the second, three days later, reported the disaster. The second dispatch reached the Ministry of Marine on 7 November, so it is likely that the first arrived a few days earlier. Even so, it is questionable whether any report could have reached Paris from Cadiz before the end of October without the use of a telegraph system, and it therefore seems unlikely that this was the motive for Captain Wright's murder. In any case, no mention of it was allowed to be published in French newspapers for another month, as it was the Emperor's policy to withhold bad news and then present it as good. Napoleon himself was told on

16 November at the Schönbrunn Palace in Vienna; his immediate reaction was said to have been, 'I cannot be everywhere.'[20] He then resumed his concentration on tactics to be employed on meeting the Austrian and Russian armies. His former military secretary, Bourrienne, still mulling over the brilliance of the French victory at Ulm, was shocked and later reflected, 'The Battle of Trafalgar paralysed our naval force and banished all hope of any attempt against England.'[21]

The consequences of Trafalgar were seen in a very different light by the respective governments of Britain and France. The British realized that the threat of invasion, which had hung over them since 1801 – with a year's interlude during the Peace of Amiens – had at last gone. Certainly the Grand Armée could march back to the coast as rapidly as it had marched into central Europe, but there now seemed no possibility of the French aspiring to the command of the Channel; equally importantly, it had given the British confidence in their own invincibility at sea. Those French who knew the extent of their defeat recognized it as a naval disaster but were focused on the development of the campaign on the Continent following the defeat of the Austrians at Ulm. Again, as Napoleon himself put it, the conflict was emerging as one between an elephant and a whale.

It was known that the Emperor was marching to engage the huge armies of two of Britain's allies, Russia and Austria, but what of Prussia? Supposedly an ally, his army probably crucial to the defeat of the French, King Frederick had not committed himself. One problem was the rivalry between Prussia and Russia over disputed territory; another was that Napoleon had offered him Hanover – the inheritance of the Hanoverian King George III – in return for neutrality. The British had in turn offered huge subsidies and other inducements to fight, and it had been decided that the only way to encourage reluctant allies, after the defeat at Ulm, was by military reinforcement. Two British expeditionary forces were dispatched to the Continent: one to Sicily to support Austria, the other to northern Germany in the hope of stiffening Prussian resolve. But the Prussians still did not march and instead issued an ultimatum to the French that, unless they agreed to a settlement of European disputes within a month, they would do so.

This gave Napoleon all the time he needed to impose his own solution.

During December rumours spread across Europe and across the Channel of a titanic battle in central Europe, somewhere east of Vienna. It was known that the French were advancing to meet the Austrians and Russians, by whom they would be heavily outnumbered. So heady had the news of Trafalgar been to the British, that a victory for their allies was forecast and 'Prinny', the Prince of Wales, declared that it was 'all over with the French and that they had been sent to the devil'.[22] Then, before the end of December, news crossed the Channel that there had, indeed, been a great battle, in which 73,000 French had routed 85,000 Austrians and Russians at Austerlitz. The Austrians were said to be ready for peace at almost any price, while the Russians were trudging back towards their own frontier and the safety of their limitless hinterland. By the beginning of 1806 the coalition that Pitt had so carefully assembled had disintegrated. He was a sick man and in no condition to work on the construction of a new alliance. When he heard the news from Austerlitz and was shown the movements of the armies on a map of Europe, Pitt declared prophetically, 'Roll up that map; it will not be wanted these ten years.'[23]

Those were not Pitt's final words, but they might well have been. Worn out by a circulatory disease, aggravated by overwork and heavy drinking, he had gone to Bath for medical treatment but there was no hope of recovery and he had begun his journey back to London when the body of Lord Nelson was borne through the streets of the capital on 9 January 1806, in a funeral procession of unprecedented pomp and ceremony, charged with emotion. On arrival at his house in the outer suburb of Putney, the Prime Minister was dying. On 23 January, aged only forty-six (a year younger than Nelson had been), he was dead.

This year also saw the death of Nelson's opponent at Trafalgar, Admiral Villeneuve. Taken prisoner by Fremantle, who had warmed to his gentlemanly manners, he was released on parole and returned to France. Longing to see his family but realizing that he would certainly be put on trial for his defeat, he decided to return to Paris. His coach stopped for the night at Rennes and there, on 22 April 1806, he was found dead in his room at an hotel. Beside him was a letter of farewell to his wife but his death had been caused by six deep chest wounds by a knife, which was found embedded in his heart. His death was officially declared to be suicide, as had been the equally violent death of Captain Wright.

Another player was about to depart. With the ending of the threat of invasion the British government had lost interest in Robert Fulton's ingenious weapons, and on 6 January the American wrote to Pitt, three days before the latter returned home to die. He was demanding substantial compensation unless the subsidy for his development of torpedoes continued, namely a down payment of £170,000 and an annual salary of £2400 for life. There was an underlying threat in his letter, as he wrote:

> Now, in this business, I will not disguise that I have full confidence in the power which I possess, which is no less than to be the means, should I think proper, of giving to the world a system, which must of necessity sweep all military marines from the ocean by giving to the weaker maritime powers advantages over the stronger, which the strong cannot prevent.[24]

Pitt was so ill that it was unlikely that he saw the letter, and those to whom it passed noted that it sounded like blackmail because £60,000 of the lump sum he demanded was to ensure that he would 'remain tranquil'[25]; the implication was that he would sell his secrets to any foreign power that would pay what he asked. The Admiralty appointed an arbitration board, which decided to pay him no more than he had already been promised: £14,000 and an annual salary and expenses of £1640. Fulton, angry and bitter, decided to return to the United States to concentrate on another invention: the steam-powered ship. A year after the Battle of Trafalgar he sailed for New York.

Pitt was replaced as Prime Minister by his first cousin Lord Grenville, a former Foreign Secretary, who formed a coalition government that became known as 'The Ministry of All the Talents', including Charles James Fox as Foreign Secretary, although he was also to die within the year. New and daunting horizons had opened. Britain might be triumphant at sea but

France was still supreme on land. Another shift in strategy had begun. Now that Napoleon was undisputed master of Europe, where would he strike next? Nobody expected another attempt at invasion, nor could he yet seriously consider any move that required naval superiority. But he had long hankered after eastern conquest: the Ottoman Empire, Egypt and the way to India, which could now be achieved overland, or by the short sea route to the Levant. The British commanders who had played their parts in the long campaign of Trafalgar now focused on the southern coasts of Europe. Among these was the newly promoted Rear-Admiral Sir Sidney Smith, who, about to take up command of the inshore squadron of Collingwood's Mediterranean Fleet, wrote to his friend William Windham, now reappointed as Secretary of State for War, from his flagship, the *Pompée*, on 12 February, urging, 'Surely Lord Nelson's death ought not to operate so disadvantageously to us to change our system into a simple and passive one of defence.'[26] A recent plan that his 'infernals' be used against Brest had been dropped but he was full of new and aggressive ideas.

> Knowing Bonaparte as I know him, I can easily imagine his thirst to realize a *speculation manquée* on Constantinople and the route to India. He cannot fail to find it increase on being nearer to the capital of the Eastern Empire than he is to his own . . . All this he can do if he is not counteracted . . . it will be a giant's labour to eradicate them from the Hellespont and Bosphorous if they once establish themselves there. I dare say I shall be looked to for the Herculean labour.[27]

So it was to the Mediterranean that Smith was sent, as also was Lieutenant-General Sir John Moore. The narrow seas between Cap Gris Nez and the North Foreland were no longer the crucible of war.

After so long this was difficult to accept. The fear and fortitude had evaporated and the drums and bugles of the militia and volunteers were no longer familiar sounds in town and village. The caricatures that had made the British laugh and bolstered their morale – Napoleon as a pilfering monkey, themselves as sturdy Jack Tars – no longer drew crowds to the windows of print shops. But one was published in Cheapside during January 1806 that may serve as a final word on the campaign of Trafalgar. Its caption ran, 'A Stoppage to a Stride over the Globe', and the drawing showed a gigantic Napoleon wearing a huge cocked hat, sabre in hand, sitting astride the earth, while a little man clings to the side of the globe, brandishing a cutlass with his right hand, his left on an island inscribed, 'Old England'. Napoleon is demanding, 'Who is it dares interrupt me in my progress?' and the little man replies, 'Why, 'tis I, little Johnny Bull, protecting a little spot I clap my hand on and d---n me if you come any further, that's all.'[28]

Epilogue

D ID NAPOLEON really mean to invade the British Isles, or was his threat a ruse to occupy British forces while he turned his attention elsewhere? Did Trafalgar really give the British the maritime supremacy that was claimed? Heavy as French losses had been, they accounted for only a fifth of their total fleet, still leaving Napoleon with about sixty ships of the line.

There was still nearly a decade of war to be fought. At the time the Battle of Trafalgar had seemed a climax to the British, as had Austerlitz to the French. There were other apparent climaxes and surprises to come. Before the end of 1806 Napoleon had put together a vastly enlarged version of the Armed Neutrality of the North known as the Continental System to stop all European trade with Britain; Portugal refused to comply and this led to the long and, for the French, ultimately disastrous war in the Iberian peninsula.

Napoleon never lost his ambition to invade England and, realizing that this could only be considered after taking control of the Channel, ordered the building of 130 ships of the line. By 1813 eighty had been completed and another thirty-five were under construction, challenging the British economy in a shipbuilding contest but never again challenging the Royal Navy in a fleet action. Nor did he forget his eastern ambitions and, realizing that he might be able to reach Constantinople, Cairo and, indeed, India only by advancing overland, he moved into the Balkans. Among those who thwarted him there were three friends of Nelson: Vice-Admiral Lord Collingwood, Rear-Admiral Thomas Fremantle and Captain William Hoste.

The British fought an unnecessary war with the United States in 1812. In that same year the Emperor expended the Grand Armée in his rash invasion of Russia in 1812 as part of his hopes of eastern conquest and, after a long, ugly struggle in Portugal and Spain, the British crossed the Pyrenees into France in 1813. Russia and the Russian winter may have broken the back of French military power, but the ultimate success of the British in the Peninsular campaigns was to be described by the historian Andrew Roberts as 'the knife's edge that opened up the oyster'. The Emperor abdicated in April the following year and was exiled to the Mediterranean island of Elba. In March 1815 he escaped, returned to France to overthrow the restored monarchy and the 'Hundred Days' began. The final climax came when the French army, led by the Emperor in person, faced the allies under the Duke of Wellington and the Prussian General Gebhard von Blücher at Waterloo, outside Brussels; it had been in Wellington's words, 'the nearest-run thing you ever saw in your life'.[1] As the battle ended in victory, the first visitor rode across the battlefield to shake Wellington's hand in congratulation; it was, oddly but appropriately, Sir Sidney Smith, unable to resist being at the kill.

The consequence for the Emperor was exile on the remote South Atlantic island of St Helena. There, more than a decade after Trafalgar, Napoleon's Irish doctor, Barry O'Meara, asked him what his intentions had been during the years of what the British had called 'The Great Terror'. 'After the Treaty of Amiens, I would have made a good peace with England', he replied. O'Meara then asked about his plans for an invasion. 'I would have headed it myself', said Napoleon, explaining his plan to entice the British fleet away from the Channel.

Before they could return, I would have had the command of the Channel for two months, as I should have had about seventy sail of the line, besides frigates. I would have hastened over my flotilla with two hundred thousand men, landed as near Chatham as possible and proceeded direct to London, where I calculated to arrive in four days from the time of my landing. I would have proclaimed a republic and the abolition of the nobility and the House of Peers, the distribution of the property of such of the latter as opposed me amongst my partisans, liberty, equality and the sovereignty of the people.[2]

Napoleon held long conversations with William Warden, the surgeon in the ship that had carried him into exile, often when in his bath, where he, plump and puffy, would lie for hours. Curiously, he talked more of Sir Sidney Smith and Acre than of Nelson and Trafalgar, partly because he had been present himself and partly because he judged their importance by soldiers' criteria. He said bitterly of Smith, 'That man made me miss my destiny',[3] but he could be generous, adding, 'Sidney Smith is a brave officer . . . he is active, intelligent, intriguing and indefatigable; but I believe he is half-mad . . . Notwithstanding that Sidney Smith had ill-treated me, I should still have a pleasure in seeing him. I should like to receive *ce gaillard là*.'[4]

Indeed, he talked more about Smith's friend Captain Wright than about Nelson. He surprised Warden with a sudden question, as the doctor remembered.

He asked me to my great surprise if I remembered the history of Captain Wright. I answered, 'Perfectly well and it is a prevailing opinion in England that you ordered him to be murdered in the Temple.' With the utmost rapidity of speech, he replied, 'For what object? Of all men, he was the person whom I could have most desired to live. Whence could I have procured so valuable evidence as he would have provided on the conspirators in and about Paris?'

He then began a lengthy narrative of the conspiracy of Pichegru and Cadoudal and Wright's part in it. Warden suggested 'There are many in England who imagine your jealousy and hatred of Sir Sidney Smith influenced your conduct towards Captain Wright.' At this, noted Warden, he 'smiled with astonishment' and exclaimed, 'Ridiculous! Nonsense!'[5]

When copies of the monthly journal the *Naval Chronicle*

reached St Helena from London, Napoleon was shown an engraving of a grandiose monument set up by Admiral Smith over Wright's grave in the Paris cemetery of Père Lachaise. This was an obelisk flanked by weeping cherubs set on a plinth with life-size veiled, mourning figures – Fame and Britannia, perhaps – holding extinguished, inverted torches. The long Latin inscription included these words:

> A while successful in his career, at length, assailed by adverse winds and on a hostile shore, he was captured and, being soon after brought to Paris, was confined in the prison, the Temple, infamous for midnight murders and placed under the most rigid custody. But in bonds and suffering severities still more oppressive, his fortitude of mind and fidelity to his country remained unshaken. A short time after, he was found in the morning with his throat cut and dead in his bed . . . To be lamented by his country – avenged by his God.[6]

Napoleon was angered and complained, 'Sidney Smith has acted in a manner unworthy of himself . . . in the epitaph, which he wrote upon Wright.' But the implied accusation preyed on his mind. 'They accuse me of the death of a poor little post-captain',[7] he complained.

> If Wright was put to death, it must have been by my authority. If he was put to death in prison, I ordered it. Fouché, even if so inclined, never would have dared to do it . . . But the fact is, Wright killed himself and I do not believe that he was personally ill treated in prison . . . Sidney Smith, above all men, knew from having been so long in the Temple that it is impossible to have assassinated a prisoner without the knowledge of such a number of persons as would have made concealment impossible.[8]

He repeated much of this to O'Meara but added, 'Now there was something glorious in Wright's death. He preferred taking away his own life to compromising his government.'[9] Napoleon was shown the long series of articles about the life and death of

Captain Wright published in the *Naval Chronicle* throughout 1815 and 1816, based on the investigations of Sir Sidney Smith after the end of the war. This only deepened the mystery. On his arrival in France Smith had gone to Paris and, using his royalist friends, who were now in positions of authority and influence, had questioned as many as he could find of the former prisoners and gaolers who had been in the Temple in 1805. This further confused the question. Early reports that Wright had been tortured were discounted, but what often seemed reliable evidence was often contradictory. Most thought he had been murdered and there were reports of strange noises on the night of the death and hints that the order had been given by Fouché, or Savary, on behalf of the Emperor.

This again angered Napoleon: 'No person asserts positively that he had seen him murdered.' But, he continued,

> If I had acted properly, I should have ordered Wright to be tried by a military commission as a spy and shot within twenty-four hours, which by the laws of war I was entitled to do. What would your ministers, or even your Parliament, have done to a French captain that was discovered landing assassins in England to murder King George? . . . They would not have been so lenient as I was with Wright. They would have had him tried and executed *sur le champ*.[10]

Then, by coincidence, a witness arrived on St Helena. One morning Napoleon was in a genial mood and asked O'Meara about a party that British officers had held the night before. 'How many bottles of wine?' he asked, 'Drink, your eyes look like drink. Who dined with you?' O'Meara mentioned some names, including that of a Captain Wallis. 'What, is that the lieutenant who was with Wright?' O'Meara nodded; it had indeed been James Wallis, once first lieutenant of the *Vencejo*. 'What does he say about Wright's death?' asked Napoleon. The doctor replied, 'He states his belief that Wright was murdered by orders of Fouché for the purpose of ingratiating himself to you. That six or seven weeks previous, Wright had told him that he expected to be murdered like Pichegru and begged of him never to believe that he would commit suicide.'[11] Napoleon then complained that, until his exile, 'this affair of Wright's made so little impression on me . . . I did not recollect it. My mind was so much occupied with grand objects that I had little time to think of a poor English captain.'[13] Now he had, and Captain Wright had come to haunt him.

Years passed and Europe was changing. On his forty-seven square miles of rock in the Atlantic, 5000 miles from France, Napoleon was sickening. Yet after five years his British guards were stronger than ever, and with reason. Inevitably there were rumours of plots to rescue him, several involving those familiar during the years of war. One was the disaffected British naval hero Lord Cochrane, who had gone to South America to fight against Spanish rule and had proposed Napoleon as Emperor of Brazil, once he had escaped. The most ingenious and bizarre possibility was rescue by submarine. Since Sir Sidney Smith's plans for unconventional warfare had been disregarded, Robert Fulton had been at work successfully on his steamships in the United States. When he had abandoned England in 1806, he had left his plans for a submarine with Captain Tom Johnstone, the ubiquitous smuggler, who repeatedly tried to interest the Admiralty in building it. Ignored by the navy, he had approached the Duke of York, who had always shown interest in the original ideas of Admiral Smith, and he had authorized the building of the submarine in secret at a boatyard on the Thames near Wallingford in Oxfordshire. As the 'Great War' faded into memory, even he lost interest but Johnstone was determined to continue with what he felt was a weapon of the future. However, like Fulton, he made the mistake of seeming to blackmail the Admiralty by suggesting that, unless subsidized, he might sell his submarine to a foreign power. Outraged, the Lord High Admiral, the Duke of Clarence, broke off all contact with Johnstone.

What exactly happened hovers on the frontiers of mythology. The Duke of York is known to have subsidized the submarine and authorized its construction at Wallingford.[14] The Duke of Clarence is known to have withdrawn all interest from the project.[15] It was reported that French Bonapartists had offered Johnstone £40,000 for the use of his submarine in the rescue of Napoleon from St Helena; it was to have been towed by sailing ship to the South Atlantic to ferry the fugitive from the island to the ship.

That would have been no more than an intriguing legend but for a manuscript discovered a century and a half later. This was an autobiographical note by the artist and waterman Walter Greaves, a friend of the American painter Whistler, in which he quoted his father, Charles Greaves, the owner of a boatyard at Chelsea on the Thames just upstream from London, speaking of the year 1820. 'My father said there was a mysterious boat that was intended to go under water . . . for the purpose of getting Napoleon off the island of St Helena', Walter Greaves wrote,

> So, on one dark night in November, she proceeded down the river (not being able to sink as the water was not deep enough). Anyhow, she managed to get below London Bridge. The officers boarding her, Capt. Johnson [*sic*] in the meantime threatening to shoot them. But they paid no attention to his threats, seized her and, taking her to Blackwall, destroyed her.[16]

Whatever the truth, any such plot would have been too late because Napoleon died on his island on 5 May 1821.

This bizarre fragment of memory illuminates an irony. The Battle of Trafalgar has been celebrated for nearly two centuries as one of the pivotal occasions in British and European history. It was, indeed, a spectacular culmination and the last great action fought at sea under sail; when a Franco-British fleet destroyed the Ottoman fleet eight years later, the latter were at anchor in Navarino Bay. Even in the age of steam and steel there were only two great actions between battleships: in 1905, at Tsushima, the Japanese destroyed the Russian fleet; eleven years later, the British and German fleets fought at Jutland in the North Sea. But never, after 1805, did two fleets of great sailing ships fight on that scale; it would never happen again.

Something else had, however, begun. In their time Smith, Fulton and Congreve – and, to a lesser extent, Wright and Johnstone – were often seen as tiresome, the former even as figures of fun. Yet in the twentieth century Smith's unconventional approach to war, whether through espionage and subversion, or in his predilection for unconventional weaponry, not only became the norm but was sometimes decisive. His expertise in clandestine war within enemy countries inspired the work of the Secret Intelligence Service and the Special Operations Executive in the Second World War; a member of the latter remembered being told by his commanding officer in 1940 that 'their business was to do to Europe what Pitt did to France before 1807.'[17] The descendants of Fulton's submarines, torpedoes and mines became of crucial importance and almost decided both world wars.

Congreve's rockets remained in service – if only seen as a peculiar type of artillery – and in the Second World War, rocket ships – descendants of those built by Smith and Congreve – were in action off the French coast they had known so well for the Normandy landings, and the weapon also grew into the long-range V2 rocket that bombarded London. In the late twentieth century the inventions of both Fulton and Congreve came together in submarines capable of firing rockets. Since the submarines were nuclear-powered and of almost unlimited endurance and could fire rockets with intercontinental range from beneath the surface of the sea, the Polaris, and, later, Trident, submarines became the capital ships of their time. The ideas of the originals and the eccentrics had, after two centuries, come into their own.

Afterwards

Fanny d'Arblay (née Burney) and her son returned to England in 1812, leaving her husband, Alexandre, in Paris. They were reunited in Brussels in 1815 and returned to London; Alexandre died at Bath three years later. Fanny died at Bath in 1840 at the age of eighty-seven, three years after her son.

Sir William Congreve designed incendiary rockets used in the attack on Copenhagen in 1807 and the action in the Basque Roads two years later. Rocket companies were formed by the army and Congreve served with them as a colonel at Leipzig in 1813 and in France the following year. He became Comptroller of the Royal Laboratory in 1814, sat as MP for Plymouth from 1818 and died in 1828 at the age of fifty-five.

Joseph Farington enjoyed wide popularity after his return from Paris to London, when engravings were made of his landscape paintings. He died after a fall from his horse in 1821, at the age of seventy-four.

Joseph Fouché continued to intrigue for and against Napoleon. He was created Duke of Otranto and was able to remain briefly in office on the restoration of the Bourbons. Dismissed as a regicide in 1816, he lived in exile until his death in Trieste in 1820, at the age of fifty-eight.

Robert Fulton, after returning to the United States, concentrated on the development of steam propulsion and also experimented with mines and a submarine gun. He again tried and failed to interest Napoleon in his inventions but, on the outbreak of war with Britain in 1812, he offered his weapons to the US Navy and his mines were used in unsuccessful attacks on British warships in Chesapeake Bay and off New York.

Finally he designed an eighty-foot submarine named the *Mute* and the *Fulton the First*, the first steam-propelled warship. He died in New York in 1815 at the age of forty-nine.

Emma Hamilton continued to live at Merton Place after Nelson's death but then moved to London with their daughter Horatia, sinking deeper into debt through extravagance. Forced into exile by creditors, she fled to Calais in 1814 and died there the following year at the age of forty-nine.

Captain Tom Johnstone continued with the development of his submarine and in 1828 again offered it to the Admiralty, hinting at the interest of foreign powers in the project. Again he was rejected and tried to promote the idea of its use in salvage or treasure-hunting, albeit without success. He died at his house by the Thames in London in 1839.

Lieutenant-General Sir John Moore commanded an expeditionary force in the Iberian peninsula in 1808 and was advancing from Portugal to Madrid when, threatened with outflanking by the French, he retreated to Corunna. There, having assured his army's evacuation by sea, he was killed in action in January 1809, at the age of forty-eight.

General Jean Victor Marie Moreau was banished to the United States by Napoleon in 1804, and lived in New Jersey until 1813. Still hoping to sieze power in France, he became a military adviser to Tsar Alexander of Russia and was mortally wounded in action at Dresden in 1813 at the age of fifty.

Sir Sidney Smith served in the Mediterranean after Trafalgar, took part in the abortive expedition against Constantinople in 1807 and became second-in-command in 1812. He campaigned against Mediterranean slavery, inspiring the British naval attacks on Algiers in 1816 and 1824. He moved to Paris after Waterloo and died there in 1840 at the age of seventy-five.

Lady Hester Stanhope made a pilgrimage to Jerusalem in 1810, after the death of Sir John Moore at Corunna, and travelled widely in the Levant, where she settled. Adopting oriental dress and habits, she became a celebrated eccentric and died in poverty at the age of sixty-three.

Notes

ABBREVIATIONS

AN	Archives Nationales, Paris	NNM	National Maritime Museum
BL	British Library	*PH*	*Parliamentary History*
NC	*Naval Chronicle*	PRO	Public Record Office

When the author's own biography of Nelson has been given as a source it is usually because the relevant manuscript is known to have changed owners and its current whereabouts is not known.

PROLOGUE

1. Nicholas, vol. 4, p. 327.
2. Fremantle, vol. 3, p. 37.
3. Fremantle, vol. 3, p. 49.
4. Nicolas, vol. 4, p. 310, n.
5. *Edinburgh Advertiser* (24 April 1801).
6. Coleridge, S.T., *The Friend* (1809), vol. 1, p. 10; Bryant, *The Years of Endurance*, p. 335.

CHAPTER 1: NELSON SPEAKING TO THE FRENCH

1. Windham, vol. 2, p. 171.
2. Pocock, *Nelson*, p. 245.

3. Nicolas, vol. 4, pp. 425–8.
4. Oman, *Nelson*, p. 471.
5. Nicolas, vol. 4, p. 441.
6. Nicolas, vol. 4, p. 446.
7. Nicolas, vol. 4, p. 432.
8. Nicolas, vol. 4, p. 432.
9. Nicolas, vol. 4, p. 454–5.
10. Pettigrew, vol. 2, p. 144.
11. Nicolas, vol. 4, p. 459.
12. Pelly family archive.
13. Pettigrew, vol. 2, p. 154.
14. PRO, ADM 51, 1437.
15. PRO, ADM 51, 1437.
16. *NC*, vol. 6, p. 155.
17. AN, *Marine* BB4/153.
18. AN, *Marine* BB4/153.
19. *NC*, vol. 6, p. 154.
20. *NC*, vol. 6, p. 156.
21. *NC*, vol. 6, p. 156.
22. *NC*, vol. 6, p. 156.
23. *NC*, vol. 6, p. 156.
24. Nicolay, pp. 279–80.
25. Nicolas, vol. 4, p. 464.
26. *NC*, vol. 6, p. 153.
27. *NC*, vol. 6, p. 154.
28. Nicolas, vol. 4, p. 472.
29. *Morning Chronicle* (18 August 1801).
30. *NC*, vol. 6, p. 231.
31. Nicolas, vol. 4, p. 485, n.
32. Nicolas, vol. 4, p. 485.
33. Pocock, p. 257.
34. Nicolas, vol. 4, p. 482.
35. Hibbert, p. 281.
36. Nicholas, vol. 4, p. 470.
37. *NC*, vol. 4, p. 172.
38. Christopher Hurst private collection.
39. Pettigrew, vol. 2, pp. 160–1.
40. Pettigrew, vol. 2, p. 166.
41. Pettigrew, vol. 2, p. 162.
42. Pettigrew, vol 2, p. 170.
43. Pocock, *Nelson*, pp. 251–2.
44. Fremantle, vol. 3, p. 31.
45. Pocock, *Nelson*, p. 253.
46. Pocock, *Nelson*, p. 254.

47. Pocock, *Nelson*, p. 254.
48. Pocock, *Nelson*, p. 254–5.
49. Pettigrew, vol. 2, p. 182.
50. Pettigrew, vol. 2, p. 183.
51. Pettigrew, vol. 2, p. 194.
52. Sueter, Murray, *The Evolution of the Submarine Boat, Mine and Torpedo* (Portsmouth, 1907), pp. 29–30.
53. Farington, vol. 6, pp. 2040–1.
54. *NC*, vol. 7, p. 351.

CHAPTER 2: A GREAT SURPRISE INDEED

1. Pocock, *Nelson*, p. 261.
2. Pocock, *Nelson*, p. 260.
3. Kelly, p. 130.
4. Hemlow, vol. 5, p. 91.
5. Chisholm, p. 199.
6. Chisholm, p. 200.
7. *The Times* (7 April 1801).
8. *PH*, vol. 36, col. 75.
9. Windham, vol. 2, p. 181.
10. *PH*, vol. 36, col. 184.
11. *PH*, vol. 36, col. 184.
12. *PH*, vol. 36, col. 184.
13. *PH*, vol. 36, col. 185.
14. *PH*, vol. 36, col. 185.
15. *PH*, vol. 36, col. 185.
16. *PH*, vol. 36, col. 185.
17. *PH*, vol. 36, col. 186.
18. Pocock, *Nelson*, p. 268.
19. Pocock, *Nelson*, p. 268.
20. Pocock, *Nelson*, p. 267–8.
21. Pocock, *Nelson*, p. 267–8.
22. *The Times* (11 November 1801).
23. PRO, 30/70/6, 383.
24. Peace, G.L., *La navigation sous-marine* (Paris, 1906), p. 208.
25. Bourrienne, vol. 2, p. 43.
26. Hemlow, vol. 5, p. 203.
27. Hemlow, vol. 5, pp. 225–6.
28. Alger, p. 24.
29. Hemlow, vol. 5, pp. 231–2.
30. Hemlow, vol. 5, pp. 231–2.
31. Hemlow, vol. 5, pp. 232.

32. Lewis, vol. 2, p. 126.
33. Farington, vol. 5, p. 1817.
34. Farington, vol. 5, p. 1817.
35. Hemlow, vol. 5, p. 243.

CHAPTER 3: A YOUNG MAN INTOXICATED WITH SUCCESS

1. Trotter, pp. 197–8.
2. Trotter, pp. 342.
3. Hemlow, vol. 5, pp. 244.
4. Granville, vol. 1, p. 396.
5. Granville, vol. 1, p. 402.
6. Granville, vol. 1, p. 401.
7. Granville, vol. 1, p. 401.
8. Julian Browning manuscript catalogue, London, 1996.
9. Farington, vol. 5, p. 1874.
10. Bury and Barry, p. 7.
11. Bury and Barry, p. 115.
12. Trotter, p. 289.
13. Trotter, p. 38–9.
14. Farington, vol. 5, p. 1853.
15. Bury and Barry, p. 104.
16. Bury and Barry, p. 500–01.
17. Farington, vol. 5, p. 1846.
18. Lewis, vol. 2, pp. 133–4.
19. Bury and Barry, p. 125.
20. Bury and Barry, p. 11.
21. Bury and Barry, pp. 129–30.
22. Hemlow, vol. 5, p. 290.
23. Farington, vol. 5, p. 1851.
24. Farington, vol. 5, p. 1861.
25. Alger, pp. 135–6.
26. Alger, p. 53.
27. Argyll, vol. 1, p. 376.
28. Granville, vol. 1, p. 379.
29. Granville, vol. 1, p. 375.
30. Romilly, vol. 2, p. 84.
31. Bury and Barry, p. 110.
32. Foner, Philip S., ed., *The Complete Writings of Thomas Paine* (New York, 1945), vol. 2, pp. 1488–9.
33. Sparrow, p. 263.
34. PRO, DRO 152M/c1803/OZ/7–14.
35. Bourrienne, vol. 1, p. 207.

36. Browning, p. 131.
37. Sparrow, p. 264.
38. Sparrow, p. 264.
39. Bury and Barry, p. 149.
40. Alger, p. 41.
41. Trotter, p. 242.
42. Mayne, p. 100.
43. Hemlow, vol. 5, p. 313.
44. Lewis, vol. 2, p. 180.
45. Brownlow, p. 8.
46. Trotter, p. 153.
47. Trotter, p. 215.
48. Trotter, p. 204–5.
49. Trotter, p. 252.
50. Bury and Barry, p. 9.
51. Trotter, pp. 265–6.
52. Trotter, pp. 266–7.
53. Granville, vol. 1, p. 362.
54. Granville, vol. 1, p. 362.
55. Farington, vol. 5, p. 1875.
56. Farington, vol. 5, p. 1961.
57. Farington, vol. 5, p. 1833–4.
58. Farington, vol. 5, p. 1906.
59. Hemlow, vol. 5, pp. 314–5.
60. Hemlow, vol. 5, p. 314.
61. Farington, vol. 5, pp. 1905–6.
62. Alger, p. 163.
63. Bourrienne, vol. 2, p. 97.
64. Mayne, p. 107.
65. Romilly, vol. 2, p. 92.
66. Trotter, p. 317.
67. Granville, vol. 1, p. 354.
68. Romilly, vol. 2, p. 92.
69. Granville, vol. 1, p. 355 [translated from the French].
70. Granville, vol. 1, p. 355.
71. Granville, vol. 1, p. 355.
72. BL, Add. MS 37, 9222.
73. BL, Add. MS 37, 9222.
74. BL, Add. MS 37, 9222.
75. Bourrienne, vol. 1, p. 237.
76. Reid, p. 420.
77. Creasy, Edward S., *Memoirs of Eminent Etonians* (London, 1850), p. 383.
78. Sartiaux, Albert, *Le tunnel sous-marin entre la France et l'Angleterre* (Lille, 1907), pp. 16–7.

79. Trotter, p. 341.
80. Memes, p. 208.
81. Memes, p. 209.
82. Trotter, pp. 285–7.
83. Bourrienne, vol. 1, p. 284.
84. Bourrienne, vol. 1, p. 329.
85. Denny, Barbara, *Hammersmith Past* (London, 1995), p. 75.
86. Maxwell, p. 8.
87. Ayling, p. 214.

CHAPTER 4: THE BUZZ OF WAR

1. Bryant, *Years of Victory*, p. 31.
2. Farington, vol. 5, pp. 1909–10.
3. Granville, vol. 1, p. 391.
4. Granville, vol. 1, p. 391.
5. Granville, vol. 1, p. 393.
6. Mayne, p. 92.
7. Bryant, *Years of Victory*, p. 42.
8. Browning, p. 116.
9. Argyll, p. 36.
10. Bury and Barry, p. 137.
11. Bury and Barry, p. 149.
12. Bury and Barry, p. 147.
13. Hemlow, vol. 5, p. 439.
14. Bury and Barry, p. 448.
15. Mayne, p. 94.
16. Browning, p. 240.
17. Oman, *Britain against Napoleon*, p. 149.
18. Bury and Barry, p. 153.
19. Leighton, Rachel, *Correspondence of Charlotte Grenville, Lady Williams Wynn* (London, 1920), pp. 81–2.
20. Bury and Barry, p. 187.
21. Farington, vol. 5, p. 1915.
22. Farington, vol. 5, p. 1915.
23. Minto, vol. 2, p. 242.
24. Morrison, vol. 2, p. 197.
25. Keate, E., *Nelson's Wife* (London, 1939), pp. 221–2.
26. Pocock, *Nelson*, p. 280.
27. Pocock, *Nelson*, p. 280.
28. Pollock, Sir Frederick, ed., *Macready Reminiscences* (London, 1875), pp. 33–4.
29. *NC*, vol. 7, p. 516.

30. Nicolas, vol. 5, p. 42.
31. Gurney and Gurney, p. 174.
32. Farington, vol. 5, p. 1982.
33. Minto, vol. 3, p. 274.
34. Bryant, *Years of Victory*, p. 34.
35. Nicolas, vol. 5, p. 67.

CHAPTER 5: A FEARFUL DAY IS PREPARING

1. *Correspondance de Napoléon 1er*, letter 7279.
2. *Correspondance de Napoléon 1er*, letter 8957.
3. Nicolay, p. 85.
4. *The Times* (4 July 1803).
5. Rémusat, Madame de, *Memoirs*, vol. 1, p. 118.
6. Nicolay, pp. 98–9.
7. Rémusat, Madame de, *Memoirs*, vol. 1, p. 121–7.
8. Schom, p. 72.
9. Phillips catalogue, London, lot 480, sale of 9 November 2001.
10. PRO, WO/30/75.
11. Nicolay, p. 18.
12. Nicolay, p. 242.
13. Nicolay, p. 243.
14. Nicolay, p. 64.
15. Nicolay, p. 64.
16. Nicolay, p. 65.
17. Crawford, p. 49.
18. Morley, Geoffrey, *Smuggling in Hampshire and Dorset, 1700–1850* (Newbury, 1983), p. 38.
19. Schom, p. 85.
20. Desbrière, vol. 3, p. 308.
21. Pasquier, Duc de, *A History of My Time: Memoirs of Chancellor Pasquier*, 6 vols. (Paris, 1893), vol. 1, pp. 177–8.
22. Wheeler and Broadley, vol. 2, p. 83.
23. Bourrienne, vol. 2, p. 145.
24. Phillips catalogue, lot 414, sale of 9 November 2001.
25. Lloyd, vol. 3, p. 31.
26. Lloyd, vol. 3, p. 59.
27. Sparrow, p. 277.
28. PRO, ADM1/1450/469,475.
29. Sparrow, p. 284.
30. Sparrow, p. 284.
31. Sparrow, p. 284.

32. Sparrow, p. 284–5.
33. Sparrow, p. 284–5.
34. Sparrow, p. 285.
35. Sparrow, p. 269.

CHAPTER 6: THEN TO INVASION BE DEFIANCE GIVEN

1. Wheeler and Broadley, vol. 2, p. 37.
2. Wheeler and Broadley, vol. 2, p. 45.
3. Bunbury, Sir H., *Narrative of the Great War with France* (London, 1852), pp. 176–7.
4. Stanhope, vol. 2, pp. 82–3.
5. PRO, WO/30/75.
6. Fremantle, vol. 3, p. 88.
7. *Bath Herald* (23 July 1803).
8. Wheeler and Broadley, vol. 2, p. 281.
9. Wheeler and Broadley, vol. 2, p. 130.
10. Fremantle, vol. 3, p. 93.
11. Granville, vol. 1, p. 426.
12. Farington, vol. 5, p. 2120.
13. Farington, vol. 5, p. 2093.
14. Harcourt, Leveson Vernon, ed., *Diaries and Correspondence of the Rt. Hon. George Rose*, 2 vols. (London, 1860), vol. 2, p. 64.
15. Farington, vol. 5, p. 2065.
16. Farington, vol. 5, p. 2112.
17. *European Magazine* (1803), p. 326.
18. FitzGerald, Percy, *Life and Times of William IV* (London, 1884), vol. 1, p. 117.
19. FitzGerald, Percy, *Life and Times of William IV*, vol. 1, p. 117.
20. Farington, vol. 5, p. 2082–3.
21. Farington, vol. 5, p. 2068.
22. Broadley, A.M., and Bartelot, R.G., *Three Dorset Captains at Trafalgar* (London, 1906), p. 148.
23. Wheeler and Broadley, vol. 2, pp. 105–6.
24. Wheeler and Broadley, vol. 2, pp. 105–6.
25. Wheeler and Broadley, vol. 2, pp. 107.
26. Oman, *Sir John Moore*, p. 322.
27. Oman, *Sir John Moore*, p. 73.
28. Farington, vol. 5, p. 2073.
29. Farington, vol. 5, p. 2100.
30. Scott, Sir Walter, *The Antiquary* (London, 1816), p. 521.
31. Wheeler and Broadley, vol. 2, pp. 135–6.
32. Farington, vol. 5, p. 2392.

33. Farington, vol. 5, p. 2280.
34. Pettigrew, vol. 2, p. 422.
35. Granville, vol. 1, p. 467.
36. Fremantle, vol. 3, p. 87.
37. *Bath Journal* (30 July 1803).
38. Farington, vol. 5, p. 2405.
39. Maurice, vol. 1, p. 367.
40. Hamel, p. 33.
41. Hamel, p. 33.
42. Hamel, p. 37, n.
43. Ehrman, p. 544.
44. Bunbury, C., ed., *Memoirs* (London, 1868), p. 33.
45. Napier, vol. 1, pp. 38–9.
46. Maurice, vol. 2, pp. 8–9.
47. Maxwell, p. 18.
48. Hubback and Hubback, p. 113.

CHAPTER 7: TO OVERTHROW THE TYRANT

1. Hall, p. 317.
2. Sparrow, p. 289.
3. Bourrienne, vol. 2, p. 237.
4. Bourrienne, vol. 2, p. 175–6, n.
5. Bourrienne, vol. 2, p. 175–6, n.
6. Bourrienne, vol. 2, p. 183.
7. Bourrienne, vol. 2, p. 185.
8. Bourrienne, vol. 2, p. 186.
9. Bourrienne, vol. 2, p. 186.
10. Bourrienne, vol. 2, p. 180.
11. Bourrienne, vol. 2, p. 138.
12. Bourrienne, vol. 2, p. 194.
13. Sparrow, p. 292.
14. Sparrow, p. 293.
15. *NC*, vol. 34, p. 441.
16. *NC*, vol. 34, p. 443.
17. *NC*, vol. 34, p. 445.
18. *NC*, vol. 34, p. 444–5.
19. Coupland, R., ed., *War Speeches of William Pitt* (Oxford, 1915), p. 332.
20. Bourrienne, vol. 2, p. 229.
21. Bourrienne, vol. 2, p. 225.
22. Bourrienne, vol. 2, p. 227.
23. Bourrienne, vol. 2, p. 227–8.

24. Bourrienne, vol. 2, p. 227.
25. Bourrienne, vol. 2, p. 228–9.
26. Desmarest, Pierre, *Quinze ans de haute police sous le consulat et de l'empire* (Paris, 1900).
27. Bourrienne, vol. 2, p. 232.

CHAPTER 8: LET US BE MASTERS OF THE WORLD

1. Bryant, *Years of Victory*, p. 77.
2. Desbrière, vol. 4, p. 11.
3. Lloyd, vol. 3, p. 31.
4. Nicolas, vol. 5, p. 438.
5. Lloyd, vol. 3, p. 54.
6. Fulton MSS, New York Public Library.
7. Lloyd, vol. 3, p. 86.
8. Popham, p. 115.
9. Crawford, pp. 55–6.
10. Crawford, pp. 55–6.
11. Popham, p. 118.
12. Crawford, p. 54.
13. Crawford, p. 59–60.
14. Crawford, p. 59–60.
15. Crawford, p. 60.
16. Bourrienne, vol. 2, p. 255.
17. Baring-Gould, S., *Life of Napoleon Bonaparte* (London, 1897), pp. 315–6.
18. *Moniteur Universel* (19 August 1804).
19. Hutcheon, p. 73.
20. Gardiner, p. 83.
21. Lloyd, vol. 3, p. 95.
22. Crawford, p. 65.
23. Hutcheon, p. 77.
24. Popham, p. 120.
25. Popham, p. 118.
26. Popham, p. 119.
27. Bourrienne, vol. 2, p. 267.
28. Bourrienne, vol. 2, p. 271.
29. Hemlow, vol. 6, p. 517.
30. Hemlow, vol. 6, p. 517.
31. *NC*, vol. 36, p. 195.
32. *NC*, vol. 36, p. 196–7.
33. *NC*, vol. 36, p. 196–7.
34. *NC*, vol. 36, p. 197–9.

35. *NC*, vol. 36, p. 197–9.
36. *NC*, vol. 34, p. 449.
37. *NC*, vol. 34, p. 199.
38. *NC*, vol. 36, p. 449.

<small>CHAPTER 9: A SWEET KISS WILL BE AMPLE REWARD</small>

1. Schom, p. 357.
2. Nicolas, vol. 6, p. 329.
3. Nicolas, vol. 6, p. 349.
4. Corbett, p. 126.
5. Corbett, p. 126.
6. Schom, p. 184.
7. Gardiner, p. 113.
8. Schom, p. 186.
9. Ruskin, John, *Praeterita and Dilecta* (London, 1908), p. 586.
10. Fremantle, vol. 3, p. 166.
11. Fremantle, vol. 3, p. 170.
12. Pocock, *Nelson*, p. 303.
13. Pocock, *Nelson*, p. 303.
14. Pocock, *Nelson*, p. 303.
15. Corbett, p. 160.
16. P. Wright, ed., *Lady Nugent's Journal* (Kingston, 1966), p. 241.
17. Frampton, Mary, *Journal, 1779–1846*, ed. H.G. Mundy (London, 1885), pp. 131–2.
18. Pocock, *Nelson*, p. 304.
19. Pocock, *Nelson*, p. 304.
20. Pocock, *Nelson*, p. 305.

<small>CHAPTER 10: LOSE NOT A MOMENT . . . ENGLAND IS OURS</small>

1. Pettigrew, vol. 2, p. 486.
2. Matcham, p. 226.
3. NMM, NWD/9594/7.
4. Silliman, B., *Journal of Travels in England* (London, 1810), p. 189.
5. Pocock, *Nelson*, p. 307.
6. Croker, p. 233–4.
7. Shankland, Peter, *Beware of Heroes* (London, 1975), p. 168.
8. Londonderry, vol. 5, pp. 86–7.
9. Minto, vol. 3, p. 363.
10. Clarke and M'Arthur, vol. 2, p. 422.
11. Glover, p. 90.

12. Crawford, p. 76.
13. Matcham, p. 234.
14. Clarke and M'Arthur, vol. 2, p. 422.
15. Nicholas, vol. 5, p. 241, n.
16. Windham, vol. 2, p. 291.
17. Londonderry, vol. 5, p. 91.
18. Londonderry, vol. 5, p. 93.
19. Londonderry, vol. 5, p. 93.
21. *Correspondance de Napoléon 1er*, letter 9115.
21. Schom, p. 295.
22. Bryant, *Years of Victory*, pp. 153–4.
23. Lloyd, vol. 3, pp. 114–5.
24. Llanggatock Papers, Nelson Museum, Monmouth, Gwent, E 244.
25. Minto, vol. 3, p. 370.
26. Pocock, *Nelson*, p. 315.
27. Nicolas, vol. 7, pp. 33–5.
28. Pettigrew, vol. 2, p. 497.
29. Egremont, p. 36.

CHAPTER 11: A GREAT AND GLORIOUS VICTORY

1. Londonderry, vol. 5, p. 91.
2. Londonderry, vol. 5, p. 95.
3. *Hythe Gazette* (6 September, 1805).
4. Londonderry, vol. 5, p. 96.
5. Londonderry, vol. 5, p. 97.
6. Londonderry, vol. 5, p. 111.
7. Londonderry, vol. 5, p. 105–6.
8. Londonderry, vol. 5, pp. 101–2.
9. PRO, WO/1/185,63.
10. Hutcheon, p. 84.
11. Russell, *Knight of the Sword*, p. 107.
12. American State Papers, US Library of Congress, Naval Affairs 1/217.
13. Hutcheon, p. 82.
14. Hutcheon, p. 82.
15. Londonderry, vol. 5, p. 108.
16. Londonderry, vol. 5, pp. 111–2.
17. Londonderry, vol. 5, p. 113.
18. Londonderry, vol. 5, p. 115.
19. Londonderry, vol. 5, p. 115.
20. Hutcheon, p. 84.
21. American State Papers, US Library of Congress, Naval Affairs 1/212.
22. Londonderry, vol. 5, p. 120.

23. American State Papers, US Library of Congress, Naval Affairs 1/213.
24. Parry, Ann, *The Admirals Fremantle* (London, 1971), pp. 69–70.
25. Parry, Ann, *The Admirals Fremantle*, p. 71.
26. Warner, p. 335.
27. Nicolas, vol. 7, p. 60.
28. Pocock, *Nelson*, p. 319.
29. Fremantle, vol. 3, p. 210–11.
30. NMM, NWD/9594.
31. Morrison, vol. 2, p. 269.
32. Fremantle, vol. 3, p. 220.
33. Harrison, vol. 2, p. 456.
34. Nicolas, vol. 7, p. 139.
35. Murray, Geoffrey, *Life of Adm. Collingwood* (London, 1936), p. 275.
36. Schom, p. 320.
37. Clarke and M'Arthur, vol. 2, p. 447.
38. Clarke and M'Arthur, vol. 2, p. 449.
39. Christie's catalogue, London, lot 272, sale of 1 November 2001.
40. Clarke and M'Arthur, vol. 3, p. 156.
41. Clarke and M'Arthur, vol. 3, p. 157.
42. Nicolas, vol. 7, pp. 245–52.
43. Pocock, *Nelson*, pp. 328–31.

CHAPTER 12: WHY 'TIS I, LITTLE JOHNNY BULL

1. Londonderry, vol. 5, p. 121.
2. Londonderry, vol. 5, pp. 124–5.
3. Londonderry, vol. 5, pp. 128–9.
4. Fremantle, vol. 3, p. 228.
5. Fremantle, vol. 3, p. 221.
6. Fremantle, vol. 3, p. 238.
7. Fremantle, vol. 3, p. 239.
8. Fremantle, vol. 3, pp. 234–51.
9. Lloyd, vol. 3, pp. 118–9.
10. Lloyd, vol. 3, pp. 118–9.
11. *The Times* (4 November 1805).
12. Crawford, p. 79.
13. *The Times* (6 November 1805).
14. Fremantle, vol. 3, pp. 216–7.
15. Fremantle, vol. 3, pp. 216–7.
16. Leveson Gower, p. 127.
17. Mayne, p. 152.
18. Farington, vol. 7, p. 2647.
19. *The Times* (7 November 1805).

20. Bourrienne, vol. 2, p. 302, n.
21. Bourrienne, vol. 2, p. 302.
22. Horne, p. 185.
23. Stanhope, Lord, *Life of Pitt* (London, 1862), vol. 4, p. 369.
24. Londonderry, vol. 5, p. 149.
25. Fulton Papers, E/807, State Department, National Archives, Washington.
26. Windham, vol. 2, p. 292.
27. Windham, vol. 2, p. 293.
28. Published by T. Clegg (London, 1806).

EPILOGUE

1. Maxwell, ed., p. 236.
2. O'Meara, vol. 1, pp. 350–1.
3. Russell, *Knight of the Sword*, p. 87.
4. Warden, pp. 184–5.
5. Warden, p. 155.
6. *NC*, vol. 36, pp. 120–1.
7. O'Meara, vol. 1, p. 182.
8. O'Meara, vol. 1, p. 417.
9. O'Meara, vol. 2, p. 24.
10. O'Meara, vol. 2, pp. 215–6.
11. O'Meara, vol. 2, pp. 217–8.
12. O'Meara, p. 217.
13. PRO, ADM 1/4783.
14. PRO, ADM 3/216.
15. Author's collection.
16. Sparrow, xiv.

Bibliography

Alger, J.G., *Napoleon's British Visitors and Captives* (London, 1904)

Argyll, Dowager Duchess of, ed., *George Douglas, 8th Duke of Argyll: Autobiography and Memoirs*, 2 vols. (London,1906)

Ayling, Stanley, *Fox: The Life of Charles James Fox* (London, 1991)

Barney, John, *The Defence of Norfolk, 1793–1815* (Norwich, 2000)

Bourrienne, M. de., *Memoirs of Napoleon Bonaparte*, 4 vols. (London, 1836)

Browning, Oscar, ed., *England and Napoleon: The Despatches of Lord Whitworth* (London, 1887)

Brownlow, Countess of, *Slight Reminiscences of a Septuagenarian* (London, 1867)

Bryant, Sir Arthur, *Years of Victory, 1802–12* (London, 1944)

Bury, J.P.T., and Barry, J.C., eds., *An Englishman in Paris, 1803: The Journal of Bertie Greatheed* (London, 1953)

Cartwright, F.D., ed., *The Life and Correspondence of Major Cartwright*, 2 vols. (London, 1826)

Chandler, David, *Dictionary of the Napoleonic Wars* (Ware, Herts., 1999)

Chisholm, Kate, *Fanny Burney: Her Life* (London, 1998)

Clarke, James Stanier, and M'Arthur, John, *The Life of Admiral Nelson*, 2 vols. (London, 1809)

Cleveland, Duchess of, ed., *The Life of Lady Hester Stanhope* (London, 1897)

Clowes, W.L., *The Royal Navy: A History*, 7 vols. (London, 1900)

Compton-Hall, Richard, *The Submarine Pioneers* (Stroud, 1999)

Corbett, Julian S., *The Campaign of Trafalgar* (London, 1910)

Correspondance de Napoléon 1er, 32 vols. (Paris, 1858–70)

Crawford, Abraham, *Reminiscences of a Naval Officer* (London, 1999)

Croker, John Wilson, *Correspondence and Diaries*, 2 vols. (London, 1885)

Desbrière, Edouard, *The Naval Campaign of 1805*, 2 vols. (Oxford, 1933)

Dickes, Christophe, *Au Camp de Boulogne, 1801–11* (Boulogne, 1999)

Bibliography

Egremont, Lord, *Wyndham and Children First* (London, 1969)

Ehrman, John, *The Younger Pitt: The Consuming Struggle* (London, 1996)

Farington, Joseph, *Diaries*, 15 vols. (London, 1978–84)

Fortescue, Sir John, *History of the British Army*, 7 vols. (London, 1899–1930)

Fremantle, Anne, ed., *The Wynne Diaries, 1789–1820*, 3 vols. (Oxford, 1935–40)

Gardiner, Robert, ed., *The Campaign of Trafalgar, 1803–1805* (London, 1997)

Glover, Richard, *Britain at Bay: Defence against Bonaparte, 1803–14* (London, 1973)

Granville, Castalia, Countess, ed., *Lord Granville Leveson Gower: Private Correspondence, 1781–1821*, 2 vols. (London, 1916)

Gurney, Joseph, and Gurney, William, *The Trial of Edward Marcus Despard for High Treason* (Dublin, 1803)

Hall, Sir John, *General Pichegru's Treason* (London, 1915)

Hamel, Frank, *Lady Hester Lucy Stanhope: A New Light on Her Life and Love Affairs* (London, 1913)

Harman, Claire, *Fanny Burney: A Biography* (London, 2000)

Harrison, James, *Life of the Rt. Hon. Horatio, Lord Viscount Nelson*, 2 vols. (London, 1806)

Hemlow, Joyce, ed., *The Journals and Letters of Fanny Burney (Madame D'Arblay)*, 12 vols. (Oxford, 1972–84)

Hibbert, Christopher, *Nelson: A Personal History* (London, 1994)

Horne, Alistair, *How Far from Austerlitz?* (London, 1996)

Howard, The Hon. E.G.G., *The Memoirs of Sir Sidney Smith* (London, 1839)

Hubback, J.H., and Hubback, E.C., *Jane Austen's Sailor Brothers* (London, 1905)

Hutcheon, Wallace, S., Jr., *Robert Fulton* (Annapolis, 1981)

James, William, *The Naval History of Great Britain*, 5 vols. (London, 1822–4)

Kelly, Linda, *Juniper Hall* (London, 1991)

Leveson Gower, Sir George, and Palmer, Iris, eds., *Harry-O! The Letters of Lady Harriet Cavendish, 1796–1809* (London, 1940)

Lewis, Lady Theresa, *Journals and Correspondence of Miss Berry*, 3 vols. (London, 1865)

Lloyd, Christopher, ed., *The Keith Papers*, 3 vols. (London, 1955)

Londonderry, Marquess of, ed., *Correspondence, Despatches and Other Papers of Viscount Castlereagh*, 5 vols. (London, 1851)

Marshall-Cornwell, James, *Napoleon as Military Commander* (London, 1967)

Matcham, M. Eyre, *The Nelsons of Burnham Thorpe* (London, 1911)

Maurice, Sir J.M., ed, *The Diary of Sir John Moore*, 2 vols. (London, 1904)

Maxwell, Sir Herbert, ed., *The Creevey Papers* (London, 1903)

Mayne, E.C., *Lady Bessborough and Her Friendships* (London, 1939)

Memes, J.S. *Memoirs of the Empress Josephine* (London, 1831)

Minto, Countess of, *The Life and Letters of Sir Gilbert Elliot, First Earl of Minto*, 3 vols. (London, 1874)

Bibliography

Monaque, Rémi, *Latouche-Tréville: L'admiral qui défait Nelson* (Paris, 2000)

Moore, J.C., *The Life of Sir John Moore*, 2 vols. (London, 1834)

Morrison, Edward, ed., *The Hamilton and Nelson Papers*, 2 vols. (London, 1893–4).

Mundy, H.G., *The Journal of Mary Frampton* (London, 1885)

Napier, Sir W., *The Life and Opinions of Gen. Sir Charles Napier*, 4 vols. (London, 1857)

Naval Chronicle, vols. 15, 34–6 (London, 1806, 1815–16)

Nicolas, Sir Harris, ed., *Dispatches and Letters of Vice-Admiral Lord Nelson*, 7 vols. (London, 1844–6)

Nicolay, Fernald, *Napoleon at the Boulogne Camp* (London, 1907)

Nicolson, Nigel, *Fanny Burney* (London, 2002)

Oman, Carola, *Britain against Napoleon* (London, 1942)

——, *Nelson* (London, 1948)

——, *Sir John Moore* (London, 1953)

O'Meara, Barry E., *Napoleon in Exile, or, A Voice from St Helena*, 2 vols. (London, 1822)

Palmer, Alan, *An Encyclopaedia of Napoleon's Europe* (London, 1984)

Pettigrew, Thomas, *Memoirs of the Life of Vice-Admiral Lord Nelson*, 2 vols. (London, 1849)

Pocock, Tom, *Horatio Nelson* (London, 1987)

——, *A Thirst for Glory: The Life of Admiral Sir Sidney Smith* (London, 1996)

Pope, Dudley, *The Great Gamble* (London, 1972)

Popham, Hugh, *A Damned Cunning Fellow: The Life of Rear-Admiral Sir Home Popham* (Cornwall, 1991)

Reid, Loren, *Charles James Fox: A Man for the People* (London, 1969)

Romilly, Sir Samuel, *Memoirs of the Life of Sir Samuel Romilly*, 3 vols. (London, 1840)

Russell, Lord, ed., *Memorials and Correspondence of C.J. Fox.* (London, 1853–7)

Russell, Lord, of Liverpool, *Knight of the Sword: The Life and Letters of Admiral Sir Sidney William Smith* (London, 1964)

Schom, Alan, *Trafalgar: Countdown to Battle, 1803–1805* (London, 1990)

Southam, Brian, *Jane Austen and the Navy* (London, 2000)

Sparrow, Elizabeth, *Secret Service: British Agents in France, 1792–1815* (Woodbridge, 1999)

Stanhope, Lady Hester, *Memoirs*, 3 vols. (London, 1845)

Thompson, E.P., *The Making of the English Working Class* (London, 1963)

Tolstoy, Nikolai, *The Half-Mad Lord* (London, 1978)

Trotter, J.B., *Memoirs of the Latter Years of the Rt. Hon. Charles James Fox* (London, 1811)

Warden, William, *Letters Written on Board His Majesty's Ship Northumberland and at St Helena* (London, 1816)

Bibliography

Warner, Oliver, *A Portrait of Lord Nelson* (London, 1965)

——, *The Life and Letters of Vice-Admiral Lord Collingwood* (London, 1968)

Wheeler, H.F.B., and Broadley, A.M., *Napoleon and the Invasion of England: The Story of the Great Terror*, 2 vols. (London, 1908)

Windham, William, *The Windham Papers*, 2 vols. (London, 1913)

Index